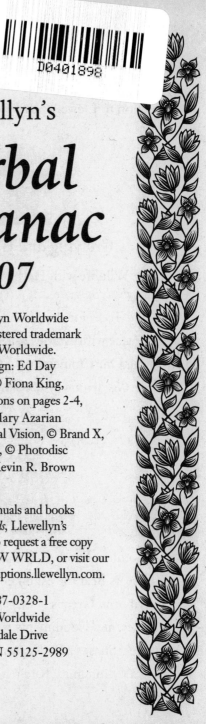

Llewellyn's

Herbal Almanac

2007

© 2006 Llewellyn Worldwide
Llewellyn is a registered trademark
of Llewellyn Worldwide.
Editing/Design: Ed Day
Interior Art: © Fiona King,
excluding illustrations on pages 2-4,
which are © Mary Azarian
Cover Photos: © Digital Vision, © Brand X,
© Digital Stock, © Photodisc
Cover Design: Kevin R. Brown

You can order annuals and books
from *New Worlds*, Llewellyn's
magazine catalog. To request a free copy
call toll-free: 1-877-NEW WRLD, or visit our
website at http://subscriptions.llewellyn.com.

ISBN 0-7387-0328-1
Llewellyn Worldwide
2143 Wooddale Drive
Woodbury, MN 55125-2989

Table of Contents

Growing and Gathering Herbs

Culinary Herbs

Herbs for Health

Herbs for Beauty

Herb Crafts

Herb History, Myth, and Lore

Introduction to Llewellyn's Herbal Almanac

Looking forward to spring is an annual rite for gardeners and schoolchildren alike. But after the thrill of parka-free frolic (in northern climates, anyway) is long gone, home-grown herbs still make a lasting impact. Llewellyn's 2007 Herbal Almanac takes a look at the year-round effects of herbs, re-examining the research on uses of herbs as medicine, as culinary spice, as cosmetics, and more. This year in particular we tap into practical, historical, and just plain enjoyable aspects of herbal knowledge—using herbs to curb memory loss; create an all-season garden; develop child-friendly crafts; and, of course, to try new recipes for tasty treats, comfort foods, and homemade liqueurs. And we bring to these pages some of the most innovative and original thinkers and writers on herbs.

Growing, preparing, and using herbs allow us to focus on the old ways—when men and women around the world knew and understood the power of herbs. Taking a step back to a simpler time is important today as terrorists, water and energy shortages, hatred, internecine battles, militant religious fervor, and war, dominate the airwaves and our consciousness—leaving precious little room for beauty, good food, health, love, and friendship. While we don't want to assign blame or cast aspersions, this state of affairs is perhaps not terribly surprising considering so many of us are out of touch with the beauty, spirituality, and health-giving properties of the natural world. Many of us spend too much of our lives rushing about in a technological bubble. We forget to focus on the parts of life that can bring us back into balance and harmony.

Though it's getting more difficult, you can still find ways to escape the rat-race—at least once in awhile. People are still striving to make us all more aware of the uplifting, beautiful ways that herbs can affect our lives. In the 2007 edition of the Herbal Almanac, the various authors pay tribute to the ideals of beauty and balance as they relate to the health-giving and beautifying properties of herbs. Though sometimes difficult to quantify, creating a community kitchen can create a valuable bond among neighbors, cultivating a container garden for fresh herbs all year, and developing new ways to satisfy your sweet tooth can clearly make a positive impact in your life.

Herbs are the perfect complement to the power of the mind, an ancient tool whose time has come back around to help us restore balance in our lives. More and more people are using them, growing and gathering them, and studying them for their enlivening and healing properties. We, the editors and authors of this volume, encourage the treatment of the whole organism—of the person and of the planet—with herbal magic. One person at a time, using ancient wisdom, we can make a new world.

Growing
and
Gathering
Herbs

Attracting Wildlife with Herbs

❧ by Elizabeth Barrette ❧

When you garden, you can face nature in one of two ways: you can work with her, or against her. You can spray the daylights out of everything and cover your garden in nets, jugs, and fences; or you can welcome wildlife into your space and enjoy the added interest. From a mystical perspective, of course, it's best to work with nature.

The principles of wildlife gardening are pretty simple. 1) Design a garden that both wildlife and people find attractive. 2) Use natural methods of pest control, fertilizer, etc., instead of harshchemicals. 3) Try to plant local native species native rather than exotics. 4) Allow natural processes to happen. Let plants go to seed. Rake leaves onto beds and stack brush into piles for tidiness, but don't haul them away. Relax, and cultivate an appreciation for imperfect things.

Herbs play an important role in a natural garden and are useful for attracting wildlife to small places where you may not have room for a whole garden. A single pot of flowering herbs can attract bees, butterflies, or hummingbirds. The magical correspondences can also help make your garden a welcoming place. Now let's look at some specific things you can do with herbs to attract wildlife. . . .

Blessed Bees

Above all other creatures, bees pay their own way. Honeybees make honey, and all bees pollinate flowers, which greatly increases fruit and vegetable yields. Their pollination services alone inspire many orchard keepers and gardeners to rent hives from a local apiary! Happily, you don't need to go that far. Just plant bee-friendly flowers and they will soon be abuzz. If you are a beekeeper yourself, be aware that herbal honey has a more robust flavor than clover or orchard honeys—dark, nutty sage honey is a specialty item, as are some other herbal honeys.

If you are allergic to bee stings, you can protect yourself by planting a small bee garden in the farthest corner of your yard. Then fill the rest of your space with plants that bees don't like. The bees will tend to stay near their favorite plants and avoid areas you frequent.

Bees need flowers from which to gather nectar. They like flowers in shades of blue, purple, and yellow. Avoid anything described as "double," which means the flowers have extra petals at the expense of pollen. Good bee flowers have flat heads or short tubes, or long, wide tubes that these insects can crawl inside. Strong fragrances, particularly lemon, also help. Bees especially need spring-blooming flowers after the long hungry winter, but they also need a steady supply of nectar through summer into early fall.

Herbs for Attracting Bees: agrimony, angelica, apple tree, basil, bergamot, blackthorn, blueberry, borage, catnip, cherry tree, chicory, chives, clover, comfrey, cranberry, crocus, currant, daisy, dandelion, dusty miller, flax, foxglove, gooseberry, hollyhock, horehound, hyssop, lavender, lemon balm, lungwort, mallow, marjoram, meadowsweet, mint, monkshood, motherwort, mullein, mustard, oregano, raspberry, rose, rosemary, rue, sage, savory, southernwood, strawberry, sunflower, thyme, valerian, willow, winter heliotrope, wormwood, yarrow.

For the Birds

Birds in the garden provide song, motion, and sometimes color. Their droppings enrich the soil. Some, like hummingbirds, are pollinators. Others eat seeds or fruit, thus helping spread seeds around. Many birds also eat insect pests that could damage plants. It's also fun to watch them build nests and raise their families.

All birds need food and shelter. Those nesting in your area also need nesting sites and materials. Bushy herbs like rose, or trellis-climbing herbs like morning glory, can offer shelter and nesting sites. Herbs like broom, straw, and thistle are good for nesting material.

Hummingbirds are the crown jewels of a wildlife garden. Unless you live in a semitropical or tropical climate, you'll only see hummingbirds in summer or early fall. They especially need nectar in the fall when they migrate. Hummingbirds prefer long, tube-shaped flowers in "warm" shades of red, orange, and hot pink. They also appreciate flowers that have no "landing zone"—this cuts down competition from bees because hummingbirds can hover. Plant in layers for vertical interest; a hummingbird garden looks great climbing up a wall or trellis. Big patches of the same color are easier to see from the air.

Herbs for Attracting Hummingbirds: bergamot, columbine, foxglove, hibiscus, hollyhock, honeysuckle, lemon tree, morning glory, nasturtium, orange tree, pineapple sage, red verbena, yucca.

Fruit-eating birds may stay year-round if they supplement their diet with other foods, but exclusive fruit-eaters usually winter in warm climates. Winter-persistent fruits are especially valuable. Many birds enjoy fruit as an occasional treat. Fruit attracts such birds as cardinals, jays, orioles, robins, tanagers, warblers, and waxwings. They prefer red fruits, but will accept other colors. Blue, black, or white fruits may be advertised with red stems or leaves. If you grow fruit for yourself, and you find it frustrating to have the birds eat all of it, try giving them a fruit patch of their own—then they'll be less inclined to press through whatever deterrents you set over your patch. Many fruits have medicinal or magical uses; some, like raspberry, have other useful parts such as the leaves.

Herbs for Attracting Fruit-Eaters: apple, bayberry, bearberry, blackberry, blueberry, cherry, crampbark, cranberry, currant, dogwood, elderberry, fig, gooseberry, grape, hawthorn, holly, honeysuckle, huckleberry, juniper, mulberry, orange, pawpaw, persimmon, raspberry, rose, rowan, sassafras, strawberry.

Seed-eating birds often stay through winter if they find enough food and shelter. Make sure you offer seeds year-round on plants or in feeders. Common seed-eaters include blackbirds, buntings, cardinals, doves, finches, grosbeaks, jays, siskins, sparrows, and towhees. Small birds like finches prefer tiny seeds such as echinacea or thistle. Larger birds like cardinals prefer meaty seeds such as sunflower. These same plants tend to attract seed-loving mammals such as squirrels and chipmunks.

Herbs for Attracting Seed-Eaters: amaranth, calendula, corn, dusty miller, echinacea, jasmine, Job's-tears, sunflower, pine, poppy, thistle, verbena, wheat.

Butterflies Are Free

Butterflies are the most colorful garden inhabitants. As pollinators, they help maintain self-seeding gardens of herbs and wildflowers. Butterflies need two kinds of plants: nectar-bearing flowers for the adults and leafy plants for the caterpillars. Each species has one or more specific plants that their larvae eat, and favorite flowers as well. If you find nibbled leaves unsightly, just hide the caterpillar plants among the showy flowering plants.

In general, butterflies like broad, flat flowerheads with single open-faced flowers or panicles of many tiny florets. They enjoy flowers with a central disc, like daisies. They will also feed from tubular flowers that are not too deep for their tongues to reach the nectar. Butterflies need a place to rest while feeding. Strong fragrances help them find flowers. Bright, intense colors attract them more than pastels. Reddish-purple, pink, and yellow seem to be favorites.

Butterflies appreciate sheltered areas for resting or hibernating too. A key factor for them is heat; they need to warm up before they can fly. So make sure your butterfly garden gets six to eight hours of direct sunlight every day. You might also want to set out several flat black stones for butterflies to bask on.

Herbs for Attracting Butterflies: alfalfa, angelica, anise, applemint, basil, bearberry, bergamot, bistort, blackberry, boneset, buckwheat, butterfly mint, catmint, chamomile, cherry tree, chicory, chives, clover, daisy, dandelion, echinacea, edible chrysanthemum, elderberry, elecampane, garlic chives, gay-feather, golden currant, hollyhock, hyssop, lavender, lemon balm, mallow, manzanita, marigold, marjoram, mint, mistletoe, nasturtium, oregano, passionflower, plum tree, red salvia, rose, rosemary, smallage, strawberry, sunflower, thistle, thyme, valerian, verbena, violet, winter cress, winter savory, yarrow.

Herbs for Attracting Caterpillars: anise, bearberry, black cherry tree, black cohosh, blueberry, borage, buckwheat, caraway, carrot, corn, daisy, dill, fennel, foxglove, hollyhock, hops, licorice, lovage, mallow, meadowsweet, mistletoe, nannyberry, nasturtium, nettle, orange tree, parsley, passionflower, pawpaw, persimmon, rue, Russian tarragon, sassafras, senna, sunflower, thistle, verbena, violet, willow, witch hazel, woolly grass, wormwood.

Waterworks

If there is only one thing you can do to attract wildlife to your garden, this is it. Always provide water, preferably in multiple ways. A small fountain or dripper helps animals find the source. Most birds seek out shallow water and will be happy with a birdbath or the margin of a pool. Hummingbirds, however, prefer a mister that sprays fine droplets into the air. Butterflies, bees, and most other insects cannot tolerate deep water—which means anything over about a quarter-inch! They drink by "puddling," sipping from moist sand or mud. Provide an actual puddle or a pond with a beach of sand or clay. For a more decorative approach, fill a birdbath with a mixture of sand, soil, a little wood ash, and a pinch of mineral salt. Keep it moist and butterflies will flock to it.

By providing water, you can attract wildlife that won't appear otherwise. Even a tiny pond, properly landscaped with animals in mind, can attract frogs, toads, salamanders, and dragonflies. Keep a few fish to gobble mosquito larvae. Water birds such as ducks or herons may stop by for a visit. Mammals like squirrels, rabbits, chipmunks, and even foxes will appreciate a pond too. Any wetland habitat will do; the more natural, the better.

Water features in the garden also let you grow new and different herbs. Some herbs like damp marshy soil, while others prefer to be submerged in a few inches or feet of water. Consider a bog garden, or a pool with several depth levels. Best of all, if you have the room, is to pipe the water from a pond through a bog garden, thus providing a natural filter. Where space is tight, even a half barrel has room for a sweet flag or water hyacinth and a couple of goldfish.

Herbs for Bog Gardens: angelica, arnica, arrow arum, basil, bog myrtle, bog violet, cattail, blue flag, blueberry, bunchberry, butterbur, coltsfoot, columbine, comfrey, crampbark, dogwood, edible chrysanthemum, elderberry, elecampane, fern, flax, gayfeather, honeysuckle, horsetail, houttuynia, Job's-tears, Labrador tea, lovage, marsh marigold, rhubarb, marsh mallow, rose mallow, smallage, sweet flag, sweet woodruff, thyme, valerian, Vietnamese cilantro, willow, winter heliotrope, winterberry, witch hazel, woolly grass.

Herbs for Shallow Water: arrowhead, calamus, cattail, coltsfoot, cranberry, four-leaf water clover, lemongrass, rice, papyrus, pennyroyal, water mint, water spinach, yerba manta.

Herbs for Deeper Water: bog bean, fragrant water lily, giant water lily, lotus, water chestnut, water cress, water hyacinth.

Magic in the Garden

Every herb has its own powers and associations. These span the culinary, craft, medicinal, and magical fields. When you want to make a garden appeal to certain creatures, you can take advantage of the associations. Herbs of the element air relate to flying insects and birds; for mammals, earth is better. Including water and fire herbs will bring balance. There are herbs for attraction and protection too, and all kinds of other things to make your sanctuary a safe and healthy place.

Herbs for Magical Appeal: apple tree (invitation), basil (protection, fire), borage (happiness), buckwheat (growth, earth), chamomile (calming, water), clover (cheer, air), coltsfoot (peace), dandelion (wishes, calling spirits, air), dill (dispel negativity), honeysuckle (protection, attraction), hyssop (consecration), lavender (awareness, air), lemon tree (attraction), lovage (attraction), mint (protection), parsley (purification, communion with Mother Earth), peppermint (get things started, water), rose (luck, healing, water), sage (longevity, purification, earth), sunflower (health), thyme (health, purification, positive energy), wormwood (protection, fire), yarrow (healing, attraction).

Putting the Pieces Together

In designing an effective wildlife garden, you must consider several things:

How much space do you have? You can attract birds and butterflies with a couple of potted herbs and a basin of water on a balcony if that's all the room you have. You could plant several modest flowering islands around an average-sized yard to attract different creatures. You could create a sanctuary spread across a sizable meadow or stretch of forest.

What is your local habitat? Forest, grassland, riverbottom, coastal, mountainous, desert? Local wildlife will more quickly gravitate to sanctuary plantings that mimic the original natural environment. Exotic arrangements, like an alpine rock garden at sea level, have less appeal. (The exception is aquatic gardens in the desert, which are a big wildlife magnet—but those can burden the local water supply, so landscape responsibly.) Also consider rainfall, soil type, lighting, and other aspects that affect what herbs will grow best in your area.

What kind of wildlife do you most want to attract? Bees and butterflies get along fine, but birds will eat insects—while foxes and other small predators will eat birds. If you want to attract several types of wildlife, you may need to plant separate areas for each, and provide extra cover.

Those broad parameters should give you an idea of your garden's structure. For best effect, plant in layers. If you're planting against a wall or other backdrop, put the tallest herbs in back, then medium ones, then short or creeping ones in front. In freestanding gardens, you can "aim" them toward a focal point by using the same pattern or take advantage of the walk-around effect by planting the tallest herbs in the center and the shorter ones all around the edges. Such arrangements provide easy access to food plants and a clear view of potential predators. They also give you a good view of your visitors!

However, critters also need shelter. If you can provide a heap of leaf litter, a brush pile, or a rotten log, terrific. Some herbs are especially good for cover. Sage forms dense, woody clumps about knee-high. All brambles (raspberries, etc.) make great cover. Plant clusters of woody "herbs"—the trees and bushes with herbal applications. Vines like grape, climbing rose, or morning glory can be trained over a trellis. Look for ways to turn eye-sores into assets, such as planting prostrate rosemary or creeping thyme in a dead stump.

Finally, consider with care the balance between the wild and the tame. A patch of herbs left entirely to its own devices is rarely attractive to people or wildlife; not only does it get weedy, but the more vigorous plants can choke out the rest. Bees and butter-flies especially like having a diversity of flowers to choose from; birds appreciate a selection of fruits and seeds. So it pays to create a partly natural, partly managed environment. A good plan typically puts the wildest areas at the edge of the lot, with the lawn and other people-heavy places toward the center. Natural gardeners speak of "editing" a sanctuary, which means removing unwelcome exotics or other invasive plants, and making sure the vigorous growers don't outpace the shy herbs. Like really good makeup, it enhances subtly, creating a tousled charm.

Recommended Resources

Apple, Heather. "Herb Gardening for Bees." *Alternative Nature Online Herbal*, 1996, 1998. http://altnature.com/library/herb.htm

Bremness, Lesley. *Herbs: The Visual Guide to More Than 700 Plant Species From Around the World.* DK Publishing, 1994.

Buchanan, Carol. *The Wildlife Sanctuary Garden.* Ten Speed Press, 1999.

Cunningham, Scott. *Cunningham's Encyclopedia of Magical Herbs.* Llewellyn Publications, 1991.

Dugan, Ellen. *Garden Witchery: Magick from the Ground Up.* Llewellyn Publications, 2003.

Evans, Erv. *Attracting Butterflies.* North Carolina State University, 2002-2004. http://www.ces.ncsu.edu/depts/hort/consumer/factsheets/butterflies/butterfly_index.html

Harper, Peter, et al. *The Natural Garden Book: A Holistic Approach to Gardening.* Fireside Books, 1994.

Hessayon, D.G. *The Fruit Expert.* Expert Books, 1990, 1993.

Kress, Stephen W. *The Bird Garden: A Comprehensive Guide to Attracting Birds to Your Backyard Throughout the Year.* Dorling Kindersley, 1995.

Long, Jim. "These Herbs Are All Wet." *The Herb Companion,* 2005. http://www.herbcompanion.com/articles/12_01_05-theseherbs

Schneck, Marcus. *Creating a Butterfly Garden: A Guide to Attracting and Identifying Butterfly Visitors.* Fireside Books, 1993.

———*Your Backyard Wildlife Year: How to Attract Birds, Butterflies, and Other Animals Every Month of the Year.* Rodale Books, 1996.

Shrubs and Trees for the Herb Garden

≈ by James Kambos ≈

When planning an herb garden, many people ignore two crucial features—shrubs and trees. It's easy to understand why. When looking for inspiration, most of us turn to garden magazines which contain lush photographs of beautifully maintained gardens filled with clouds of Russian sage in bloom or thyme creeping across a stone path. Shrubs and trees, unfortunately, are frequently used as little more than backdrop. But herb gardeners shouldn't forget to include the largest members of the herb kingdom in their garden plan. Not only are many shrubs and trees classified as herbs, but they add structure and form to the herb garden.

There are many reasons to add shrubs and trees to the landscape as

you plan your herb garden. To begin with, if you plan ahead, shrubs and trees can add privacy and can often take the place of fences. They can screen unsightly views and reduce street noise. You can also use shrubs and trees as focal points or to create "rooms" within your herb garden.

Above all, shrubs and trees bring year-round beauty to the herb garden. Many produce beautiful flowers while others have interesting foliage and form. Some also develop fruits and berries, which are important food sources for birds and other wildlife. Best of all, during the quiet months of winter, while smaller perennial herbs die back, herbal shrubs and trees add visual interest.

Selecting Shrubs and Trees for Your Garden

To help guide you in selecting the proper shrubs and trees, I've compiled the following list of shrubs and trees appropriate for an herb garden. All the plants listed are classified as herbs and I have personally found most of these shrubs and trees to be tough, reliable performers in my Zone 6 herb garden.

For each shrub and tree I've included information on their mature size and why they are useful in the herb border. Where possible, I've included some history and herbal lore. Any medicinal information provided is for personal enrichment only. Many of the following shrubs and trees are quite toxic and should be used solely for ornamental purposes.

This is certainly not a complete list of shrubs and trees, but the plants I've listed are easy to find at most garden centers. Including only a few of these shrubs and trees in your herb garden will provide you with years of carefree beauty.

Shrubs

Let's begin by taking a look at shrubs suitable for the herb garden. These shrubs are truly the foundation of any well-planned herb garden and, in some instances, can take the place of a small tree.

Boxwood

This evergreen is one of the most popular shrubs used in herb gardens. It is suitable for sun or shade and was once used to treat high fevers; however, it is highly toxic and can be fatal if ingested. Boxwood usually grows to two feet high and may be used to define certain areas of the herb garden. They are easy to prune to any shape. To create a unique look, try planting small ornamental grasses or variegated liriope in front of boxwood for a contrast of color and texture. In the home, it has many decorative uses; its stems combine beautifully with other herbs for holiday accents.

Daphne

This family of shrubs is noted for striking evergreen to semi-evergreen foliage, which on certain varieties can be variegated. Most daphnes grow three to five feet high and wide; they prefer light shade and rich, well-drained soil. Their fragrant flowers are white or pink and will perfume your herb garden from spring to early summer. Daphne was once used for medicinal purposes ranging from rheumatism to skin disorders, but the plant is poisonous. These smaller shrubs are ideal for restricted spaces. Varieties such as 'Carol Mackie' and 'Somerset' are hardy, easy-to-grow selections for the home gardener to try.

Hydrangea

Long ago, the Indians of North America relied on the roots of wild hydrangea to treat many forms of bladder disorders. Modern science has proved them correct. Today, however, the herb gardener can use hydrangeas to add great beauty to the herb border. They flower, have beautiful foliage, and grow under a wide range of light conditions. The only problem is deciding which cultivars you want to grow. There are roughly twenty varieties from which to choose.

The one I selected is *Hydrangea arborescens*, 'Annabelle,' which is closely related to the wild form and attains a height and width of four feet. The large white flower heads bloom in June and mature to pale green. When my garden was selected for a garden tour, 'Annabelle' was a big hit. It blooms profusely in part-sun to full shade. Some hydrangeas bloom better when cut back; check with your local garden center to see if the variety you choose needs this. And depending on your soil type, some hydrangeas may bloom with pink or blue flowers.

Lespedeza

Pronounced (less pee DEE zuh): This little-known, but very easy-to-grow, shrub is a member of the pea family. In grandma's day, lespedezas were common in many gardens and are now slowly regaining popularity. The shrubs have an attractive arching growth habit; foliage is oval and soft-green. In late summer, when few shrubs bloom, lespedezas are covered with white or rose-pink flowers similar in shape to sweet peas. They grow with equal vigor in sun or shade, and reach four to six feet in height/width. Although they aren't fussy about soil, cut them to the ground in early spring to achieve best bloom. A specimen known as Japan clover was once raised in the south and was used as a fertilizer.

Lilac

Cherished for their fragrant clusters of spring-blooming flowers, lilacs are a favorite among herbal shrubs. This relative of the olive was originally planted near the home to repel evil. In the herb garden, the lilac can grow from five to twenty feet high, which makes a dramatic sight planted as a specimen, or in a group. The flowers can be white, pink, yellow, or the beloved light purple. Smaller varieties include 'Marie Frances' (pink), 'Little Boy Blue' (light blue), and 'Miss Kim' (light lavender). These lilacs grow to about six feet in height.

Mahonia

Commonly called the Oregon holly grape, mahonia has a long history as an important herb. Ingredients in the roots were once used to treat psoriasis and the leaves were used for dyes. Unfortunately, this tough evergreen shrub has been ignored by herbalists as a landscape plant. The leaves are thick, glossy, and dark green. It blooms in early spring with sweetly fragrant yellow flowers and produces blue fruits in the summer. Easy to grow in dry, shady locations, it matures to about four to six feet high and wide. This attractive shrub deserves more attention.

Sambucus

Also known as elderberry, sambucus is quickly becoming a popular shrub in the herb garden. Delicate feathery foliage ranging from gold to black, lemon-scented white or pink flowers, and clusters of berries give this shrub great appeal throughout the growing season. The flower umbels have been used to make elderflower wine and a nonalcoholic syrup. Medicinally, elderflowers were added to herbal teas to treat the flu. The raw berries have a laxative effect, but when they are cooked to make jams, this property is eliminated. The berries are also a popular food for many songbirds. There are several sambucus which have ornamental value. They include: 'Sutherland Gold' (with yellow foliage), 'Black Beauty' (with deep burgundy foliage), and 'Madonna' (a variegated form with gold margins on the leaves). Sambucus grow eight to ten feet high and wide. Many gardeners cut these shrubs back to a foot from the ground in the winter. This shouldn't hurt their vigorous growth, and keeps their size in check.

Viburnum

Spring flowers in white or pink, lush summer foliage, and dramatic blue or red berries in winter make the viburnum family of shrubs a great choice for any herb garden. Ranging in height from five to ten feet, viburnum can be used as shrubs or small trees in the landscape. The raw berries are poisonous, but when cooked they are said to become edible and years ago were made into jams. The bark is also toxic, though it was once used in very small amounts to induce labor. Herbalists today can rely on these tough hardy shrubs to add beauty to the herb garden. One popular hybrid is 'Mohawk.' 'Mohawk' is one of the most fragrant shrubs you can plant. The pale pink flowers will perfume an entire garden with a clovelike scent in early spring. It remains compact and rounded in habit, reaching seven feet high and wide. A viburnum I've enjoyed in my herb garden is 'Compactum.' The flat, white flower heads are followed in late summer by clusters of red berries. And it is a beautiful sight on a snowy winter day to see cardinals helping themselves to this banquet as snowflakes swirl around outside my window. 'Compactum,' as the name suggests, is good for a small garden and seldom grows more than five feet high. There are many more viburnum species available. Contact a nursery or consult garden catalogs to see which viburnum would best fit your herb garden.

Trees for the Herb Garden

Trees add vertical interest to the herb garden. They can also add beauty with their flowers, foliage, autumn color, bark, and overall shape. Trees look splendid when planted in the center of an herb bed as a focal point. The trees listed below have been selected because they remain small and won't overwhelm a small garden.

Cherry (Malus)

Spring-flowering cherry trees are ideal additions to the herb garden. They offer spectacular floral displays, hardiness, and interesting bark, all on small trees that seldom grow above thirty feet. There are several cultivars to choose from. Two favorites that I've grown are 'Kwanzan Flowering Cherry' and 'Snowcloud.' The Kwanzan cherry grows to about twenty-five feet and has an attractive vase shape. The pink flowers that smother the tree in April are a highlight of my garden during the spring. 'Kwanzan' doesn't seem to be bothered by wind, ice, or snow. They are rugged and long-lived. Cherry 'Snowcloud,' on the other hand, is a lovely miniature which grows to only six to eight feet. Its blooms are pure white and the tree has a rounded shape. For further interest, in late autumn the foliage turns brilliant orange. 'Snowcloud' is a beautiful, unique tree for even the smallest garden.

Crabapple (*Malus*)

One of the pleasures of working in my herb garden in early spring is being surrounded by the sweet scent of the flowering crabapple trees I planted years ago. The new varieties available today are mostly pest and disease resistant. Flowering in shades of white to deepest pink, crabapples bring a casual charm to the herb border. And many cultivars produce gold or red fruits that persist well into early winter, which many birds enjoy. Some varieties to consider are 'Leprechaun,' a small tree, eight feet tall/wide. Flowers are white and fruits are bright red. 'Coralburst' reaches heights of twelve to fifteen feet and blooms with coral-pink flowers. It is very cold hardy. And don't forget the old-time favorite, 'Royalty.' Somewhat hard to find today, 'Royalty' grows to about twenty feet, has leaves tinged with bronze, and produces the traditional yellow-green crabapple fruits popular years ago.

Dogwood (*Cornus*)

This is one of America's favorite native trees. In spring, the dogwood stars the landscape with white or pink flowers. In late summer, the oval berries turn bright red; autumn turns the leaves a beautiful scarlet. Most dogwoods are slow growing and seldom exceed twenty-five feet high. For a beautiful combination in the herb garden, plant blue-flowering trailing myrtle (vinca) around the base of a white-blooming dogwood. They usually bloom at the same time and make a stunning combination. Ask a local garden center to help you select the proper dogwood variety for your region.

Hawthorn (*Crataegus*)

If you have room for only one tree in your herb garden, let it be the hawthorn. Few shrubs or trees have such a distinguished history as a healing herb. There was a time it was once used to treat the symptoms of diarrhea. But modern science has recognized the hawthorn as a valuable source of remedies used to treat various heart disorders. Both the flowers and fruit (haws) have been found to contain medicinal properties which can aid in the treatment of circulation, angina, and irregular heartbeat. The hawthorn is not only a beneficial herb, it is also a lovely ornamental. Most hawthorns grow eighteen to twenty-five feet high. Since they bloom in late spring, hawthorns help extend the season for flowering trees. Their delicate white flowers are followed by small fruits called haws. The haws turn a rich burgundy in fall. The branches of most hawthorns have long straight thorns. However, there is a newer introduction called 'Ohio Pioneer,' which is thornless, but does produce attractive haws. Hawthorns grow easily in most soils. They are trees of beauty, and should be a welcome addition to any herb garden.

Shrubs and trees form the foundation of the herb garden. They create a sense of permanence, and as they mature, give the herb garden an established appearance. Their floral, fruit, and foliage displays announce the changing seasons. And whether you plant shrubs and trees in your herb garden for beauty, or for their herbal properties, you'll be making an investment in your landscape which will be enjoyed for generations.

Mail Order Sources

Klehm's Song Sparrow Farm and Nursery/13101 East Rye Road/Avalon, WI 53505. Phone: 1-800-553-3715. www.songsparrow.com

Rare Find Nursery/ 957 Patterson Road/Jackson, NJ 08527. Phone: 1-732-833-0613. www.rarefindnursery.com

Wayside Gardens/ 1 Garden Lane/Hodges, SC 29695. Phone: 1-800-845-1124. www.waysidegardens.com

Making Peace with Nettles

⊰ by Dorothy Kovach ⊱

By the time you see nettles, it's usually too late—some part of your body is already tingling. *Urtica dioca*, better known as stinging nettles, is true to its name. Even the tiniest sprout can leave a violent sting when it touches skin. When brushed, they will send an electronic charge that rips through one's system.

This can be quite a jolt! Don't let the heart-shaped leaves fool you—it is their jagged edges that tell the true tale. Hidden throughout its leaves are hairy spines, which when touched release an acidic substance that is responsible for that sudden burning sensation. One thing is certain, stinging nettles demand respect! Just barely touching them can bring burning welts on the part of your body that dared to come too close. You might say that stinging nettles have a passion for revenge. Perhaps they want to get back at us for all our weeding and rearranging.

Like its ruler Mars, it is not only sneaky, but it is also a competitive plant. When found in open fields, it will spread along the ground, never getting much higher than your knee, but when it encounters a bush, as if rising to the occasion, it will climb as high as the nearby shrub. Nettles thrive in rich loam that is high in nitrogen, and are often found growing in swales, near stream beds in sandy soil. Deep green in color, it seems to hide—intertwining itself in other plants, so as to surprise you. Because of its sharp sting, most gardeners try to eradicate it. This can be tough because it spreads by both seed and underground root. If folks knew that this subtle little plant is one of the most valuable in the plant kingdom, they might want to keep it around.

Well Traveled, Well Used

Nettles are found throughout the world. They were said to have originally come to England via ancient Roman soldiers. From there, the English are said to have brought them to America. Roman soldiers believed that nettles protected them from the intolerable climate of England. Preferring welts to being cold, they would rub the leaves on their hands and legs to keep warm. The practice of flogging for punishment reportedly originated from a desire to warm the body in the winter. The ancients believed that striking the body with nettles could increase circulation, thereby warming the body and protecting against arthritis and rheumatism. This might not be as far-fetched as it seems.

Today, doctors are beginning to find that the ancients might have been on to something. The highly respected British journal of medicine, *The Lancet*, reported that Dr. Colin Randal of Plymouth University applied nettles to the damaged joints of twenty-seven arthritis patients, who had never tried nettles before, for one week. They then applied a sting-free white nettle for a week as a placebo. Those tested reported a much lower level of pain and disability after the stinging nettle treatment. Other than the sting, they found no other appreciable side effects. More importantly, they also found that their subjects were less reliant on their traditional medications. Given the potentially deadly side effects of some arthritis medications, that burning sensation might be a small price to pay. And in light of the prices we are now paying for energy, using nettles to keep warm may come back in vogue!

Nettles are astringent in nature and were often used by the ancients to help slow bleeding. A small piece of paper towel soaked in nettle juice placed inside the nostril will often help a severe nosebleed. It has also been used to help stop internal bleeding when the cause was not known. Rich in vitamins and minerals including iron, copper, silicon, and manganese, nettles may promote general health. Nettles are considered a terrific blood purifier, akin to garlic in the ability to clean toxins from the blood and help bring down cholesterol levels. A mild diuretic, nettles should not be overlooked by the middle-aged male. It is no secret that by age fifty, one out of every two men will have had an enlarged prostate gland, which can cause havoc to both a man's sleep and his relationships. And by age eighty, the number of men with prostate problems jumps up to 80 percent. But the ancients used stinging nettle roots as a tonic to shrink an enlarged prostate gland.

And as they say in commercials, "That is not all!" May flowers are a joy to many, but to the allergy sufferer, spring is a time of endless torment that brings red itchy eyes and runny noses, not to mention the potentially life-threatening effects of asthma. Recognizing their healing properties, our forebears kept nettles, which contain natural histamines, on hand to clear the sinuses and chest of congestion. When ingested orally, nettles reportedly help build up a tolerance to the irritating effects of airborne pollen. This is important if you smoke or ever used to smoke. Nettles and deep breathing have done wonders to heal damaged lungs. A tea made with nettles taken twice daily at the outset of spring will do wonders to keep allergies at bay.

Gather and Enjoy

Stinging nettle leaves should be gathered on a clear spring morning after the dew has dried, when its energy is at its highest, and before it flowers. The root, on the other hand, is harvested at twilight on an overcast, but otherwise dry, crisp autumn day. When gathering, remember that nettles give off venom, so dress accordingly. Wear gloves, long sleeves, and pants. You will find nettles growing in rich soil, often near a pond or a stream. After picking the leaves, wrap the stems in bundles and hang them to dry. When it is time to harvest, don't forget to put those gloves back on! Nettles still pack a punch even when dry! Their ability to burn is quelled only by heat, so you will need to clean any clothes that brush against nettles in hot water.

So pay attention when harvesting your nettles. Don't make the same mistake I did—I wore wool while gathering nettles. That sweater stung so much afterward that it was rendered useless. Only heat can cool down nettles, but heat shrinks wool—a Catch-22. Since then, I always wear cotton at harvest time.

Last but not least, you can enjoy an easy recipe for nettles. Bon appetit!

Nettles Garlic Soup

1 quart nettle tops, thoroughly washed
2 cloves garlic
1½ cups beef broth or consommé
2 tablespoons butter
¼ cup flour
salt and pepper

Place ingredients in a pot and cook on the stovetop until nettles are tender. Remove from heat and strain or chop the nettles into a fine composition. Return mixture to the stove and bring to a boil, then simmer. While simmering, add 2 tablespoons butter and slowly add about ¼ cup of flour, which must be stirred all the time or it can go lumpy. Add salt and pepper to taste. Serve.

Cultivating Our Connection to Cacti

❧ by Tammy Sullivan ❧

There is no other plant family that encompasses such a large variety as cacti. From beautiful blooms and delicious taste to mind-altering shamanic potions, the cacti family has a long and storied history.

Cactus was so important to the Aztec people that they named the very heart of their kingdom Tenochtitlan, which means "home of the cactus people" or "cactus on a stone." The area was chosen for settlement based on the vision of an eagle perched atop a cactus. The leaders took this as a sign from their gods that they had reached their promised land. Today that area is Mexico City.

Cacti are native to the Americas, but some species are known across the globe. Here, we focus on the three most recognized: saguaro, peyote, and prickly pear. Believed to be thirty million to forty million years old, cacti are relative newcomers in the plant world. But, the legends and lore that surround these fabulous plants are unparalleled. Consider this strange, but true, event involving a man and a saguaro cactus. Apparently, the man shot a hole through a giant saguaro and the cactus retaliated years later by falling over on the man and killing him. Needless to say, I would be very careful not to wound or somehow offend the spirit of the saguaro.

The spirit of the saguaro also has warmer connotations. Legend has it that a beautiful young girl once sank into loose sand. She raised her arms up, reaching for help, as she sank. Sadly, she died. From that exact spot, the first saguaro emerged—also with its arms lifted skyward. Indeed, many saguaros seem to have an eerie resemblance to humans. In fact, folklore tells another tale of the cardon cactus (a very large saguaro relative) that walks the desert at night. People were said to wake and find the huge cactus had moved to an entirely new spot.

Saguaro

The saguaro, or *Carnegiea gigantean*, is best known for its magnificent size. The body can grow up to two feet in diameter and up to fifty feet tall. Consisting of more than 90 percent water, they frequently weigh in at eight tons or more. Each spine measures two inches.

A slow grower, saguaros typically grow about one inch a year, but they live for hundreds of years. The saguaro is a protected plant due to the difficulty in propagation and its slow growth. Thankfully, it is a hardy plant that can withstand frost. It will normally produce flowers and fruit after thirty years, but will not develop arms until seventy-five to eighty years of age.

The saguaro is a night bloomer with flowers three inches or larger in width. The blossoms are most often pure white, but can be yellow tinted. These beautiful and fragrant flowers have been adopted as the official state flower of Arizona.

In order to successfully set fruit, the saguaro cactus requires cross-pollination, usually accomplished by the whitewing dove or the lesser nose bat. The resulting edible fruit bears red pulp, looking and tasting like a three-inch watermelon.

Saguaro fruits are harvested by knocking the fruit from the arms of the cactus with a long stick called a kuipad. Careful collection is required because the fruit will often split while on the plant. When this happens, it is left for wildlife. With the yield suitable for human consumption, Native Americans frequently use the fruit to make special jelly and wine. The abundant small black seeds are usually dried and ground into flour.

Among some tribes, the collection of the saguaro fruits is a ritual. Before collection can proceed, the cactus and the person harvesting must be blessed. A single fruit is opened and rubbed on the chest (over the heart) of the harvester as they ask for clarity and pure intentions. The fruit comes into season just as all other food and water sources have dwindled away. As a result, many tribes depended upon it for survival.

The husks of the open fruit are said to bring rain and are often left on the ground to encourage this. Entire festivals are created around this tradition. Saguaro wine is made and consumed at the festival with the belief that as the body becomes saturated with wine, the clouds become saturated with water. Traditional dances are performed and the participants sing to the clouds in hopes of bringing plenty of wet weather.

The saguaro is also synonymous with new beginnings, as the fruit harvest marked the New Year for many southwestern tribes. For many, a tribal tradition is for new mothers to be fed gruel from the saguaro fruit, which is said to help the mother's milk flow more easily. The saguaro's inedible woody ribs were used to start fires and help build fences, houses, and furniture.

The Gila monster and gilded flicker hollow out places in saguaro trunks to make a home. These creatures' nests formed the saguaro into perfect vessels, which were then used by the Native American tribes for decades. These hollowed-out containers are called "desert boots."

The saguaro is treated with the highest respect. The Native Americans held them to be human relatives and a member of the tribe. To harm a saguaro was to harm one of your own.

Peyote

The peyote cactus is best known for its mind-expanding, hallucinogenic uses. As such, it has been used as a religious sacrament for more than ten thousand years. It is featured prominently in the works of Carlos Castaneda.

Peyote is a small, spineless, low-growing plant. Generally growing about one inch tall, the peyote crown usually measures about four inches across, with flowers budding from the crown's center, and sports a hairlike tuft. The crowns, also called buttons, are harvested by slicing them from the roots and drying them in the sun. The roots will then grow new buttons.

Harvesting peyote for sacramental use requires that certain ceremonies be followed by many tribes. A purification ritual and a confessional-type ritual are prerequisites. The procession continues with the participants being introduced to the "clashing of the clouds" and the "opening of the clouds," both being symbolic gates in the astral. Only after passing through these gates may peyote be collected and consumed, thus ensuring a spiritual experience. Singing and dancing take place all night as the participants pray. The area is constantly smudged with tobacco, sage, and cedar because peyote is known to have a foul smell and unpleasant taste.

To the Aztecs, consuming peyote was viewed the same as praying, allowing them to experience the Great Spirit within themselves, which was considered a gift as well as their right. They prepared for the peyote ritual very carefully, routinely undergoing a multiday fast to cleanse themselves in preparation for the sacrament. One of the first effects felt after consuming peyote is nausea, which was seen as further purging of the body to make way for the Great Spirit.

Peyote is also believed to be a very protective plant. The

ancient Aztecs saw the plant as the flesh of a god, specifically a warrior chief known as Peyotl. Peyote was divided into two types, a blue-green variety called the peyote of the god and a yellow-green variety called the peyote of the goddess. They are actually the same plant, but the peyote of the goddess is harvested earlier so the taste is not as bitter and the effects are not as strong.

Few doubt the importance of peyote to Native American tribes as a religious sacrament, but how often do we hear about its use as an antibiotic cream? Or as a flu treatment? Peyote was also an important medicine for arthritis and snake bites, and a cure for an overdose of another ethnogenic plant—the datura.

Prickly Pear

The prickly pear cactus (one of over 360 species in the Opuntia genus) boasts beautiful blooms, edible leaves, magical vibrations, and medicinal benefits. Both a fruit and a vegetable, it has been cultivated and consumed for centuries and is one of the world's most useful plants. But, don't let the cutesy folk names of bunny-ears or beaver-tails fool you—the spikes are sharp!

Opuntia, the oldest cultivated crop in Mexico, has a historical pedigree that extends back to the Aztec empire. Aztec legend states that animals taught humans about the prickly pear. People would watch and see the livestock graze on the plant and soon followed suit, using opuntia as water in times of drought and making a special fermented drink from the fruit for celebrations. Only recently has this plant been introduced to commercial cultivation. It is touted as having great economic potential as a fruit crop.

A hardy evergreen perennial known to reach heights of several feet, the prickly pear has a very interesting growth pattern. A segmented plant, its central stem consists of pads linked together in a chainlike fashion. The prickly pear usually enjoys a life span of around twenty years, becoming a part of the habitat.

Wrens are known to make nests in the prickly pear. Grazing animals also enjoy dining on the plant and it is often used as food for livestock. In parts of Mexico where droughts are extended, the opuntia is the only plant that can withstand the rugged conditions. Durable and fast-growing, it is frequently used in Mexico as hedging among its multiple uses around the home.

Prickly pear leaves are prepared for cooking by trimming and removing the spikes. This must be done carefully, as the prickly pear has two types of spikes. Besides the large, visible spikes, it also has tiny, hairlike spikes called glochids. Removing glochids from the skin can prove to be painful, if not impossible. The preferred method is to burn them off. The glochids tend to shrink when singed, much like human hair, but the plant's flesh is remarkably fire resistant. A spikeless species of prickly pear, the *Opuntia ficus-indica*, is extensively used for culinary purposes.

The prepared cactus pads, called nopales, are frequently available in grocery markets. Nopales are harvested throughout the year because the young, tender growth is the best for culinary purposes. They can be eaten raw, tossed in a salad or sauce, boiled in soup, fried, or prepared any way you like. They are often cooked in the same manner as green beans. When raw, a nopale has a quality reminiscent of okra and feels a bit slippery in the mouth, but the taste will make up for it. When you dice a nopale, it is then referred to as nopalito. Regardless of preparation method, nopales are extremely low in calories, loaded with vitamins and minerals, and have no cholesterol or saturated fat.

The fruit of the prickly pear, commonly called the "Indian Fig," is edible as well. These fruits make deliciously sweet preserves, drinks, jams, jellies, syrups, and even pickles. However, Indian Figs are most often enjoyed uncooked. Even the seeds of this plant are edible and may be ground into flour. The prickly pear fruit is usually harvested in mid-September. To locate Indian Figs in your local market, look for a fruit called "tuna."

Prickly pear blossoms range in color from red or orange to pink or yellow. After the blooms fade, the fruits begin to form. To juice the fruit (a process required for making jelly), despike it, clean it, cut it into small pieces, and crush it. Add about a cup of water to the pulp. Boil the mixture for ten minutes. Strain out the cactus pulp. To make a syrup suitable to sweeten drinks like margaritas, simply continue boiling until thickened.

The sap from the prickly pear has been used as mosquito repellent, a cure for warts, a glue, a treatment for lung problems, a way to dissolve kidney stones, and a first-aid salve (similar to aloe vera). As a mosquito repellent still used in Central Africa, its effects are said to last a whole year if applied with water.

The same nopale pads prepared for cooking were also historically used as poultices and bandages. Warmed pads placed on the body were said to shrink swollen tissues and sterilize the area.

The pads are often ground and used as a laxative, but the most surprising medical benefit of the prickly pear is its ability to treat certain forms of diabetes. While research is ongoing, Aztec lore suggests it was used as a diabetic cure until the sixteenth century and is an accepted traditional treatment in Mexico. Other medicinal uses may yet be discovered. New research indicates that prickly pear extract may prevent hangovers.

Besides culinary and medicinal uses, the prickly pear could also play a role in the garment industry. The fruit attracts an insect used in making a traditional Aztec scarlet red dye. Spanish settlers could not believe the clarity and vibrance of the colors the Aztecs wore. Since their own culture offered no such brilliant shade of red, they arranged a trade. At one point, the dye was second only to silver as a Mexican export. In fact, this dye was used on the famous red coats worn by the British army.

Australia introduced the prickly pear onto rangeland in an effort to join in on the dye trade. Before too long, more than sixty million acres were covered with prickly pear. Needless to say, this plant can be highly invasive if allowed to grow freely.

The nopales of the prickly pear grown in a home garden can be harvested up to six times a year. And the more fruit you harvest, the more fruit the plant sets. As each pad can weigh about a half pound, you can easily expect a twenty pound harvest of nopales. To keep the prickly pear healthy and growing, fertilize monthly and provide plenty of light. The prickly pear can absorb more water than most cactus, but is also fairly drought tolerant.

Legend also asserts the prickly pear cactus is magically gifted, possessing the qualities of healing, purifying, chastity, banishing, and protection. Its ruling planet is Mars and it falls under the element of fire. The spines are used to scratch symbols into candles, to fill a protection bottle, or in poppet magic. Frequently, these cacti flank the entry and guard the home. To bring a bit of cactus magic into your home, try the following recipes:

Pickled Paddles

Ingredients: Garlic cloves; fresh dill; fresh, sliced prickly pear paddles; 3 cups water; 3 cups vinegar; 6 tablespoons salt.

Drop one clove of garlic and a few sprigs of dill into each jar. Pack with sliced paddles. In a medium saucepan, combine the water, vinegar, and salt. Heat over high heat until boiling. Allow the mixture to boil until the salt is dissolved. Fill the jars with the liquid and seal. Process in a hot water bath for ten minutes.

Prickly Pear Jelly

Ingredients: 3½ cups prickly pear juice, the juice of 1 lemon, 1 package pectin, 8 cups sugar.

Combine juices and pectin in large saucepan. Heat to boiling, stirring constantly. Add sugar all at once and boil for 1 minute. Pour into hot jars and place in a water bath for 10 minutes.

Prickly Pear Fritters

Ingredients: 1 egg, sliced nopales, yellow corn meal.

Beat the egg. Dip sliced nopales in the egg. Dust with corn meal. Deep fry until golden brown. Serve with salsa.

Dessert Fritters

Prepare dessert fritters in a similar way except use the fruit, not the nopales. After frying, roll the fritter in confectioners' sugar. Serve with honey.

Container Gardening

❧ by Chandra Moira Beal ❧

Gardeners have been growing plants in containers for centuries. The practice may have begun as a way of nurturing treasured rarities or plants charged with a special religious or mystical significance. Many of the frescoes and paintings of antiquity show that the decorative value of container-grown plants has always been appreciated.

Container gardening has remained relatively unchanged over the years. We grow many of the same plants that were loved by gardeners hundreds of years ago, although the introduction of new plants from the wild and developments in cultivation mean that today we have a wider choice of plants to fill any containers we choose.

Modern gardeners are increasingly reliant on containers for growing herbs, as more of us live in towns and cities and have less room for conventional gardening. Growing herbs in containers offers great imaginative scope when working with a limited space such as a patio, roof, terrace, or balcony. Even in large and mature gardens, container gardening can offer variety and allow you to introduce plants that otherwise might not grow in the native soil. Containers also enhance areas such as a flight of steps, a doorway, a paved patio, a pergola, or a window ledge.

Container Herbs and The Elements

In cooler climates, placing your herb containers in the full sun is ideal. But when the sun really shines, containers can dry out quickly. In very hot weather, herbs may need watering several times a day. An area that gets some shade while catching the sun in summer for at least half the day is ideal. Most sun-loving plants will do well in these situations, although they tend to produce slightly more leaf growth than they would in optimum conditions. If you have a mix of sunny and shady areas, periodically changing the arrangement of your containers could be worthwhile. Many plants that like full sun will quite happily tolerate a few days in the shade.

Container-grown plants are vulnerable to wind damage because of their exposed position. Even the containers themselves can suffer damage in strong winds and topple over. For exposed positions, choose sturdy plants of short stature.

The keys to growing herbs in containers is choosing the right plant for the right place and giving it conditions for optimum growth. Container gardening is one of the easiest ways to provide growing conditions for specific plants because the growing medium can be adjusted to suit their requirements and the containers themselves can be moved. Most herbs, especially the culinary and aromatic ones, are native to the Mediterranean and grow best in warm, sunny conditions with well-drained soil.

The care and management of plants in containers is essentially the same as for plants in an open garden, but the container gardener must be more vigilant to make sure herbs get a regular supply of water. Some plants are much more tolerant of dry soils than others. Adjusting the potting compost can help meet a plant's requirements for moisture, but you need to take into account its exposure to wind and sun, which speeds up evaporation. Plants that can be grown in shaded, sheltered positions will retain moisture longer.

The number of plants competing for the water supply is also important. Water loss can be slowed down by mulch spread over the layer of soil. There are water-absorbent gels available now that can be added to soil, but if you can't water containers regularly, it is best to grow drought-resistant plants such as thyme and sage. Plants are divided into three basic categories:

Annuals are plants that complete their life cycle in a season.

Biennials are plants that flower and die the year after they're sown.

Perennials are plants that produce flowers and seeds more than one time in their lifespan.

You should plant biennial and perennial herbs in the spring and annuals at the beginning of summer, shortly after the last frost, to enjoy the longest growing season. Pinch back any flowers if you want to keep the herbs going longer and to encourage leaves to develop rather than the seeds.

Choosing a Container

A container's size, weight, and material are relevant considerations. A smaller container will hold less soil and need more frequent watering. Consider the weight of the container if you are going to move it about when it's full of soil and plants or if it's going on a balcony or rooftop. Stability can be a problem with lightweight plastic or fiberglass pots, as well as with heavy containers that have narrow bases.

The classic rounded pot shape allows you to easily remove

the plant and its root ball if you want to re-pot it or plant it in the garden. Square pots, which hold a greater volume of potting mix, are useful for plants with extensive root systems. With urns and jars, make sure that the container has a sufficiently wide planting area for your needs.

All containers should have adequate holes for drainage, because most plants will become sickly if grown in stagnant or water-logged soil. It must also be the right size for the plant. If the container is too small, the compost will dry out quickly and the nutrients will soon be exhausted. Plants in small containers quickly become root bound, but plants in an oversized pot develop root growth at the expense of top growth.

The first containers for plants were almost certainly made of terra cotta, a material that many find the most sympathetic to plants. As one of the most popular materials, there is a plethora of designs to choose from. The rich, earthy color combines well with plants and weathers gracefully so that its appearance often improves with age. Because it is porous, it quickly soaks up water, so remember to water frequently. Pots imported from the Mediterranean have a tendency to crack and flake, so if you live in a cold area make sure they are frost resistant.

To give terra cotta and stone a weathered look, you can speed up the distressing process by painting the outside with some live cultured yogurt. Place the painted pots in a shady place and, in about a month, green moss will grow over the surface. Or place the treated pots in the sun and the salts in the clay will leach out, forming a white patina.

Wood is attractive for tubs, troughs, and window boxes. Beer and wine barrels have always been a popular choice, and they are now made especially for the gardener in a variety of shapes and sizes. Make sure the metal hoops around the barrel are fixed and that there are no signs of warping. In damp regions, wooden containers may have a limited life unless they are made from hardwood such as maple, beech, oak, or walnut. Softwoods, such as cedar, redwood, or pine, can be treated with a clear wood varnish or colored paint (just make sure it's not toxic to the plants) to halt decay, or you can line wooden window boxes and tubs with plastic sheeting to limit rotting caused by watering.

Lead and copper containers are especially attractive when they develop a green-blue or gray patina from exposure. Although metal containers are expensive and very heavy, they last a lifetime. Antique shops and auctions are a great place to pick up uncommon metal containers.

Stone is also beautiful, but can be cumbersome. Reconstituted stone or concrete is a cheaper alternative, but can look harsh when brand-new. When treated with cultured yogurt, it soon resembles sculptured stone.

Window Boxes and Other Containers

If you go with a window box, keep in mind which way the windows open and whether the box will sit on the sill. When boxes sit right against windows, rain can splash soil against the glass or plants may block out valuable light. Also, make sure there is reasonable access for watering. You can fit metal brackets below the window so that the box is supported and the top growth comes level with the sill.

Window boxes are ideal for growing culinary herbs you want within easy reach of the kitchen. Besides being tasty, many herbs have aromatic leaves or attractive flowers. The traditional cottagers' garden usually had a little plot near the kitchen for culinary herbs. A window box gardener can easily cultivate a miniature version of this plot. The smaller perennials—such as chives, burnet, marjoram, thyme, winter savory, and prostrate rosemary—are the most suitable for window boxes. Larger herbs such as hyssop, rue, and sage do well together, though they may need pruning to keep their top growth under control. Annuals and biennials such as basil, chervil, parsley, and summer savory are also good choices.

But don't limit yourself to traditional containers. Many household items can be converted into herb containers that lend a quirky charm to the garden. Just make sure they have good drainage holes, which are easy to drill. Some possibilities include an enameled colander, unusual metal or wire baskets, wheelbarrows, old sinks, porcelain bathtubs, buckets and pails, painted tin cans, wine barrels, concrete chimneys, wooden tubs, and stone troughs.

Before filling them with plants, all containers need to be prepared. To give your plants the best possible start, remove any old soil and scrub out the inside with disinfectant to prevent pests and fungal spores or bacteria that might be present on the porous surface. Cover the drainage hole with broken pieces of crockery, concave side down, to help water escape through the bottom.

Choosing and Planting the Herbs

Many herbs grow happily in pots and tubs, which are both decorative and useful. Taller culinary herbs such as rosemary, bay, and tarragon do well in window boxes. Angelica and fennel can be grown as ornamental plants for their handsome foliage. Aromatic herbs make lovely mixtures in tubs and half barrels. Mints should stand alone because they are so invasive.

Ordinary soil isn't a good choice for container gardening as it may harbor pests, diseases, or weed seeds. Also, soil with an unbalanced composition may lack some nutrients or have an excess of others. The ideal compost is a sterile mixture that is both free draining and water retentive, and has a well-balanced supply of minerals including nitrogen, phosphorus, and potassium, along with trace elements. The commercially prepared mixtures in prepackaged quantities from garden centers are most convenient. You can vary the mixture to suit the requirements of your plants, especially those that like drainage, by adding coarse sand to it.

You can buy plants as young stock in the spring either in individual pots or trays. Look for plants that are vigorous and healthy with no weeds or yellow leaves. Avoid stunted or lanky growth, dry soil, or limp foliage. Plants that have been in their containers too long may have roots growing out through the bottom, or may have formed a choking spiral of roots inside the container. Poke the soil around the edge gently with your finger, up to your first knuckle, to get an idea of whether the plant is root bound. (If you feel large, thick roots at this depth, gently slide the plant and root structure out of the pot for a further look. If the larger roots are spiraling up around the sides of the pot, it is too root bound.) Also, make sure you check the underside of leaves for signs of aphids or other pests.

Some people enjoy growing herbs from seeds, and it is a relatively inexpensive way of getting a good number of plants. Start them early in warm conditions such as a greenhouse, windowsill, or enclosed porch.

In autumn, raise containers up on stands or bricks so they don't stand in water. In winter, most containers need insulation—move them to a greenhouse, carport or porch, or even a shed or garage temporarily. If you can't bring them inside, you could sink the containers up to their rims in soil, or push them all together in a sheltered spot and fill the gaps between them with bark chippings. Then pile some more bark over the top of the pots to act as an insulating quilt.

Which Herbs to Grow?

Angelica: This hardy biennial that can grow five feet to eight feet tall with handsome, aromatic leaves and large heads of greenish-yellow flowers in mid- to late summer needs a moisture-retentive soil mixture. Best grown alone. Plant in a tub with full to partial sun.

Basil: A tender annual of great culinary value. There is a range of cultivars from sweet basil to purple Thai or lemon basil. The large-leaved plant grows up to two feet high. Nip the tips regularly to keep plants leafy instead of going to seed. It is suitable for pots or window boxes, and does well when planted with marjoram, lemon balm, and parsley. Because basil requires full sun and loves warmth, it must be moved inside for winter.

Bay: An evergreen tree with aromatic leaves that is best grown in a large container. Bay likes sun or semishade and well-drained, rich potting soil. Keep it slightly moist and water through the winter, except when temperatures fall below freezing.

Borage: A hardy annual that grows eighteen to thirty-six inches high with starlike blue flowers that attract bees through summer and fall. Borage grows well with rosemary, rue, and sage. Plant it in a tub in full sun.

Chervil: A delicate plant with fine fernlike leaves that have an anise flavor. This is a short-lived annual growing about six inches high. It puts on seeds within a few months, so pick all the leaves you can use before it flowers.

Chives: A hardy perennial with onion flavored tubular leaves about eight inches high. The pink flowers that appear in summer should be removed from plants intended for culinary use. Likes to grow with parsley, marjoram, and mint. Good in a window box, tub, or pot. Chives need full sun and plenty of water.

Coriander/Cilantro: A fast-growing annual that reaches twelve to fourteen inches high. The leaves look similar to flat-leaf parsley, but the flavor is peppery. Great for making salsas and using in Mexican food. The seeds are good in curries; grind them in a peppermill. Needs full sun and moist, well-drained soil.

Dill: Resembles fennel with feathery leaves and yellow flowers that bear seeds. If you're growing dill for the leaves, keep it closely cut to delay flowering; if you want the seeds, let the plant grow to about a foot high and let the seeds ripen on the stems. Dry them by hanging the heads upside-down in paper bags in a cool, airy room.

Fennel: A tall, hardy plant with feathery, anise-flavored leaves. Fennel attracts butterflies, beneficial insects, and birds. The sweet and bronze varieties may grow to six feet tall. The entire plant is edible, and the seeds and their essential oil are used medicinally. Collect the seeds in August and September when they are ripe and dry them like dill seeds (see above). Fennel needs full sun with plenty of water and good drainage.

Lavender: An evergreen shrub with many cultivars that grows one to three feet with spikes of blue flowers in summer. A good companion plant to thyme, rue, or sage. Good in a window box or tub, and needs full sun.

Marjoram: Tender perennial grows twelve to eighteen inches high. Plant it with basil, chives, parsley, or thyme. Does well in a window box, tub, or pot in full sun. Needs to be moved inside for winter.

Mint: An aromatic perennial with many varieties, such as apple mint and spearmint. Grows two to three feet. Mint does best alone in moist soil, but can get along with chives and parsley. Grow in a pot in full to partial sun.

Oregano: Frost-hardy aromatic herb whose delicate, spicy flavor is used for cooking. Likes sun. Cut back old plant stems during spring.

Parsley: Classified as a hardy biennial, but during the second year it only comes up to flower, then turns to seed right away. Grows ten to eighteen inches high with flat-leafed (more flavorful) and curly leaf (more decorative) varieties. A good companion to basil, calendula, chives, marjoram, or mint. Parsley can be grown in a hanging basket, window box, tub, or pot in full to partial sun.

Rosemary: An evergreen shrub that grows either tall or spreading, with narrow leaves and small blue flowers in spring. Good for window boxes or tubs, but needs full sun. Rosemary can be grown with borage, rue, sage, tarragon, and thyme.

Sage: A drought-tolerant evergreen shrub with gray-green foliage. Grows to about two feet. Good companion plants are borage, rosemary, rue, tarragon, and thyme. Grow in a window box or tub in full sun.

Sorrel: Sorrel looks like curly dock, which has long green leaves like dandelions without the serrated edge, but on a smaller scale, with shorter leaves that resemble spinach or arugula. The flower stems are about three feet high. Pick the tender young leaves to use in salads or omelets, or cook like spinach. Larger, tougher leaves can be used as homegrown tinfoil to wrap things on the barbecue.

Tarragon: This hardy perennial is not very decorative but has good culinary value. It does well with sage, rosemary, or rue. Grows to two feet in a tub with full sun.

Thyme: An evergreen which grows as a bushy shrub or a creeping plant. Highly aromatic with summer flowers. Likes to grow with marjoram, rosemary, rue, and sage. Perfect for a window box, tub, or pot in the full sun.

Culinary
Herbs

Herbal Comfort Foods

by Dallas Jennifer Cobb

When I need comforting, I turn to food and drink. I am sure that I learned this from my mother and grandmother, both British. For them, tea was not just a drink, but a time of day and a medical intervention.

In my childhood home, tea time was both a ritual and a right. Midmorning we would gather in the kitchen for tea and toast, or tea and a bickie (biscuit). When body or feelings were hurt, a "cuppa" tea and a shortbread, or a warm bowl of soup with steaming bread, was the healing balm.

So now, when I am stressed and in need of comfort, I find myself turning to the very foods my mum and grandma gave to me for comfort.

Like me, many people reach for particular foods to comfort and sustain them when they are stretched thin—

foods that hold an emotional association or memory of good times. What are your comfort foods? When you are stressed, what do you reach for?

If you are like most people, you reach for stimulating substances like caffeine, chocolate, alcohol, and sugar. But even if you crave these foods and think that they will provide you with comfort, most of them provide a very short-term positive effect, but can contribute to some really negative effects.

Choosing healthy foods to comfort us can help to counteract and reduce the negative biochemical and physiological effects of stress. Also note that when you eat is almost as important as what you consume. Having three to five small meals a day can help to reduce stress on the digestive track and give us more stable blood-sugar levels throughout the day. Drinking lots of water will maintain an optimum level of hydration, counteracting stress by circulating the available nutrients within the system.

For the sake of this article, consider comfort foods to be those that are nutritious, nurturing, wholesome, and satisfying —foods that ease the stressors on mind, body, and spirit.

When I am stressed or overwhelmed, I often reach for foods associated with historic comfort. Whether it is a cup of warm herbal tea that reminds me of the nurturing feeling of my grandmother's kitchen, or the quick-to-whip-up dinner biscuits that satisfy my longing for a warm, full tummy, most of my most satisfying comfort foods have herbs in them.

I want to welcome you to come and sit in my kitchen, and let me share some herbal comfort with you. Many of my tried-and-true recipes are included, plus a list of recommend herbs for uplifting you on a low day, and reminders of other simple practices you can use to wrap yourself in a warm blanket of comfort. Whether you are worn out, sad, or just need some loving care, these recipes will help you to reach for comfort foods that will truly uplift you, adding to your health.

The Uplifting Effect of Herbs

Herbs have generally high levels of antioxidants, compounds found naturally in foods that manage and remove damaging free radicals. Though oxygen is necessary for life, it also has a damaging quality. The way that oxygen can cause rust on metal, or the browning of an exposed fruit, oxygen can also cause damage within our bodies. Similarly, oxidization within our bodies produces free radicals—molecules or parts of molecules caused by the metabolic process of oxygen.

Free radicals can damage cells and destroy their function, causing genetic damage, tissue degeneration, aging, and susceptibility to disease. An antioxidant is something that slows or prevents this damaging process within our bodies. Most natural antioxidants come from fruits, vegetables, and herbs.

The most powerful herbal antioxidants are green tea and grape-seed extract, closely followed in efficacy by rosemary, sage, lavender, clove, allspice, sweet marjoram, nutmeg, lemon grass, turmeric, and coriander.

Overcoming Stress

Stress is our internal reaction to our external environment, and can be physical, mental, emotional, or spiritual. For an internal stress response to be triggered, we must perceive the external stimuli as something dangerous. Within our bodies, stress induces a complex biochemical and hormonal response.

This stress response stimulates our body to use nutrients more rapidly to meet the increased biochemical needs of metabolism. Stress can deplete us of essential nutrients, causing internal imbalance and greater susceptibility to illness or disease.

Common responses to stress include increasing adrenal production, suppressing the immune system, and stimulating the production of free radicals. Stress has also been shown to decrease the naturally occurring protective antibodies within our systems, and deplete nutrients and antioxidants.

Because stress depletes our body's nutrients, we need to choose foods that are nourishing and nurturing. Herbs that are nutrient rich and full of antioxidants help us overcome the effects of stress.

Herbal Comfort Food Recipes

When you reach for comfort foods, remember to honor your body and your health. Choose foods that hold both a psychological comfort value and a physical comfort value. Choose foods that uplift spiritually, emotionally, and physically, foods abundant with antioxidants. Let the comfort food be part of a solution to stress rather than contribute to further stressing your system. Junk food will not satisfy your nutritional needs, or your body.

I have included a few recipes that hold emotional resonance for me, and contain herbs with high antioxidant and micronutrient values.

Sweet Treats
Gingersnaps

Need some real quick uplifting? Take a pass on the caffeine and grab one of these. A little spicier than your usual gingersnap, these delicious cookies pack a stimulating boost. In addition to antioxidants, ginger, clove, and cinnamon are known for their stimulating qualities, plus have added immune boosters. They can aid circulation, help break up phlegm, and generally warm the body. Blackstrap molasses is high in iron in an easy-to-assimilate form, plus its complex sugars give us a boost without the big letdown that comes from highly refined sugar.

  1   cup butter

  1   cup sugar

  ¼   cup blackstrap molasses

  1   egg

  1   teaspoon vanilla extract

  2   cups all-purpose flour

½ teaspoon baking soda

1 teaspoon cinnamon

½ teaspoon powdered ginger

½ teaspoon powdered cloves

¼ teaspoon salt

Preheat over to 350 degrees F. Cream the butter and sugar, then add molasses, egg, and vanilla and mix well.

Sift the dry ingredients together, then add these slowly to the creamed mix. Drop dough by tablespoons onto a nonstick cookie sheet. Bake 15 minutes or until golden brown.

Luxurious Lavender Shortbread

Because shortbread is a tradition in my home at Christmas, I associate it with good family times. When I need some serious comfort I often reach for this recipe. My healthy modifications include using whole grain flour for added fiber and complex carbohydrates, and adding beneficial herbs.

1 cup butter—do not use margarine

½ cup powdered sugar

3–4 heaping tablespoons fresh lavender flowers, finely chopped

2 cups whole-grain flour (wheat or spelt)

Preheat oven to 300 degrees F. Take the butter from the fridge—it needs to be cold. Cut butter into pea-size chunks; place in a large bowl. Thoroughly cream lavender and sugar into it with a fork.

Add flour quickly, mixing thoroughly. Try not to use your hands because they heat the dough up and make it tough. Refrigerate the dough again for about 20 minutes.

Turn the cookie dough out on a floured board and roll to ¼-inch thickness. Cut into hearts or some other comforting shape. Bake at 300 degrees F on a nonstick cookie sheet for about 25 minutes or until golden brown.

Other herbs to use in shortbread:

Ginger—substitute ¾ cup crystallized ginger, finely chopped.

Rosemary—substitute 3–4 tablespoons fresh rosemary, finely chopped.

Lemon balm—substitute 5 tablespoons fresh lemon balm, finely chopped.

Lovely Licorice

Licorice root is known as a natural laxative, plus it helps alleviate colds and flu, and calms frazzled nerves. The blackstrap molasses is an easily absorbed natural source of iron that is sweet tasting.

 1 cup blackstrap molasses
 1 teaspoon ground licorice root
 1 teaspoon ground anise root
  Whole grain flour (wheat or spelt)

Warm molasses in a large saucepan on low heat. Add 1 teaspoon each licorice and anise root.

Use about 2 parts spelt to 1 part whole wheat flour. Too much whole wheat will give the licorice a bitter taste. Add flour until you have a dense consistency that you can roll into snakes. Cut snakes to desired length.

The licorice will harden as it cools, and keeps for a long time in the refrigerator. Make a big batch, and stow some away for a rainy day when you will really need it.

Savory Treats

I heard a rumor that real estate agents will sometimes go to a home prior to an open house and bake bread in the oven to fill the home with the luscious scent of fresh baked bread. They do this because so many of us have deep, positive associations with the smell of fresh bread.

Whether it is bread or biscuits, cookies or cakes, the effect of fresh baking is universal. It warms the soul, and sometimes even warms a wintry house.

So if you need some comfort, heat the oven, let the kitchen warm up, and get to the task of baking. Metaphorically speaking, you may find yourself uplifted by the leavening bread.

Whole Grain Herb Bread

⅔ cup water

2 teaspoons sugar

⅔ cup skim or soy milk

2 teaspoons dry active yeast

3 egg whites

3 tablespoons olive oil

1 teaspoon salt

½ teaspoon dried basil, oregano

4½ cups whole grain flour (wheat or spelt)

Bring the water to a boil in a small pot. Remove from heat, stir in sugar, milk, and yeast. Mix well. Let this stand for 10 minutes or until it is slightly frothy.

Combine egg whites, oil, salt, basil, and oregano in a large bowl. Add yeast mixture to it and blend well. Add 4 cups of flour, ½ cup at a time, mixing well after each half cup.

Knead the dough one a floured board until it is smooth and elastic. Add more flour if it is too sticky. Form into a ball and cover with a cloth. Let dough rise in a warm place for about 1 hour. Divide into 2 pieces and place in bread pans. Let rise in a warm place until doubled in size. Bake at 350 degrees F for 30 to 35 minutes.

Slather with butter while it is hot, and enjoy some soul comfort.

Herbed Homemade Biscuits

A versatile recipe. Try substituting your favorite herbs, or those herbs whose tastes complement the dish you will serve the biscuits with.

    2   cups whole grain flour (wheat or spelt)
    3   teaspoons baking powder
    1   teaspoon salt
    ½   cup butter, cut to pea size
  ⅔–¾   cup milk, soy milk, or buttermilk

Variations:

1 large clove garlic and ¼ cup finely minced fresh oregano,
    (1 tablespoon dried); or

¼ cup tomato paste and ½ cup finely minced fresh basil,
    (2 tablespoons dried); or

¾ cup shredded cheddar cheese and ¼ cup minced fresh sage
    (1 tablespoon dried)

Sift all the dry ingredients in a large bowl. Add the butter. Add milk and mix well. Herbal ingredients go in last, and are mixed throughout dough. Roll out to ½-inch thickness, and cut into interesting shapes. Bake at 450 degrees F for 12 to 15 minutes.

Enjoy these biscuits with soup or stew, or on a really bad day. Slather them with butter.

Rosemary Bread Sticks

    ⅔   cup skim or soy milk
    2   teaspoons baking powder
    1   teaspoon salt
    ½   teaspoon black pepper

½ cup finely chopped chives
1 teaspoon finely chopped fresh rosemary (or dried)
1½ cups whole grain flour (wheat or spelt)

Combine milk, baking powder, spices, and herbs. Stir in flour, ½ cup at a time, mixing thoroughly. Knead until smooth and elastic. Add more flour if it is too sticky. Cover and let stand for 30 minutes in a warm spot. Divide into 12 little balls, then roll these long and thin.

Bake on a nonstick cooking sheet, at 375 degrees F for 12 minutes, then flip them over and bake 10 minutes on the other side, or until golden brown.

Healthy Herb Butter

½ cup unsalted butter
1 clove garlic, minced
1 tablespoon chives, finely diced
   Pinch of salt
   Shake of pepper

Bring butter to room temperature. Fold in herbs and blend carefully. Scrape mixture into a small bowl and refrigerate. Serve with hot bread or biscuits.

Garlic helps to stimulate the immune system, fights infection, and warms the system. Chives and black pepper also have antibacterial and warming properties.

For a little variety, keep the garlic in the recipe above, but substitute the following herbs for the chives, salt, and pepper:

1 teaspoon minced basil
½ teaspoon minced oregano
1 teaspoon minced marjoram
½ teaspoon minced sage

Nurturing and Nutritious

While you are longing for comfort foods, remember that savory may be as satisfying to the soul as sweet. The following recipes allow you to indulge in something comforting and nurturing—but also good for you. Don't be fooled, vegetables *can* be comfort food.

Dill and Potato Cakes

2 cups whole grain flour

1 tablespoon finely chopped fresh dill

1 cup mashed potatoes

3 tablespoons butter, softened

   Pinch of salt

2 tablespoons milk or soy milk

Sift all the dry ingredients into a large bowl. Add dill, butter, mashed potato, and milk, and mix. It should make a soft malleable dough. Roll out to a ½-inch thickness and cut with cookie cutters. Place on a nonstick bake sheet and bake at 450 degrees F for about 20 to 22 minutes or until golden brown.

Herbed Grilled Mediterranean Vegetables

½ cup fresh herbs—any combination of parsley, thyme, rosemary, oregano, and basil

½ teaspoon sea salt

2 tablespoons olive oil

1 small eggplant

1 red pepper

1 yellow pepper

1 green pepper

3 zucchinis

1 fennel bulb

Cut all vegetables into bite-size chunks. In a large bowl, mix vegetables with olive oil until all have a thin coating of oil. Sprinkle herbs and salt into the bowl and mix thoroughly. Grill for 10 to 15 minutes, or until lightly browned on both sides.

Herbed Roasted Root Veggies

3 large potatoes

3 sweet potatoes

6 carrots

2 onions, peeled and cut into wedges

3 tablespoons olive oil

1 garlic, separated into cloves and peeled

¼ cup minced rosemary

¼ cup minced thyme

Salt and pepper to taste

Cut all the vegetables into bite-size chunks. In a large bowl, toss the veggies first with oil, then add herbs and toss until the veggies are evenly covered with herbs. Place these on a large nonstick baking sheet and bake at 400 degrees F for about 1 hour, stirring occasionally. When everything is golden brown, remove from the oven.

Autumn Harvest Herb Soup

3 large leeks, sliced thinly

4 tablespoons olive oil

8 cups water

2 large potatoes, diced

3 large sweet potatoes, shredded

1 butternut squash, peeled and shredded

1 clove garlic, minced

¼ cup fresh thyme

3   tablespoons fresh sage, finely chopped

Salt and pepper to taste

In a large pot, fry leeks in oil until they soften. Add water, bring to a boil. Add all veggies and herbs and simmer for about 45 minutes. Use a hand blender or masher to blend out lumps. Add salt and pepper to taste. Serve with chunks of homemade bread or hot biscuits for dipping and wiping out the bowl.

Comfort

Though stress is a part of everyone's life, it doesn't have to destroy us, or our good health. Take the time to create small satisfying rituals that can nurture and sustain you through times of stress. Make little lists of your favorite foods, and give yourself permission to enjoy as much as you want of the fruits, vegetables, and herbs on that list.

Whether it is the antioxidants found in herbs that hold an uplifting vibration, the superior nutritional content, or the deep emotional context of their remembered scents and tastes, remember that herbal ingredients have a deep connection to comfort. I hope you will find some tasty recipes for comforting treats that will get you through the long winter ahead, or a tough day.

Eat well, find comfort in everyday, simple pleasures, and let that comfort infuse your life.

Herbal Treats Beat the Summer Heat

≈ by Elizabeth Barrette ≈

Among their many powers, herbs can help us maintain harmony with our environment. The most flexible are "adaptogens," which help the body adjust to different challenges. Especially relevant are "refrigerants," which lower body temperature, impart a cold sensation, or otherwise make hot weather seem less oppressive. Cold foods and beverages, particularly made with the right herbs, can improve comfort while providing a nutritious, culinary pleasure. Here are some herbs with cooling properties:

Anise has a sweet, fresh smell similar to licorice—a popular flavor in candies and cookies. Used sparingly, it soothes digestion.

Basil has a spicy-sweet smell and goes with almost everything. It reduces fever and headaches.

Borage stands out with its hairy leaves and blue, star-shaped flowers. It has a faint cucumber flavor. Borage also eases dry coughs and lowers fever.

Catmint has a mellower smell and taste than its relative catnip. It soothes headaches and reduces fever. Add tender leaves to salads.

Catnip is intoxicating to felines, but relaxing to humans. It relieves nausea and promotes restful sleep. Catnip makes an excellent tea.

Celery is juicy and refreshing. It helps keep the body hydrated. Chop stalks and add to salads, cheese spreads, etc., for a crunchy texture.

Chamomile smells like fresh-mown hay warmed by the sun. Use it to prevent nightmares and bring peaceful sleep. Chamomile makes delicious tea.

Cilantro has a pungent, spicy character. Chop its feathery leaves for use in sauces, sandwiches, and taco toppings.

Coconut has a mellow, sweet flavor and fragrance that creates a tropical mood. Coconut milk, coconut cream, and shredded coconut are soothing and cheering. Use liberally in desserts.

Coriander is the dried seed of cilantro plants and has a mild spicy flavor. It aids digestion and reduces flatulence.

Cucumber refreshes and rehydrates. Its crisp flavor makes it a favorite in salads, but it is also delicious in beverages.

Cumin is among the cooling herbs in Ayurvedic tradition. Its strong flavor adds interest to mild herbal dishes.

Dandelion may be the most widely available herb of all. Use tender young leaves in salads. The flowers make dandelion wine.

Dill has a tangy flavor, stronger in the seeds and milder in the feathery leaves. It reduces stomach pains and hiccups. Use in pickles and dips.

Echinacea is best known for strengthening the immune system, but has broader normalizing effects on the body. It reduces fever and allergies.

Fennel has a mild licorice flavor with a greener note. Chew the seeds to aid digestion. Leaves may be added to salads or dips. Bronze fennel adds a red hue to herbal vinegar.

Ginseng increases the body's efficiency. American ginseng is more relaxing than oriental varieties. Use in tea and desserts, when appropriate.

Hibiscus lends a rich tangy flavor to tea. It helps cool the body. The flowers make a lovely edible garnish.

Lavender has a sweet-sharp, musky fragrance. It soothes anxiety, and relieves flatulence and halitosis. The flowers flavor tea, jelly, cream, vinegar, and desserts.

Lemon is famed for its intensely sour, bright flavor and fragrance. It adds zest to salad, tea, dessert, and dishes of all kinds. Lemon uplifts the spirit and stimulates thirst.

Lemon balm is both lemony and minty. Use in tea, or candy the leaves.

Lemongrass has a subtle grassy-citrus flavor. Relieves diarrhea and stomachache.

Licorice appears most often in candied form, with its dark spicy taste. It reduces allergies and asthma.

Lime belongs to the citrus family, with a greener flavor. It relieves anxiety and depression. Use in tea, desserts, and anywhere that calls for lemon juice.

Linden is sometimes called limeflower, though it is not citrus. Its flowers and honey have a light, sweet quality that make them ideal for tea and desserts.

Peppermint is more cooling than spearmint, with a mellower, bluish taste. It soothes and refreshes. Use in tea and desserts.

Raspberry leaves have cooling and antispasmodic properties. Tea made from them tastes similar to green tea. Sweet, juicy raspberry fruit stars in many summer jams, ice creams, and other desserts.

Rose needs an intense, sweet scent to function as an herb. It revives and rejuvenates. Candy the petals and use the hips in tea or jelly.

Saffron has a mellow, nutty-spicy flavor. It lowers fever and stimulates the libido.

Sarsaparilla is rich and spicy with a faint medicinal taste. Its cooling properties make it popular in tea and soda.

Sorrel starts out bland in spring, but summer heat gives it a sharp tangy bite. It quenches thirst and reduces fever. Use in salads, soups, and sauces.

Spearmint has a sharper, greener taste than peppermint. It cools and invigorates. Use in tea and glazes, especially with meat.

Thyme comes in many flavors, such as musky and nutty; it also mimics herbs like caraway and lemon. It reduces indigestion and flatulence. Use in spreads and vinegars.

Watercress has a crisp, pungent flavor. Use in salads or soups. It also makes a great bed for serving other things, such as cheese spread.

Wintergreen has a strong minty-medicinal flavor. Its leaves and berries are good for toothpaste and tea.

Edible herbal flowers: angelica, bergamot, calendula, carnation, chicory, chrysanthemum, clover, daylily, dianthus, elderflower, jasmine, lemon, marjoram, nasturtium, pansy, primrose, rose, sage, viola, violet.

Freezing Herbs

One good way to preserve herbs is to freeze them. Frozen herbs may be added directly to soups, stews, or sauces. For uncooked foods, first defrost and drain the herbs.

Herbs with tough stems and leaves should be separated before freezing. Pick off leaves and brush them clean. Don't wash them; too much water dilutes flavor. Spread leaves on a cookie sheet, and place in freezer overnight. Then transfer to freezer cartons or bags for storage.

Delicate herbs like fennel or thyme may be frozen as sprigs. Snip off pieces of uniform length and shake gently to clean. Pack them in layers in a freezer carton to prevent crushing.

You don't have to freeze whole herbs. They can be chopped, then frozen in ice cube trays or other small containers. You can also purée juicy herbs such as basil or cilantro. Mince in a food processor, and slowly add olive oil to form a paste. Freeze the paste in ice cube or popsicle trays.

Take this opportunity to combine herbs that you use together. Some excellent cooling blends include basil, Italian parsley, and thyme; dill, mint, and lemon balm; peppermint, spearmint, and wintergreen; dill and fennel; catmint and lavender.

Ice Cream and Sorbets

The food that most symbolizes summer is ice cream and its luscious relatives. Ice cream uses heavy cream as a base, often with eggs added. Though usually sweet, it can be savory, and is the richest of frozen desserts. Sherbet is moderate, using milk mixed with fruit or juice. Sorbet is lighter, made from water or fruit juice blended with pureed fruit. Granita is a delicate fluff of ice crystals flavored with fruit or fruit purée. Herbs lend their flavor to sweet and savory frozen treats.

Basil Ice Cream

Pour 1 cup milk into saucepan and simmer until bubbly. Remove from heat; add 1 cup fresh basil leaves and 1 teaspoon coriander. Allow to sit for a half hour. Run mixture through a food processor until smooth. Strain and discard solids, then set basil mixture aside. Combine 1 cup milk, 2 cups whipping cream, and ½ cup sugar; cook in saucepan over medium heat until bubbly, stirring constantly. Remove from heat. Beat together 7 egg yolks and ½ cup sugar, then add to hot mixture, stirring constantly. Stir in basil mixture. Cook over medium heat, stirring constantly, until mixture thickens enough to coat a spoon (about 5–7 minutes). Allow to cool, then freeze in ice cream maker per manufacturer directions. Garnish with sprigs of fresh basil, and serve.

Minty Melon Sherbet

In a small saucepan, add 1 teaspoon lime Jell-O to ¼ cup water; wait 1 minute. Then add 2 tablespoons coarsely chopped mint leaves, 2 tablespoons lime juice, 2 tablespoons light corn syrup, and ⅓ cup sugar. Cook over low heat until Jell-O dissolves, then remove pan from heat. Cover and let stand for at least 1 hour. Strain out the mint leaves and discard them. In a metal-bladed blender or food processor, purée together 1 cup honeydew melon cubes and 1 cup cucumber cubes. Stir purée into the mint mixture; then stir in 1 cup milk. Freeze in ice cream maker. Garnish with sprigs of fresh or candied mint, and serve.

Rose-Coconut Sorbet

In saucepan, combine 1 cup sugar and 1½ cups water. Stir over medium heat until sugar dissolves, then bring to a boil for 5 minutes. Remove pan from heat. Carefully stir in ½ cup coconut cream and 2½ cups fresh red or pink rose petals. Allow to cool for 2 hours. Strain syrup to remove petals, then add a dash of lemon juice. Freeze in an ice cream maker. Garnish with candied rose petals, shredded coconut, and/or rose syrup.

Wonderful Lemonberry Granita

In saucepan, combine ½ cup sugar and 1½ cups water; bring to a boil. Reduce heat; simmer until sugar is fully dissolved. Stir in 1 cup fresh red raspberries and 1 cup fresh yellow raspberries. Allow to cool. Run through a food processor until smooth. Strain and discard solids. Stir 2½ tablespoons lemon juice into raspberry mixture. Pour into a shallow metal pan and cover. Freeze for 1 hour, then scrape crystals away from pan edge. Freeze again, scraping and stirring the ice as it forms, until granita is completely crystallized. Serve immediately. Garnish with raspberries, lemon slices, or fresh or candied lemon balm leaves.

Toppings

In summer, you don't want to cook any more than necessary. Herbs perk up cold foods to make them more exciting. Herbal vinegars and salad dressings are the perfect complement for a bowl of tossed greens. Syrups and glazes accent ice cream or fruit. Butter and cheese spreads go well with crackers or bread.

Better Butter

To 8 ounces softened butter, add 2 tablespoons chopped cilantro, 1 tablespoon caraway-flavored thyme, ½ teaspoon cumin. Beat herbs into butter. Add 1 tablespoon lemon juice, and salt to taste; mix until smooth. Pack into butter mold or dish; chill before serving.

Changeable Cheese Spread

In a bowl, stir together 16 ounces cream cheese (softened) and 8 ounces small-curd cottage cheese. Add a blend of chopped fresh herbs, such as 1 tablespoon each of lemon thyme and dill; 2 tablespoons celery, 1 tablespoon cilantro; or 1 tablespoon English thyme, 1 teaspoon coriander, 1 clove garlic. Serve on a bed of watercress or stuff into edible flowers such as daylily or hibiscus.

Elegant Vinaigrette

Combine 3 tablespoons olive oil and 1 tablespoon cider vinegar in a clear glass jar; shake well. Add one clove garlic (crushed) and a dash of salt; shake. Add fresh chopped herbs: 1 tablespoon thyme, 1 tablespoon basil, 2 teaspoons fennel, 1 teaspoon coriander. Shake well, then let it sit for a half hour. Shake again before serving.

Ginseng-Mint Glaze

In small saucepan, combine ⅔ cup water, 2 tablespoons clover honey, 2 teaspoons cornstarch and mix well. Add ⅛ cup each of fresh spearmint and peppermint, and a 1-inch piece of ginseng root. Boil over medium heat, stirring constantly, until mixture begins to thicken. Cool for 10 minutes. Use slotted spoon to remove leaves and root. Stir in 2 tablespoons lime juice. Chill 1 hour, then drizzle over fresh fruit and serve.

Herbal Vinegar

Gently warm (do not boil) 3 cups white cider vinegar. Into a glass bottle, put 6 sprigs of bruised herbs, such as borage, cilantro, dill; spearmint and catmint with coriander seed; rose petals, violet petals, and lavender; dill, lemon thyme, and nasturtium. Allow vinegar to cool, then cover and store in a cool, dark place.

Many Lemon Sauce

In a saucepan, heat ¾ cup sugar and 4 tablespoons water until syrupy. Add 1 tablespoon each of lemon balm and lemongrass. Cook for five minutes, then remove leaves. Add 2 tablespoons butter, juice of 1 lemon, and a pinch of salt. Stirring constantly, cook until syrup reaches desired consistency.

Beverages

Drinking soda—or worse yet, alcohol—will not keep you cool and hydrated in summer. For that, drink water. Herbal tea is also a good choice, especially when made with cooling herbs. Herb/fruit blends also work well. Sweeten minimally or enjoy plain.

Moon Tea

A magical version of "cold infusion" is Moon Tea. For this you need 1 cup of fresh herbs (not tightly packed) and 1 quart room-temperature water. You may also add a slice of fresh lemon or dried licorice root. Place the herbs in a clear glass container and pour the water over them. Close the lid. Set the container where moonlight can reach it for a mystical touch. Let the herbs steep overnight, and drink your Moon Tea the next day.

Berry Good Tea

Fill a muslin tea satchel with 5 tablespoons rose hips, 4 tablespoons hibiscus flowers, 3 tablespoons blackberry leaves, 3 tablespoons raspberry leaves, 1 tablespoon raspberries. Prepare as Moon Tea. Uplifting and refreshing, this is a good breakfast drink.

Citrus Sipper

In a saucepan, combine 1 tablespoon chopped lemon balm, juice of 1 lemon, ¼ cup lime juice, 2 tablespoons sugar, 2 cups water. Heat and stir until sugar dissolves. Cool at least 3 hours, then strain. Makes two 1-cup servings. This sprightly tea stimulates thirst and cheers the spirit.

Cool Head Tea

Combine in a mug ½ teaspoon each of dried chamomile flowers, dried linden flowers, fresh lavender flowers, and fresh catnip flowers. Add 1 cup boiling water, cover, and steep for 5 minutes. Strain and drink. This soothing tea calms mind and body.

Doublemint Fizz

Start with 4 tablespoons spearmint and 4 tablespoons peppermint. Add the juice of 2 lemons, and set aside. Combine 2 tablespoons sugar and ½ cup water in a small saucepan; heat until sugar dissolves. Cool and put in a glass jar; then add the herbal mixture. Allow to steep overnight in refrigerator. Strain out the herbs. Add 2 quarts of ginger ale, pour over ice, and serve.

Desert Cooler

Blend 2 teaspoons dried hibiscus flowers and 1 teaspoon dried mint. Add 2 cups boiling water, cover, and steep for 5 minutes. Strain out and discard herbs. Add a dash of roseflower water or rose syrup to taste. Divide into two 1-cup servings and drink. This exotic floral tea refreshes and rehydrates.

Garnishes

Finally, use herbs to dress up special summer dishes. Parsley is fine, but sprigs of any cooling herb work as accents—consider frilly cilantro, dill, spearmint, the striking color of golden lemon thyme. Robust lavender stems make pretty stirrers in drinks. Some herbs, such as watercress, make an excellent bed for serving fish, fruit, or other foods.

For a decorative touch in beverages, freeze edible flowers or herb leaves into ice cubes. Choose single leaves or flowers that fit into the holes of an ice cube tray: lemon balm, spearmint, borage flowers, and violas are ideal. Gently shake them clean. Place one item into each space, fill the tray with water, and freeze overnight. If items floating on the water is a problem, try filling the tray just halfway; freeze for half an hour to an hour, then fill the rest of the way and return to freezer. For a spectacular effect in punch bowls, lay sprigs of herbs and edible flowers in a ring mold, fill with water, and freeze to make a colorful ice ring.

Candied herbs or edible flowers have a delicious "frosted" look. Some herbs are famous for this: borage flowers, peppermint, rose petals, spearmint, and violets. Use them to garnish cakes, ice cream sundaes, fruit salads, beverages, etc. Pick leaves or flowers on a sunny day and brush clean. Separate 1 egg white and beat until it starts to stiffen. Dip items in egg white, or paint the egg on with a pastry brush. Hold each item over a small bowl of sugar, and sprinkle sugar over it until fully coated. Place sugared items on a sheet of waxed paper, on a wire rack. Bake at 225 degrees F until dry and crisp. Store in airtight container.

Afro-Caribbean Greens

⇜ by Stephanie Rose Bird ⇝

Greens are a highly sought after soul food beloved in Jamaica as Callaloo, and in the United States where collards, mustard, and turnip tops are simply called "greens." Numerous healthy recipes abound in the Motherland itself for various leafy greens as well. This article explores the phyto-nutrients contained in greens, and ways of growing, preparing, and using greens that are easy enough for everyone to try.

One reason people often reserve greens—collard, mustard, and turnip, or even spinach and kale—for special occasions is the challenge of cleaning them. I remember my grandmother and mom soaking them overnight in the bathtub or sink. While following in their footsteps, I also found that soaking your greens in the sink and adding vinegar to the water accelerates the cleaning process—no more overnight soaking. For those craving convenience, more and more shops carry precleaned and chopped greens and spinach.

A Historical Healing Connection

Orisha of the Greens
Ewe O, Ewe O
My plants; my plants!

—From *Odu of Ifa*, the word of Osayin, told by the Griot

Understanding gods, goddesses, angels, and nature spirits can help us understand a great deal about cultures and their healing ways in connection to foods. Practitioners of Ifa, a faith with origins in Nigeria, believe a variety of orishas (deities) populate the world. Today, there is popular discussion and appreciation of about a dozen orishas; however, there are at least six hundred.

A curious orisha every herbalist should know is Osayin, the patron of the herbal arts. Unlike most orishas, whose birth is of orisha parents, Osayin sprang forth from the womb of Mother Earth herself like a seedling. He stayed hidden within the forests and learned all there is to know about plants. Still, Osayin was the servant of Ifa, and, as such, he taught herbalism to Ifa and those knowledgeable of that particular path.

These days we would call this orisha physically challenged. He is called lame, as he has one arm, a very large ear that does not hear at all, and a tiny ear that hears extraordinarily well. This orisha has a high-pitched voice that is so irritating it is difficult to listen. Osayin is one-eyed and misshapen, according to griots who teach us through oral tradition. This complex orisha shows us what can become of greed and admonishes against hoarding our gifts. In modern language, his story is a cautionary tale to herbalists who become intoxicated with power, retaining it rather than sharing.

We know Osayin as the African Green Man, Yoruban orisha of herbal medicines of the forest, and patron of herbalists—known as curandeiros by the African-Brazilian people. Green is the color of health and healing in nature. Thanks to the chlorophyll that makes plants green, they are able to use the sun's energy to generate food through photosynthesis, a process that converts carbon dioxide and water into carbohydrates while releasing oxygen. Our Green Man, Osayin, is orisha of wild crafted herbs, berries, flowers, bark, and wood. One of the chief orishas, his presence has always captivated my imagination.

According to the griots, Osayin collected all the medicinal herbs of the forest as well as the knowledge of how to use them. As spiritual herbalist, he tucked all of his botanicals and knowledge in a guiro, or calabash. There were numerous other orishas with helpful characteristics to the business of the world, but Osayin wanted to keep the knowledge of herbs out of their reach—high up in a tree, hidden in a calabash.

Oya, orisha of weather and changes, generated a huge wind, followed by a storm that knocked the calabash of herbal knowledge down to earth. She did this with the blessing of numerous orishas who desired herbal wisdom. In the Americas and Caribbean, a path influenced by Ifa called Regla de Ocha (Rule of the Orisha), Osayin is represented by the güiro (gourd) that hangs in the Santeria ile (house-temple). Tribute needs to be paid to Osayin before his herbal medicine can be used in ceremony, spells, and cures. Osayin's symbols include the gourd where his spirit resides and a twisted tree branch, as well as his color—green. In Catholicism, St. Benito, St. Jerome, and St. Joseph represent his spirit.

As herbalists, we celebrate the magic held within the calabash, but we also realize that this earth wisdom should be available to all—this is the lesson of Osayin and the calabash. With no choice left, Osayin's calabash of herbal information, recipes, rituals, and ceremonies for health and spiritual well-being is now open to all. If you dare to look deep within the calabash, who knows what knowledge might be waiting inside?

Osayin's Green Bounty

While the family Cucurbitacea and calabash tree fruit brings Osayin's calabash immediately to mind, there are a few other precious gifts that are of him as well. These soul foods include greens. Green is Osayin's color and also represents the verdant essence of Mother Earth. Osayin's array of greens represents fertility, vitality, and health. Greens also instill these traits in us, building our resistance to illness and strengthening our entire body system.

In West Africa the preferred green is called bitterleaf, which is washed to remove its bitter taste. Cassava leaves are enjoyed, as are ewedu, red sorrel, yakuwa, lanṣun, and pumpkin leaves. Jamaica has made callaloo a much-loved vegetable and seafood stew featuring their unique greens called, variously, dasheen, Chinese spinach, taro tops, or callaloo bush. In Africa and the diaspora, beet tops, kale, and spinach are some other vegetable greens enjoyed. Here is a recipe for callaloo:

Callaloo

1	lb. callaloo leaves (can substitute spinach)
4	slices thick-cut, naturally cured bacon
1	medium vidalia onion
3	cloves garlic
¼	cup fresh thyme
1	teaspoon sea salt
1	teaspoon ground peppercorns
32	ounces organic free-range chicken stock
8	ounces crab meat
4	ounces coconut milk
1	cup young okra
	hot sauce (Tabasco) to taste

Wash callaloo or spinach well. Chop and set aside. Cut bacon into ½-inch squares. Chop onion finely. Add bacon to Dutch oven or heavy-bottomed saucepan over medium high heat. Fry for about 4 minutes. Add the onion and sauté until translucent. Mince the garlic. Wash, pat dry, then chop the thyme. Add thyme to pan, along with salt and pepper; cook another 3-4 minutes. Add the chicken broth. Allow this to deglaze the pan, then cover and cook on medium low for 10 minutes. Add the crab, coconut milk, and okra. Cook another 10 minutes. Check seasonings; add hot sauce if desired.

New Image for a New Age

When once people thought greens, such as collard, mustard, and turnip (tops), were a lowly food, now people all around the world celebrate the nutrient-rich gift of Osayin's greens. Greens are especially high in lutein, chlorophyll, and antioxidants. Lutein is the main antioxidant that helps the eyes. Greens are showing promise as a deterrent for macular degeneration. This ailment consists of a deterioration of the sensitive central region of the retina, which weakens the field of vision. The green vegetables with the highest concentration of lutein, in order, are kale, collard greens, and spinach.

Collard, mustard, and turnip greens need not be overcooked or fatty to be tasty. The soul food we enjoy is packed with anti-oxidant vitamins and minerals—especially wholesome when not overwhelmed by animal fat. In Asian cuisine, such as Thai, collards and other greens are stir-fried and they are delicious, showing there is no real need to cook the greens until they are dull and lifeless. Try your leafy vegetables (collard, mustard, and turnip greens) seasoned with apple cider vinegar, or sautéed in olive or palm oil with onion and cayenne. If you want to cook them more in accord with tradition, which amounts to stewed greens, by all means drink the broth (pot liquor) for additional optimal health benefits. Greens can also be braised with light olive oil, a dash of salt, apple cider, or balsamic vinegar, seasoned with cayenne and garlic, and simmered in chicken broth for about 20 minutes to retain their goodness. Traditionally our people have enjoyed cooking these vegetables in a cast-iron skillet, which is why I recommend a Dutch oven for cooking the callaloo. Cooking greens in cast iron and adding a dash of vinegar or splash of lemon makes them even richer in iron than they normally are, since some of the iron is leached from the pan. Some folks cook them with tomato, and the citrus interacts with the cast iron in the same way as vinegar or lemon, again enhancing their iron rich quality. Greens are an excellent food for young people who are having growth spurts, as well as pregnant women and the elderly, because they are high in calcium.

Lowly vegetable no more, greens in their various array of shapes, sizes, and shades are warming, energizing, tasty, healing foods. A gift for all seasons from Osayin!

Jams, Jellies, and Condiments

❧ by Tammy Sullivan ❧

A meal just doesn't seem complete without a few choice condiments. Salads seem naked without at least a little bit of dressing—and who wants French fries with no ketchup or salt? If those condiments happen to be fresh or home-preserved, so much the better.

Salt has been man's primary condiment since before recorded history. Other condiments have been around since at least 5000 BC, when the early Greeks began cultivating the olive. They soon developed a method to cold press the olives with a stone wheel and bottle the oil. Homer called olive oil "liquid gold."

Condiments are chosen for their ability to complement or enhance the flavor of various foods. Some possess intentionally overwhelming flavor because their past function was to

hide the fact that the food may not be fresh. Liquamen was an extremely popular condiment in ancient Rome—so popular, in fact, that it was the first mass-produced condiment with more than one ingredient. Liquamen, a salty fish sauce, is the precursor to the popular Worcestershire steak sauce.

Similarly, ancient China has manufactured soy sauce since the twelfth century BC and it has survived with a few minor changes. They also developed dipping sauces and the precursor to modern-day ketchup. Surprisingly, both ketchup and soy sauce originally were fish-based too.

Ancient Greece developed the forebear to modern gravy with a flour, water, and spice paste used to thicken stews. The ancient Greeks also used grape leaves in their food and would frequently wrap meats in them before cooking to add flavor and keep the meat juicy.

Mustard was another important herb for the ancient Greeks. With a diet consisting of plenty of fresh seafood, mustard leaves were frequently thrown into the stewpot or the seeds were ground and added to wine for a sauce. Mustard is known to have been used throughout ancient Egypt and Asia as well.

Yogurt and cheese came to be known around 5000 BC through accidental creation. Without a cool storage spot, milk would often begin to curdle within a few hours. Depending on the temperature, the resulting yogurt could be creamy or coarse. If it was coarse, it was used to make a soft cheese, as the process of making butter was not discovered for another 2,000 years. Butter is the only manmade condiment deemed fit for the gods.

Honey, a pure substance that required only human discovery, is the only other condiment the ancient Greeks deemed fit for the gods. Fittingly, the first recorded use of honey dates back to Egypt circa 5500 BC, when the ancient Babylonian and Sumerian cultures used it as an offering to the gods. Honey wine, also called Mead, was thought to be the earthbound equivalent of "Nectar," the drink of the gods.

Some Native American tribes rarely used salt, preferring sugar as their primary condiment. Each spring they would tap the maple trees and cook down the sap until they had a fine syrup they called "sweet water." This tradition carries on today with maple syrup being among the most popular of syrups.

Mankind's search for an earthbound ambrosia surely precipitated the continued creation of condiments. The desire to consume foods thought to impart magical qualities must have played a part as well. Early man must have thought he had stumbled upon true ambrosia when sugar was discovered. In 510 BC, Persian Emperor Darius spoke of the honey from the "reed without bees." He was speaking, of course, about cane sugar. Cane sugar took the place of fruit juice, date syrup, and honey as the primary sweetener almost as soon as it became available—and remains one of the most heavily cultivated crops in trade.

The condiment world really began to heat up with the discovery of horseradish root. Horseradish root made its debut around 1500 BC and the discovery is credited to none other than Apollo himself. According to legend, the Oracle at Delphi told him the root was "worth its weight in gold." Vinegar was usually added to the ground root to create a sauce. Eventually, it made its way to Japan and became the fabulous wasabi paste and dipping sauces of today.

The ancient Egyptians are credited with the invention of the first pickled items. In 500 BC, Herodotus wrote about the pickled fish and fowl that was frequently consumed by the ancient Egyptians. The popular pickled cucumbers that we enjoy today date back more than 3,000 years and originated in India.

As new types of herbs became more widely known due to seafaring tradesmen, new ways to prepare food followed. People no longer found it necessary to cover the taste with an overwhelming sauce when it could be improved by adding a few spices. Spices became highly sought-after items and frequently were used as currency. In fact, pepper was once demanded as a ransom payment in ancient Rome. Pepper was seen as the ultimate status symbol, for only the truly rich could afford it. Likewise, cinnamon was highly prized by the Romans, who considered it sacred because of its delightful aroma.

Ancient civilizations also prized their grapes. Fruit pectin was not understood yet, so most grapes were preserved as wine. Pliny the Elder researched and developed methods to keep wine from turning to vinegar. Today, flavored and wine vinegars are considered veritable staples on the spice shelf. Later on, spiced wine became all the rage in France and Spain.

Through the years, exciting new foods would be added to the rapidly growing list of condiments. In the late 1700s, condiments were revolutionized with the advent of home canning. It was now possible to taste sauces, relishes, and syrups from faraway lands, thanks to the longer shelf life.

Jelled sauces had been served since before recorded culinary history, although fruit pectin was not fully understood until the late 1800s. In the early 1800s, pioneers would boil their cider until it had a syrup consistency. Once the cider cooled, it formed into a jelly.

With so many varied condiments throughout the world, choosing new ones to try can be quite intimidating. Many go way beyond famous and into the infamous category. For instance, do you know what the leading sandwich spread is in Australia? I'll bet you can name at least one brand of hot sauce. Both condiments have been mentioned in numerous hit songs. Sugar and honey have become so synonymous with all things sweet that they are used as pet names for those we love—and let's not even discuss the many songs that feature them.

When you make your own condiments, you can tailor the recipe to suit your palate. An equally important consideration in making your own condiments is home preservation.

Why Preserve?

While it is certainly possible to make a small amount of a condiment, it is just as convenient to make several pints and save some.

It's also practical if you are using vegetables, herbs, or fruits from your own garden—I have yet to see anyone consume an entire tomato harvest in one sitting.

When you preserve the food from your home garden, you are in control from planting the seed to preparing the finished dish. You know exactly which ingredients were used and what pesticide system you implemented.

How Do I Preserve?

There are many methods of food preservation available today. Whether canning, freezing, dehydrating, vacuum packing, or storing in a root cellar, you can be assured of fresh-tasting food all year round. Let's begin with the easiest.

Freezing

Assuming that you already own a refrigerator equipped with a freezer, the only additional item you need for this preservation system is a box of plastic baggies. Jams, jellies, and pie fillings are easily stored in the freezer along with the vegetables. Frozen food retains its moisture content, color, vitamins, and most importantly, its full flavor.

Most vegetables only need to be cleaned and sliced before sliding into the baggie. Berries and other fragile items should be frozen in a baggie with water added to it. The water will form an ice block and keep the berries from being crushed. Certain vegetables keep best when blanched a few minutes before packaging for the freezer.

The downside to freezing is if you don't package the food correctly, it could get freezer burn. Also, the frozen food must be maintained at a subzero degree temperature, so a prolonged power outage could damage your stock.

Canning

Home canning has many benefits. Along with a long shelf life, canned food can be stored at room temperature. Canning is appropriate for many types of food including sauces, soups, vegetables, relishes, fruits, butters, and pickles.

The home-canning system requires a small investment. You will need glass jars, lids, rings, and a large pot. The rims of the jars should be fully submerged under water and processed in a water bath. A water bath is basically boiling the jars to ensure that no bacteria remain to spoil the food.

If making jelly, you will also need fruit pectin and a strainer bag. The jars and rings can be used over and over, but the lids must be replaced each time. The United States Department of Agriculture says the only truly safe canning procedures are those that include processing in the water bath with new lids for a tight seal.

Dehydrating

Dehydrating is the oldest form of food preservation known to man. Primitive cultures would place berries, grasses, and herbs upon large rocks and leave them lying in the sun until they had thoroughly dried. Although modern society has many choices when it comes to preserving food, dehydration is still the preferred method for herbs, flowers, apples, and potatoes.

Dehydrated food takes up little space and can be stored at room temperature. The initial cost of a food dehydrator is minimal, but is also optional. Tomatoes that are dehydrated in the sun are considered a delicacy.

There are no chemicals needed for food dehydration. No added sugars or salts. All you need is a sharp knife and trays (these can be made from window screens) for your dehydrating unit. Slice the herbs, fruit, or vegetables and slide them into the unit or arrange them on the screen trays. Now, either place the trays in the sun or turn the unit on. That's it! That is all there is to it! Let the sun or unit do its job while you relax. Once the food is completely dry, simply bag it in plastic baggies and store. This is a fantastic method for making nutritious snacks for children.

Vacuum Packaging

Vacuum packing requires the most expensive initial investment. Along with the machine, you must also purchase bags. While the bags are reusable, they are not cheap. But the process itself is simple and straightforward. Place the food in the bag, turn on the machine and—presto!—you're done. Coffee is best preserved in this method. While this preserves shelf life, some items should also be frozen.

Herbs are best kept in dehydrated form or frozen in water. If choosing to freeze, freeze whole leaves fully intact. Chop or grind after thawing.

There are many books and websites to guide you through the process step by step (no matter which preservation system you choose), or you can contact your local county home economist. Since this article is about the condiments themselves instead of the preservation systems, let's get to the recipes!

The jam, fruit butter, and jelly recipes are prepared for use with the home canning system. It takes time for the jelly to "set" or to gel properly.

Mayonnaise

1 egg
1½ cups olive oil
3 tablespoons lemon juice
1 teaspoon salt
1 teaspoon sugar

Combine all ingredients and whip until the right consistency. Add other spices as desired.

Ocalee's Dandelion Jelly

1 quart tightly packed dandelion petals (petals only)
2 quarts water
2 tablespoons fresh lemon juice

1   package fruit pectin
    Pinch of orange zest
    Squirt of fresh orange juice
5½ cups sugar

Rinse the petals thoroughly. Boil them in water until the water turns yellow, which normally takes 3 to 4 minutes. Remove the petals and squeeze the remaining moisture into the liquid. Take 3 cups of the petal liquid and add the pectin, lemon juice, and orange juice in a large boiler. Bring to a full boil and then add the sugar all at once. Boil for 2½ minutes. Pour into hot sterilized jars and process in the water bath for five minutes.

Blackberry Jelly

3½ cups blackberry juice
1   package fruit pectin
5   cups sugar
½   teaspoon butter

Sanitize the jars by placing them in boiling water for at least 10 minutes. Allow them to remain warm while you cook the jelly. Combine the juice, pectin, and butter over high heat. Stir constantly until it begins to boil. Add sugar all at once and continue stirring. Bring the mixture to a full rolling boil and allow it to boil for 1 minute. Remove from heat. Skim the foam off the surface. Ladle the liquid into the jars and place the lids and rings on them. Process in a hot water bath at least 10 minutes.

Yield: Seven 8-ounce jars.

Caramel Apple Butter

3   pounds apples
1   bag caramels
2   cups sugar

¼ teaspoon cloves

¼ teaspoon ginger

½ teaspoon cinnamon

Peel and puree the apples. Take 7 cups of the fruit pulp and cook it in a Crockpot along with the sugar. Allow the mixture to cook for 3 to 4 hours or until the consistency of applesauce. Stir in the caramels and spices. Resume cooking until the caramel has thoroughly melted. Place in hot jars and set in a water bath for 10 minutes.

Banana Butter

3 cups mashed bananas

¼ cup lemon juice

6½ cups sugar

Cherries or pineapple chunks (optional)

1 package fruit pectin

Combine all ingredients except the pectin in a large pot. Stir constantly until it comes to a full boil. Boil hard for 1 minute. Add pectin and stir. Skim off foam and pack into hot jars. Process 5 minutes.

Flora's Rose Petal and Champagne Jelly

1½ cups rose petals

Juice of 1 lemon

¾ cup champagne

1 package fruit pectin

1½ cups sugar

¾ cup water

Place the rose petals, lemon juice, and champagne in a blender and blend until smooth. Place the remaining water in a saucepan and add the sugar and pectin. Stir constantly and bring to a boil. Allow the mixture to hard boil for 1 minute. Pour the hot mixture into the blender and blend all of the ingredients together. Pour into hot jars. Process 5 minutes.

Southern Style Chow-Chow

1	head of cabbage
2	cups chopped green tomatoes
3	cups sliced cucumbers
2	cups sliced green peppers
1	cup sliced red peppers
1	tablespoon salt
1½	cups sugar
2½	cups vinegar
1	teaspoon each of the following spices: black pepper, onion powder, white pepper, and dill

Place all the vegetables in a large boiler, sprinkle with salt. Let them rest for a few hours. Drain, rinse, and drain again. Combine sugar, vinegar, and spices in a saucepan and bring to a boil. Simmer for 10 minutes. Add vegetables and simmer 10 more minutes. Pack into jars and process 10 minutes.

Greta's Pepper Relish

1	red onion
1	yellow bell pepper
1	red bell pepper
	Olive oil, tarragon, pepper

Slice or dice the onion and peppers. Pour a little olive oil in a skillet and toss in the vegetables. Throw fresh tarragon over the mixture. Stir-fry over medium heat until the red onion takes on a translucent appearance. Scoop the mixture from the oil and serve immediately.

Roman Vinegar

Fill a decorative bottle about ¼ full with garlic cloves, basil, thyme, and oregano. Heat red-wine vinegar in a small saucepan. Pour the vinegar over the herbs.

Honey-Vidalia Marinade

Place one whole Vidalia onion in a blender. Add three tablespoons honey and blend on high. Continue adding honey until the mixture is the same consistency as a runny applesauce. Pour over meat and baste as needed.

Greek Garlic Dressing

1 quart yogurt
2 cucumbers: peeled, seeded, and diced
2 cloves garlic, minced
3 tablespoons fresh dill, chopped fine
  salt and pepper to taste

Combine all ingredients. Serve as a dip or a salad dressing.

Pesto

Place 2 large cloves of garlic in your blender or food processor. Add 3 cups packed basil leaves, ½ cup black olives, 2 tablespoons Parmesan cheese, and ½ cup olive oil to the garlic. Blend mixture until crumbly. Add nuts if desired. Blend a few minutes more.

All-Purpose Seasoning Salt

Peel and slice garlic cloves. Run them through the dehydrator and grind. Add salt and pepper to the ground garlic. You may add a bit of powdered onion as well. Delicious on everything!

Roasted Garlic

Pop a head of garlic in a small baking dish. Add a bit of water and a bit of olive oil. Bake at 400 degrees F for 30 minutes. Squeeze the garlic flesh out of the papery shell.

Bouillon Cubes

To make your own bouillon cubes, keep the stock from any homemade soup. Boil it down until it is a bit thicker and freeze in an ice cube tray. Each cube is equal to one cube of store-bought bouillon. Keep in mind that yours will not be so highly concentrated in salt, so season accordingly.

Herbal Butters

To make herbal butters, allow the butter to soften at room temperature. Add in the herbs of choice and blend until it has a spreadable consistency.

Healthy Snacks To Go: A Few Options

Sliced bananas, dipped in honey and dehydrated.

Sliced apples and coconut, dehydrated and tossed with fresh grapes.

Nuts and dehydrated strawberry slices.

The fruit pulp left over from jelly making can be used in the dehydrator to make fruit leather.

Sweet, Sweet Stevia

❧ by Dallas Jennifer Cobb ❧

With increased awareness of the rise in obesity and diabetes in North America, many of us are looking for a natural, healthy alternative to sugar.

Stevia rebaudiana has so much sweetness packed into its leaves that it can be used in place of sugar. One leaf of stevia is ten to fifteen times sweeter than an equal amount of sugar. Plus, it contains no calories and has an effective glycemic index of zero.

Extracts of stevia, commonly used as sweeteners in Japan, China, and South America, are now finding their way into the mainstream markets of North America.

Stevia also has other health benefits. It is said to help fight tooth decay and gum disease by inhibiting oral bacteria, restoring pancreatic function

STEVIA

and correcting blood sugar problems, lowering high blood pressure, helping relieve nausea, softening skin and healing acne, and lessening cravings for sweets and smoking. With a repertoire so extensive, you may wonder why stevia is not widely used in North America.

The History of Stevia

The Guarani Indians of Paraguay, South America, have used stevia as a sweetener for centuries. Traditionally called Kaa-he-he (sweet herb), the Guarani gathered the wild stevia shrub and used it to sweeten their mate, a traditional tealike beverage. In the 1800s, Stevia use was documented throughout the region, in Paraguay, Brazil, and Argentina. Through trade links, stevia came to the attention of Europeans in the 1800s, was documented for analysis in a Hamburg, Germany, research laboratory, and noted in U.S. government releases of 1918.

Stevia rebaudiana was named by Dr. Moises Santiago Bertoni, director of the College of Agriculture in Asuncion, Paraguay, in 1887. He named the herb in honor of a Paraguayan chemist named Rebaudi, the first to extract the plant's sweet constituent, stevioside.

Historically, stevia, a native herb, was wild-crafted. The first commercial crop in 1908 yielded a ton of dried leaves. Following that, plantations producing stevia grew throughout Paraguay and similarly spread to Brazil and Argentina. During World War II, stevia was planted and used in England because of sugar rationing. In the 1960s, Japan strictly regulated the use of artificial sweeteners, but allowed the use of stevia as a replacement for sugar and other synthetic sweeteners.

Current Commercial Considerations

In 1991, the U.S. Food and Drug Administration banned the sale of stevia products. In 1994 they approved their sale as dietary supplements, meaning that they can carry claims of providing health benefits, but they cannot be marketed as conventional foods or food additives. Because of this, stevia still cannot be sold as a conventional food or sweetener, but may be purchased in a health food store and used at home in place of sugar.

While American authorities have refused to recognize stevia's potential as a conventional food or sweetener, it is currently grown and used widely in South America, Japan, China, Germany, Malaysia, Israel, and South Korea. In Canada, stevia is available only as a dietary supplement, but the department of agriculture has been conducting tests to determine the commercial viability of stevia as a crop and sweetener.

Growing Stevia

Stevia rebaudiana is a perennial shrub from the daisy family, native to mountainous areas of South America. In its naturalized environment, stevia is semitropical. Because stevia enjoys heat, it can be grown as a perennial in Zone 7 or warmer climates. In other climates and zones it can be grown as an annual, planted in a summer garden and harvested in the fall.

Stevia prefers a sandy loam with a slightly acidic to neutral pH. During the summer months, or through periods of intense heat, stevia enjoys light watering frequently. A generous layer of compost around the base of the plant will provide added protection and nutrition for the shallow feeder roots near the surface, preventing them from drying out. Though sensitive to drying out, stevia also dislikes too much moisture, so soil with a high sand content will ensure good drainage.

Stevia grows about two to three feet tall. The bushes have many branches bearing slightly serrated, opposing leaves. It also forms small white flowers at the end of summer, which must be removed to concentrate sweetness in the leaves.

While stevia can be grown from seed, it is a difficult and time-consuming process. Stevia seedlings can be ordered from herb nurseries and planted directly into your garden when soil temperatures exceed 65 degrees Fahrenheit. With one healthy plant you can make your own cuttings, by removing a three-inch tip, dipping it in rooting hormone and inserting it in sandy loam. Plant stevia in rows 20 to 24 inches apart, with about 15 inches between plants to accommodate their bushy growth. In addition to pinching off flowers, prune and pinch off leggy growth to encourage a bushy shape.

Feed stevia about once a month with a balanced fertilizer, either an organic compost or a compost with a lower nitrogen content than phosphoric acid or potash content. Organic fertilizers work best because they release nitrogen slowly.

Stevia seems to have an insect-repelling quality that deters grasshoppers. Though nontoxic, stevia is thought to repel insects by its very sweetness.

Where to Get Stevia Plants

It is important to buy stevia plants from reputable retailers to ensure that you get plants that are high in stevioside content, the natural sweetener in Stevia. Some recommended mail order sources are:

Herbal Advantage: Rte. 3, Box 93, Rogersville, MO 65742
Phone: 800-753-9929

Richter's Herbs: 357 Highway 47, Goodwood, Ontario L0C-1A0. Phone: (905) 640-6677 or fax: (905) 640-6641

Well Sweep Herb Farm: 205 Mt. Bethel Road, Port Murray, NJ 07865. Phone: (908) 852-5390

Harvesting Stevia

Glycosides, specifically stevioside, are the substances responsible for stevia's sweetness. The glycosides are concentrated in stevia leaves just before flowering, a process triggered by the shorter days of late summer and early fall.

Since the shorter days and cooler weather of autumn promote the formation of stevioside and intensify the sweetness of stevia, harvest as late as possible in the fall, but before the first killer frost. Continue to pinch back flowers and monitor the weather, timing your harvest for peak levels of stevioside.

If you live in a climate colder than Zone 7, you can either pull the plants from the ground, or use pruning shears to cut the stalk of the shrub near ground level.

If you live in a Zone 7 or warmer climate, your plants should be able to survive the winter outside. For these perennial plants, prune branches only—not the main stem—leaving about four inches of the branch. The first year's harvest may be minimal, but you will enjoy an abundant harvest the second year. But after this, the older a plant gets, the less productive it will be. Try to start new shoots of stevia each year so you always have some two-year-old plants in peak production.

Drying Stevia Plants

After harvesting stevia, the leaves need to be dried. Plants can hang upside down in the sun for a few hours on their branches before removing the leaves. When you remove the leaves, spread them on a screen or net for good air circulation. Because stevia doesn't require high temperatures to dry, air circulation is more important than excessive heat. Place the net or screen in the sun for a full day in warm autumn weather. Longer drying times may lower the stevioside content of the leaf. After drying, the dried leaves can be stored in a jar or airtight plastic container.

Using Stevia

Dried stevia can be stored as a leaf, or ground up in a food processor, coffee grinder, or with a manual mortar and pestle and stored as a powder. You can also make a liquid version by adding a cup of boiling water to about ¼ cup of finely powdered leaves. Let it set for 24 hours, then strain and refrigerate the liquid.

With these homemade products, you will need to experiment to determine the appropriate amount of ground stevia, or stevia liquid, to use in your recipes. Variances depend upon the concentration of steviosides in the plant.

Commercially produced stevia products are more reliable because they are commonly produced from plants containing a high level of stevioside. With these powdered extracts, you need only a miniscule amount of stevia to flavor a cup of tea or coffee. If you notice a bitter aftertaste when using these products, that is most often caused by using too much. Try reducing the amount of stevia and experimenting with taste. Brands higher in steviosides will provide a sweeter taste with less bitterness.

Stevia Conversion Chart

Although different stevia products offer different levels of sweetness, the chart below is based on the most common white powder extract form of stevia. When substituting stevia for sugar, use the following chart to determine proper amounts.

Granulated Sugar	Stevia Powder Extract
½ cup	⅛ teaspoon
¾ cup	⅕ teaspoon
1 cup	¼ teaspoon
10 pounds	⅘ ounce

Cooking with Stevia

Stevia can be used fresh, in its dried form, in its liquid version, or in a commercially produced white powder. One leaf of fresh stevia can be added to a glass of lemonade, ice tea, hot tea, or coffee. It can also be dropped into the cooking pot to sweeten sauces, jams, jellies, and sweets.

Most recipes requiring sugar can be adapted to use stevia. But because much less stevia powder is needed for the same sweet taste, you must adjust recipes to balance the liquid and dry ingredients. While many stevia products vary, in general, ¼ to ½ teaspoon of stevia powdered extract equals 1 cup of sugar.

Reducing the sugar in your diet helps reduce calories consumed and lowers the glycemic index of the baked or cooked food item. Mixing stevia with sweeteners like honey or maple syrup can provide a reduction in sugar and calories while maintaining good taste.

The most important thing to remember is not to use too much stevia. Start with a small amount, taste the effect, and then add more stevia to suit your taste. When you use too much stevia, you run the risk of adding that bitter aftertaste to your baking or cooking.

As stevia is sweeter than sugar, the dry volume of stevia used will be much less than sugar. So when you substitute stevia for sugar, recipes will need to be adjusted to maintain the same relative moisture content and consistency.

Stevia Drinks
Stevia Lemonade

2 cups fresh squeezed lemon juice

8 cups water

¼ to ½ teaspoon stevia powder

Combine lemon and water in a large pitcher. Add ¼ teaspoon of stevia powder and stir. Add additional stevia to taste. Add ice, garnish with mint leaves or fresh lemon if desired, and serve in tall glasses.

Stevia Iced Tea

½ cup fresh squeezed lemon juice

8 cups brewed tea, cold

¼ to ½ teaspoon stevia powder

Combine lemon and tea in a large pitcher. Add ¼ teaspoon stevia powder, and stir. Add additional stevia to taste. Add ice and garnish and serve in tall glasses.

Stevia Hot Chocolate for Four

3 tablespoons cocoa powder

½ teaspoon powdered stevia extract

¼ cup boiling water

4 to 5 cups soy milk or milk

2 tablespoons honey or maple syrup

7 mini marshmallows (optional)

In a saucepan, mix cocoa and stevia. Add boiling water and stir. Add the soy milk or milk. Keep at medium heat—do not boil. Add honey or maple syrup to taste. Garnish with mini marshmallows.

Stevia Snacks

Stevia Chocolate Chip Walnut Cookies

1 cup butter

1 egg

1 teaspoon stevia powder

1 teaspoon vanilla

2¼ cups whole grain flour (whole wheat or spelt)

Pinch of sea salt

1 teaspoon baking soda

2 cups semisweet chocolate chips

1 cup chopped walnuts

Preheat the oven to 375 degrees F. In a large bowl, blend the butter, egg, stevia and vanilla, creating a creamy mixture.

In a medium bowl mix the dry ingredients.

Add the dry mixture to the creamy mixture slowly, stirring well after each addition. Add chocolate chips and walnuts and stir well. Drop heaping teaspoons of dough onto a nonstick cookie sheet. Bake at 375 degrees F for 10 to 13 minutes, until the cookies are golden brown. Yields about 4 dozen.

Stevia Apple Crisp

1½   cups rolled oats
1   cup whole grain flour (whole wheat or spelt)
½   cup butter melted
¼   teaspoon salt
1   teaspoon nutmeg
2   teaspoons cinnamon
1½   teaspoons stevia powder
   Dash of vanilla

6   medium apples: peeled and cored, sliced thin
¼   cup applesauce
¾   cup raisins (optional)
½   cup walnuts (optional)

Preheat oven to 375 degrees F. Mix the first 8 ingredients together. Use about ¼ of the mix to line the bottom of an 8 x 12 baking dish. Spread apples and applesauce evenly, add raisins and walnuts if you choose. Cover with the remaining dry mixture. Bake at 375 degrees F for 30 minutes, then turn up to 450 degrees F for 5 to 7 minutes to brown the top.

Brian's Stevia Banana Bread

2   very ripe, brown spotted medium or large bananas
1   egg
½   teaspoon powdered stevia
¼   cup oil
¼ to ⅓   cup soy milk or milk
2   cups whole grain flour (whole wheat or spelt)
2   teaspoons baking powder
½   teaspoon baking soda

1 teaspoon cinnamon

1 teaspoon mace

½ cup walnuts (optional)

Mash the bananas in a large bowl. Preheat oven to 350 degrees F. Beat in the egg, oil, stevia powder, and milk. Combine all dry ingredients in a large bowl.

Fold dry ingredients into the wet ingredients, stirring as little as possible. Add walnuts, stir briefly. Pour into a nonstick loaf pan. Bake at 350 degrees F for 50 minutes to 1 hour until a toothpick comes out clean. Yield 1 loaf.

Stevia Pumpkin Pie

10 to 12 ounces soft or silken tofu

¼ cup oil

1 15-ounce can plain pumpkin

2 tablespoon maple syrup

⅛ teaspoon stevia powder

½ teaspoon stevia extract

¼ teaspoon salt

1 teaspoon cinnamon

½ teaspoon ginger

¼ teaspoon nutmeg

Blend all ingredients until smooth and creamy. Pour into an unbaked pie shell. Bake at 350 degrees F for 1 hour. Cool and serve.

Whether you try these recipes or experiment and develop your own, you will find stevia to be a versatile, sweet herb. May you find sweetness, one recipe at a time, and not feel that you have to forego sweet treats in order to invest in your health.

Happy cooking with sweet, sweet stevia.

Creating a Community Kitchen

❧ By Kaaren Christ ❧

There is nothing new about women coming together around some heat-producing element to feed our families. We have been doing it for generations, long before the oven, the stove-top range, or the microwave. From time immemorial we have gathered around fires, clay ovens, and fire pits to tend to the tasks of feeding ourselves and those we love. We traveled in groups following food, and we prepared meals with what the seasons offered.

Before all of the modern conveniences we take for granted today, "feeding" was a task that took all day, every day. When we weren't actually preparing the food that would nourish our families, we were thinking about it. We would discuss the availability of ingredients with other womenfolk, collect the wood needed

for the fire, and, finally, tend to cooking the actual meal. In days gone by, the cooking and sharing of food was the event that organized people's activities every day. It brought us together. If you didn't come home to eat, you simply didn't eat. No one else was going to feed you. Villages were often separated by miles, and there were no convenience foods to fill an empty stomach.

The experience of coming together to prepare food is almost nonexistent for many women today. Although many of us still sit down with our loved ones at the end of the day to share a meal, it is quite likely that we made it happen all by ourselves.

The experience of eating together has changed, too. Preparing the food is no guarantee that our families will come home to eat it with us. There are many other options that simply didn't exist years ago. Food can be found on every corner—full meals, snacks, and an endless array of convenience food. If you live in a big city center, the choices are endless. We no longer rely on our families to eat. Cooking and eating have become solitary pursuits.

Not only has cooking and eating become a rather lonely event, it doesn't demand as much thought and attention. Because our survival no longer depends on growing our own vegetables, raising our own animals, or grinding our own grain—and since we can be fed without stoking fires or tending pots—the time we actually spend on tasks to feed ourselves and our families is only a tiny fraction of what it once was.

Even without fast food restaurants, just take a quick trip down the grocery store aisle and you'll find a wide variety of prepackaged meals to choose from—lasagna, stir-fries, roasted chickens, etc. In the three minutes it takes to get from one end of the aisle to the other, our task is half complete!

From there, it only takes a quick scan of the packaging for cooking time and temperature, a quick punch of a button, and the work happens without us. It's quick—it's hard to argue that. It's convenient too, but perhaps something has been lost. When that lasagna finally reaches the table, it arrives without fanfare or celebration, without a history that has meaning or emotion. What's to say about it? Maybe you liked the picture on the box. Maybe it was a brand you have had good luck with before. Maybe it was on sale.

How It Started

I didn't think of any of these things until I became a new mom. I was living on a beautiful gulf island off of the coast of Vancouver Island, British Columbia. I had followed a dream that I was lucky enough to be living: a little piece of land to call my own, a log cabin, and acres of giant Douglas Firs, Hemlocks, and Western Cedars. During my pregnancy I had a wonderful midwife, and through her met many other mothers who were also following dreams and living in this secluded island paradise.

During that time, adult company was easy to find and good meals were often shared at dinner gatherings. There were long conversations with friends over pots of tea at the local bakery and many potluck meals that lasted well into the evening.

But one by one our babies were born, and those days of leisure seemed to vanish along with all of those communal eating experiences. Our mornings now began when babies awoke, and we fell into bed not long after they fell asleep in the evenings. It seemed we were forced into the seclusion of our own homes, separated by miles, with only our babies to keep us company.

Babies—don't get me wrong—are wonderful company. But I was so hungry for adult companionship after three months that I would have eaten company if they had found me! But I was also hungry in a very literal way, and during this time I became painfully aware of my growing need for good food.

As a breastfeeding mother, I was almost as voracious as my daughter. My motivation coalesced one particularly chaotic afternoon when all the chores on my list remained as incomplete as they had been at 9:00 A.M. Laundry formed mountains on the couch, dishes filled the sink, and there was a pot of plums stewing on the woodstove I already knew I would never find time to preserve. And there I was, standing at the counter bouncing a fussy baby on my hip and eating cold tuna out of a can with a fork, almost faint with hunger. "I need to eat better than this."

I began to talk to others about being lonely. And about being hungry. Not long after I became aware of my loneliness, my midwife suggested I start a community kitchen with other new moms. "That way you get good company and good food," she had said.

A community kitchen? That was crazy! How would we manage? I barely had enough time to add mayonnaise to a can of tuna! How could a group of women all in the same situation ever manage to get anything done? My mind was reeling, imaging the potential chaos, the mess, the … the … food!

I suddenly realized I was just hungry enough to try it.

The following is for anyone who has ever experienced the same hunger.

What Is a Community Kitchen?

A community kitchen is simply people coming together to share the task of preparing food. The kitchen itself doesn't matter much, although it should be safe and clean. Beyond that, what it looks like is entirely up to the group. It may be in someone's home, at a community center, or in a church basement. There can be as few as two people cooking or as many as fifty participating on a rotating schedule. Some kitchens are very organized and have regularly scheduled meetings and committees while others happen occasionally, whenever members can get together in an ad hoc fashion. Some groups meet twice a week, some weekly, others monthly. Some have well-crafted menus, others work with whatever food happens to be available that day.

Why Start a Community Kitchen?

The reasons for cooking together are as individual and different as each member. My decision was born out of two needs: the need for adult companionship and the desire to continue enjoying tasty and nutritious meals amid the rigors of motherhood. But there are many other reasons: an attempt to share recipes and cooking skills, a desire to save money on the weekly grocery bill, a longing to try a wider variety of food, a way to save time.

In some groups, the goal is simply to learn to cook. Each kitchen shares one thing: together, people share the work and pleasure of creating food, which is divided and shared among them when finished cooking.

Let's Get Cooking

Sometimes an organization will start a community cooking group. Generally, these groups are advertised and open to the public. They tend to happen in a community building of some sort and often have a fully equipped kitchen. The organization that hosts the group might receive funding, which usually means that the cost to the participant is quite reasonable. Sometimes the organization will target a particular group of people, like new mothers or seniors.

Other community kitchens get started when one woman gets tired of eating tuna out of a can. She makes two or three phone calls out of desperation, and the kitchen is "born." Our kitchen was born when four women with new babies and similar needs decided to get together once a week at each other's homes and cook.

We met for a few weeks and enjoyed it so much we wanted to share the experience. We didn't advertise, we just started telling other mothers with young babies what we were doing. Within six months we had grown to a group of twenty women, with each of us cooking twice a month on alternate Wednesday mornings, at two different homes.

Structure

There are a number of ways to structure a group if you wish to start one. It's not a bad idea to start with four or five people until you get a sense of how you will work with one another's schedules and divide tasks, and, of course, what you will cook! Have an initial meeting over tea. Brainstorm recipes, taking into account dietary needs of all members. In the beginning, we all happened to be vegetarians and shared similar tastes. As the group grew, women joined who were not vegetarians, but we continued to prepare vegetarian meals because while vegetarians did not eat meat, the meat eaters still enjoyed eating vegetables.

Because we all had babies who were most often with us, we decided that the best way to manage was for one of us to take "baby duty" each week, and rotate this responsibility. Whether you were on baby duty or cooking duty, you still received your share of the food prepared for that week. One of us would set up shop in the living room to play with the children while the rest got cooking.

Sometimes a family member who wasn't interested in cooking would help out with the little ones, which was very helpful. Finding a young teenage girl who lives nearby and eager to begin babysitting is also a good idea—for a couple of dollars each, four babies can enjoy playtime with a fresh face, and four mothers have the assurance of being in the next room if needed. It was a wonderful arrangement for everyone.

Menus

Our group usually made three or four dishes each week. We had only one firm "rule"—our weekly menu had to include some kind of soup. In addition to the soup, we would prepare one more main dish—maybe a vegetarian lasagna, enchiladas, ratatouille, or stuffed peppers. The other two food items varied depending on what was in season, as well as the collective whim of the group.

Sometimes we would bag all of the dry ingredients needed to make a spice cake or a banana bread, and need only to add eggs, milk, or butter at home. Other times we would make loaf or cookie batter completely, leaving only the baking to do at home. Some groups compile a little recipe book for their members, so that there is some valued predictability to their "tried and true" favorites, even when members change on occasion.

Supplies

You don't need a lot of supplies to have a community kitchen. We found it helpful if each person had their own little "kitchen kit" to bring to each cooking session. This included a favorite cutting knife, a good-sized cutting board, a wooden spoon, and a tea towel.

Each person brought their own containers to put their portion of the prepared food in as well. Some brought Tupperware, others reused plastic margarine containers or brought tinfoil. This way, no one person needed to have a fully stocked kitchen, and each person came prepared to work.

Our group invested in only one piece of communal equipment—a high-quality stockpot for making the large batches of soup. This pot traveled with the group week to week. For most other menu items, the regular-sized bowls and utensils found in most kitchens were enough to satisfy our needs.

Ingredients

When we initially planned our group, we found it helpful to decide on a number of standard menu items that we all enjoyed and create a monthly menu so we could plan in advance. We were fortunate to live near a food cooperative that sold many of the ingredients we regularly needed in large quantities for a good price. At the end of each session, we would look ahead to the next week's menu, collect the money necessary to purchase next week's ingredients (many everyday ingredients like salt, common herbs, spices, etc., were contributed by members who hosted), and decide who was going to pick up the groceries. Sometimes we would make a decision to buy a large bag of brown rice, for instance, with the understanding that one member would keep the rice at their home and be responsible for bringing rice if it was required the next week.

The cost to participate will vary widely depending on the group's tastes and preferences. When there were four of us and we used a lot of seasonal produce that we came by in various "creative ways," we found that $10 to $20 per week was more than enough, and allowed us to create dishes that were truly delightful—with high-quality ingredients and special additions that most of us would never have indulged in by ourselves. Leftover ingredients would be housed by one member, and reappear weeks later when needed. There was a wonderful mixture of planning and spontaneity.

One of the most wonderful benefits of being a part of a community kitchen is the way you can enjoy the bounties of each season. Often, Mother Nature offers much more than any one of us could manage on our own, but together we were able to enjoy all of Her blessings, year-round. If you start a group, ask yourselves—what's in season? What produce is ready to harvest? Are there local farmers or orchards that regularly have excess produce that they might offer the group for free or at a reduced rate?

Cooking with the Seasons

When parsley was bursting into bright green bunches in the herb garden, that was the time to make tabouli and couscous salads. After a long winter of hot soups and stewed vegetables, we would anticipate those early spring salads with delight;

eaten cool, full of crisp celery and radishes, chickpeas, lemon juice, and enough parsley to turn it as green as spring itself. In June, we would stew plums and cherries that grew along old homestead roads and make jams. Sometimes we would simply wash large amounts of fresh lettuces and radishes, drying and portioning the freshly harvested vegetables. Other times we would grate up a batch of carrots or other vegetables and put them into little containers so that once home, we simply needed to toss the prepared fresh produce together to enjoy a complete salad, something none of us ever felt we had time to do during the day.

Summer brought batches of tomato salsa and cold cucumber soup, and when the nights turned cold, we would cook up French onion and potato and leek soup. In our area, an orchard owner would offer people all the windfall apples they could gather, just so the apples didn't rot on the ground. This led to a monthlong apple blitz—making homemade apple sauce, vats of apple squash soup, and apple jelly. One member who had a food dehydrator made apple rings for everyone.

There are as many kinds of community kitchens as there are communities. Each has its own birth story, its own childhood, and its own life cycle. Despite the differences, there is something that unites them all.

Those weekly cooking sessions brought previously isolated women together for only three hours each week, but the benefits—the gifts—we received were felt every day and could not be measured. Parenting tips were shared over stew, sad stories shared during the chopping of onions. We learned about one another's ambitions and heartaches, and supported each other through many life changes. Occasionally, when someone in our midst would become ill, have a family crisis, or give birth to a new baby, our little group would take food to the family.

As our babies grew into toddlers, we made time to sit together for a little bowl of soup before washing the dishes at the end of our session. Our little ones learned about the pleasures of sharing food that had history—and heart. When they were yet a little older, they learned to wash lettuce or butter buns. We were relearning something that had been lost when we were each alone in our own homes, something important. When we gathered to make food for ourselves and our families, we weren't simply cooking—we were cooking up community.

Herbs for Health

All About Arnica

❧ by Chandra Moira Beal ❧

A rnica Montana is a highly useful herb with many applications. Appreciated and used
for generations, the plant's properties
act on the veins, capillary vessels, and
the skin to produce a wide range of
anti-inflammatory and anti-neuralgic
effects, making it an essential item in
the household first-aid kit.

Arnica in History

In countries where arnica is indigenous, it has long been a popular remedy. Preparations of arnica were listed
in the *United States Pharmacopoeia* (the
official listing of approved drugs in the
United States) from the early 1800s
until 1960. The species was described
in 1814 by the eminent German botanist Frederick Pursh in his monu-
mental collection *Flora Americae*

Septentrionalis. Pursh was the first to publish works about the many new plants collected by the Lewis and Clark Expedition of 1804 to 1806.

It may be no coincidence that arnica grows in rocky slopes and mountains—just the type of place where people and animals are most likely to fall and bruise themselves. Arnica was introduced to European folk medicine when shepherds, who pastured their sheep in the alpine slopes of the mountains, noticed that when sheep fell and bruised themselves, they nibbled on the leaves of the arnica plant. Hence, it is called "fallkraut"—literally the "fall herb"—in German.

Allopathic and traditional Western physicians began using arnica extensively in the nineteenth century to treat external lesions such as those caused by a blow, a fall, or a contusion. The homeopath Teste, writing of the physicians of this era, noted that "Arnica is undoubtedly one of those drugs, the therapeutic properties of which have been most justly valued by allopathic physicians."

In North America, the flowers are used more often than the roots. A legend goes that mountain climbers used to chew the fresh arnica plant to relieve sore, aching muscles and bruises from falls. Preparations made from the flowering heads have been used in homeopathic medicine for hundreds of years. It is extremely popular in Germany, and more than 100 drug preparations are made from the arnica plant alone. Large quantities of arnica were marketed during World War II.

Plant Characteristics

Arnica, a perennial herb indigenous to Central Europe that grows mainly in woodlands and mountain pastures, is also found in England and southern parts of Scotland and Siberia. After being imported to North America, the plant is now widespread where it grows wild, particularly in moist soil conditions in mountains and valleys at elevations between 3,500 to 10,000 feet.

Arnica is a member of the economically important sunflower family, *Asteraceae-compositae*, the largest plant family in North America. Primarily cultivated in central and western North Dakota, Colorado, northeastern California, and Canada (in areas spanning from Saskatchewan to British Columbia), the plant has been collected at elevations as high as 11,000 feet in the Rocky Mountains.

It is also known as Mountain Arnica, Mountain Daisy, Mountain Tobacco, Leopard's Bane, Wolf's Bane, and Sneezewort. The origin of the generic name is unknown, but is possibly is a corruption of *ptarmica*, which is Greek for "causing to sneeze."

The bright green leaves are narrow and four to six inches long. They form a flat, clustered rosette. The upper leaves are toothed and slightly hairy, while the lower leaves have rounded tips. A large stem, round with stiff, short hairs, rises from the center about one to two feet high. The center stem ends in one to three flower stalks, with each stem bearing one to three flower heads about two inches wide. When the plant flowers each year around May to July, it produces blooms that are bright orange and yellow, similar in appearance to daisies. The flowers are hermaphroditic (they have both male and female organs) and are pollinated by bees, flies, moths, and butterflies. The seeds have a tuft of grayish white hairs. The rhizome, or root, is dark brown, cylindrical, usually curved, and bears brittle wiry rootlets on the undersurface.

Growing Arnica

Although you can buy arnica remedies in natural food stores, try growing your own plants to create your own customized remedies. Don't expect any flowers the first year. Be patient. The plant must first develop roots to ensure that you have flowers for years to come.

Arnica thrives in moist soil, usually in the open woods and

especially under stands of aspen and pine. It prefers a well-drained soil mixture that is lime-free, but rich in loam, peat, and sand. The plant does well in acidic, neutral, and alkaline soils—even growing in highly acidic soil or nutritionally poor soil. Grown in full sun, arnica plants can reach a height of one to two feet, but can also grow in partial shade, preferably a mottled shade with no afternoon sun exposure. Possible locations for a plot of arnica are woodlands, cultivated beds, sunny garden edges, or areas with dappled shade. Arnica is hardy to Zone 6 and is not frost tender.

The plants may be propagated by root division or from seed. For best results, sow seeds in early spring and plant out in May. Divide plants in the spring. Arnica seeds are available online at www.johnnycyberseed.com or from Rocky Mountain Rare Plants at www.rmrp.com.

Harvesting Your Own Arnica

When harvesting arnica flowers, some rules apply:

- Harvest after a dry spell, as rain can dilute the flowers' potency.

- Take no more than half of a single plant or stand of plants. Because arnica flowers often come up in threes, take only one flower from a plant.

- Harvest flowers on the Full Moon to capture their full potency.

- Pick flowers in their prime. Avoid old or bug-infested flowers.

Actions

Arnica contains a bitter, yellow crystalline substance called arnicin. Tannin and phulin are also present. The flowers are thought to contain more arnicin than the root, but no tannin. The active components in arnica are sesquiterpene lactones, which reduce inflammation and decrease pain. Other active principals are thymol, which acts as an antiseptic, local anesthetic, cooling agent, and preservative (it's also found in Listerine mouthwash!); flavonoids, water-soluble plant pigments that strengthen capillaries and other connective tissue, and act as anti-inflammatory, antihistaminic, and antiviral agents; inulin, a storage food in the plants of the Composite family which may promote good digestion; and carotenoids, natural plant pigments such as beta carotene and lycopene.

How It Works

Arnica works by stimulating white blood cells, which perform much of the digestion of congested blood, and by dispersing trapped, disorganized fluids from bumped and bruised tissue, joints, and muscles. Its discutient property helps dissolve unwanted buildup such as tumors and its antibacterial function helps ward off illness. Arnica is also known to stimulate blood circulation, especially in the coronary arteries. Combined, such qualities can improve your general well-being or shorten recovery time for injuries, relieving fatigue and stiffness from overexertion or trauma.

Having applications for a wide range of physical and emotional shocks and injuries, arnica makes an excellent all-around first-aid remedy. Many topical preparations containing arnica are available commercially, but you can also make your own from homegrown flowers (see recipes below). Arnica is most commonly prepared as a tincture, which can also be used as the base for creams, liniments, ointments and salves, and compresses and poultices. Homoeopathic tinctures have been used successfully to treat epilepsy and seasickness (taken before sailing and every hour on board until comfortable).

Arnica also comes in diluted homeopathic forms for topical and oral use. A number of homeopathic remedies are available in oral pill, topical, or intravenous forms.

Homeopathic preparations of arnica have a remarkable effect on tissue injured due to trauma or surgery: there is less discoloration from bruises; reduced bleeding, aches, and swelling; and the general effects of the injury are lessened. Unlike aspirin, homeopathic arnica is active topically (as a gel, cream, or ointment) as well as when taken internally (oral pellets). When used together, the topical and internal forms have a better effect on healing.

The cream, gel, or ointment is typically rubbed on the skin to soothe and heal bruises and sprains, and to relieve irritations from trauma, arthritis, and muscle or cartilage pain. Applied as a salve, arnica is also good for chapped lips, irritated nostrils, and acne. The plant is also used externally for arthritis, burns, ulcers, eczema, and acne.

As an anti-inflammatory, it's useful before, during, or after competitive sports; with intense, sustained effort such as long-distance driving or lengthy airplane trips to prevent deep vein thrombosis; and during physical therapy, or even before or after dental extractions and surgery, as arnica promotes rapid healing of damaged tissues.

There are no known side effects or drug interactions, unlike acetaminophen, aspirin, and ibuprofen, which can contribute to liver toxicity, impair kidney function, increase bleeding, and irritate the gastrointestinal tract. Camphor or menthol rubs are great for sore or tired muscles but have no effect on deep muscles, often have a strong odor, and can't be used with heat. On the other hand, arnica acts on the whole body and can be used safely with heat.

For instance, the tincture has been used as a paint for chilblains when the skin is unbroken. For tender feet, a foot bath of hot water containing a half ounce of the tincture is said to bring great relief. Applied to the scalp, it encourages hair to grow. Arnica oil may also be used in topical preparations.

There are many more ways to effectively use arnica—by itself, or as part of a compound. Among others, arnica flowers are sometimes prepared with other Compositae family flowers. Those that work especially well with arnica are:

- Pot marigold (*Calendula officinalis*)
- British elecampane (*Inula brittanica*)
- Joseph's flower (*Kragapogon pratensis*—similar to salsify)
- Viper's grass (*Scorzonera humilis*)

Take Precautions

As with all herbs, care should be taken with their use and application. If you are pregnant or breastfeeding, consult with your physician before taking any medication, including herbs.

The only exception is that arnica can be taken internally in suitable homeopathic dilutions. Homeopathic doses are very diluted and generally considered safe for internal use when taken as directed on the product label.

Used topically, arnica is generally safe. However, prolonged use may irritate the skin, causing eczema, peeling, blisters, or other skin conditions. Arnica should not be used on broken skin, such as leg ulcers.

While arnica has also been used internally as an herbal remedy for certain heart disorders, it should only be used this way under the supervision of a health care provider. An experienced clinician may recommend arnica as an herbal remedy for heart conditions, angina, or coronary artery disease.

Arnica in herbal form is primarily restricted to external use because it can cause serious side effects when it is used internally, such as dizziness, tremors, and heart irregularities. It may also irritate mucous membranes, induce weakness, and cause vomiting. Arnica should only be used internally under the supervision of a professional clinician who understands the risks and benefits of this herb.

Making Your Own Arnica Remedies

The following is a sampling of generally safe topical treatments, all of which are intended for external use only.

Arnica Liniment

Fill a wide-mouthed jar with fresh, clean flowers. Fill to the top with rubbing alcohol. Shake at least once a day for fourteen days; twice a day is better. Strain off the liquid and throw out the flowers.

Swab the liniment on skin with cotton wool or fingers two to three times a day. You can also dip a cloth in the liniment, lay it on the skin and cover it with a bandage.

Arnica Massage Oil

Anti-inflammatory as well as relaxing to the nerves.

- 4 ounces sweet almond oil
- 4 ounces sunflower oil
- 1 tablespoon arnica extract
- 10 drops lavender oil
- 1 tablespoon St. John's Wort extract

Combine all ingredients in a jar and shake well. Leave to steep for a day, then bottle and label. Apply as a massage oil to tired and achy muscles.

Arnica Sports Oil

This blend is great for sports injuries, muscular pain, and inflammation.

- 4 ounces sweet almond oil
- 4 ounces sunflower oil
- 1 tablespoon dried arnica flowers
  or arnica powder

Combine all ingredients in a jar and shake well. Leave to steep for a day, then bottle and label. Rub into joints before and after sports activities, and to accelerate recovery after injury or strain.

Topical Arnica Tincture

Use as a liniment or as a base for arnica creams and salves.

6 ounces powdered arnica flowers
(available from herbal suppliers or at some health food stores)
8 ounces grain alcohol (180 proof)
A glass jar with a screw-top lid

Add the powdered arnica to a glass jar containing the grain alcohol. Mix well by stirring constantly for about ten minutes. Screw the lid on the jar and allow the mixture to set overnight. This allows the arnica flowers to dissolve more completely in the alcohol. The next day strain the mixture using cheesecloth as a filter. Bottle the resulting fluid and label. While this is not a pharmaceutical-grade tincture of arnica, it is a very effective preparation for taking the extreme soreness out of bruises. Apply externally only.

Arnica Tea Bath

Place one tablespoon of the powdered arnica flowers in a cup of boiling water and steep for ten minutes. Pour the liquid through a cheesecloth to filter out any powdered solids. The warm solution of arnica tea may be applied directly to the bruised area, or poured into a bath for a therapeutic soak.

Antibiotic Oil

1 full dropper of arnica flower tincture
2 tablespoon sesame seed oil
5–10 drops rosemary oil

Combine all the ingredients in a small bowl, then pour onto cotton gauze to treat a cut or bruise. Keep the gauze over the cut for three days, changing the gauze daily. On the fourth day, allow the cut to air dry.

Breathe Easy

❧ by Sally McSweeney ❧

E veryone has heard the old adage "you are what you eat," but how many of us realize that we are also what we breathe? Every minute, we inhale and exhale approximately ten to fifteen times, extracting oxygen from the air and releasing carbon dioxide and water back into the air. Oxygen is vital for our bodies—our very survival depends upon the efficiency of this unconscious process, especially when we are compromised by illness or unfavorable surroundings.

Healthy lungs need a healthy environment. When we breathe polluted air, we contaminate our lungs. The subsequent irregular, interrupted, or inefficient breathing can result in respiratory infections and diseases. There are two major forms of respiratory diseases: congestion and spasm. Congestive problems, such as

bronchitis, coughs, and pleurisy, are the result of mucus buildup; spasm-related conditions, such as asthma, nasal catarrh, colds and influenza, and sinusitis, generally arise from allergens and pollutants in the environment and at home.

In either case, the first step against this is prevention. A good diet and exercise regimen can bolster your immune system. You can also take steps to improve the air you breathe every day. According to the Environmental Protection Agency, people in the United States spend more than 90 percent of their time indoors where, amazingly, concentrations of certain pollutants are higher than outdoors!

Fortunately, indoor-air quality can be enhanced with some relatively simple measures. HEPA filters (widely used in hospitals for years, but now readily available in stores) can filter out minute harmful air particles. Vacuuming regularly, or getting rid of carpets, if possible, eliminates larger particulates. Take special care of your bedrooms because you spend all night there. Wash your bed linens in hot water to kill dust mites and consider switching to hypoallergenic pillows. Animal lovers should try to keep pets out and bathe them once a month to reduce dander (despite the vociferous objection of most cats). Other considerations include acquiring a dehumidifier for the home if it is excessively damp or purchasing a humidifier, which regulates humidity in a safe, water vapor form, if dry air is a problem. Houseplants provide oxygen to the environment, but can also produce mold from the damp soil, so choose plants like Boston ferns that do not require a lot of water.

However, as hard as you try to maintain a healthy lifestyle and environment, it is not always possible to escape pesky pollutants or bacteria. In those instances, herbal remedies can greatly benefit the respiratory system. These herbs belong to several major categories:

Anti-catarrhal: Herbs such as boneset, coltsfoot, and elder help the body to get rid of excess catarrh or mucus.

Demulcents: Corn silk, flaxseed, marshmallow leaf, and slippery elm are among herbs that contain mucilage, which has a "slippery" quality that enables them to lubricate, and therefore protect, inflamed mucus membranes.

Respiratory Stimulants or Expectorants: Herbs that stimulate the nerves and muscles of the respiratory system and remove excess mucus include elecampane, hyssop, lobelia, and mullein.

Respiratory Relaxants: Sensitive lung tissues are relaxed by herbs like aniseed, thyme, and wild cherry bark, which often promote expectoration.

Pectorals: Herbs that strengthen the whole respiratory system include echinacea, garlic, goldenseal, hyssop, and mullein. It is advisable to always have several on hand.

Congestion-Related Respiratory System Diseases

Congestion is a result of excess mucus production and is often caused by infection. Many doctors are happy to hand out antibiotics to combat the symptoms, but do not address the cause or prevention. Remember "we are what we eat"? Many foods are mucus forming and when we overindulge, we experience mucus build-up, and therefore, congestion. Also, antibiotics will destroy the "good bacteria" in our digestive system, which can lower resistance to subsequent threats to our immune system. The circle is now complete; we are now more susceptible to infection. Maintaining a mucus-free diet is not easy; you should limit dairy products, eggs, many grains—especially wheat, oats, and rye as they contain gluten—and starchy vegetables such as potatoes.

Bronchitis

Bronchitis occurs when the bronchi, the inner walls that line the main air passages of the lungs, become infected and inflamed. It is best treated with pectorals or expectorants and demulcents.

Elecampane root (*Inula sp.*) is an excellent expectorant and anti-bacterial specifically used where there is an excess of catarrh and accompanying cough. This herb has a long-standing medicinal reputation and was referred to by Dioscorides and Pliny and in Anglo-Saxon herbal treatises. It is most effective when made into a decoction and given in small, warm doses (1 teaspoon to 2 ounces of water), three times a day. It is good for children, especially for chronic respiratory disorders, but should not be taken when pregnant or nursing.

Hyssop (*Hyssop officinalis*) is an antispasmodic, expectorant, and antiviral herb. It was referred to by Hippocrates and is a great remedy for all lung complaints, particularly bronchitis, which results in lung weakness. Do not use during pregnancy.

Lobelia (*Lobelia inflata*) is a jack-of-all-trades that can be used as a respiratory stimulant to ensure expectoration and as a relaxant to soothe the muscles of the system that have been overtaxed by the painful coughing that bronchitis involves. It is also an antiasthmatic. However, it may have some toxic effects, so should not be used without professional consultation.

Blood root, coltsfoot, comfrey root, flaxseed, marshmallow, mullein, pleurisy root, thyme, and **white horehound** are all effective herbs in the treatment of bronchitis. Antimicrobial herbs are also invaluable to help prevent infection; the best and most well known of these is **garlic** (*Allium sativum*). It can be taken raw or in capsules, and has been used for thousands of years for its healing properties. As the volatile oil in garlic is mostly excreted through the lungs, it is also highly effective in combatting catarrh, frequent colds, influenza, and whooping cough. Garlic can, however, irritate the stomach and should also be avoided during pregnancy and nursing.

Echinacea and eucalyptus are also popular antimicrobials. **Echinacea** (*E. angustifolia*) is also an immune system stimulant and antibiotic which helps the body against bacterial and viral attack. **Eucalyptus** (*Eucalyptus globules*) is the primary ingredient in a steam inhalation and can be used for bronchitis as well as asthma, catarrh, coughs, sinusitis, and throat infections. To make a steam inhalation, put three teaspoonfuls of eucalyptus leaves in a basin and pour on four pints of boiling water. Put your head over the basin, covering with a towel to prevent the loss of the volatile oils. Carefully breathe the vapors for about 10 minutes through the nose. Do this three times a day. You can also make up a "tea" to add to your bath water. Take two tablespoons each of eucalyptus and thyme leaves, pour two pints of boiling water over them, and steep for 30 minutes. After straining, add the liquid to the bath water so you can breathe the vapors while you relax.

Coughs

Coughs accompany many respiratory problems. **Coltsfoot** (*Tusilago farfara*), whose Latin name means "cough dispeller," has also been referred to as "coughwort" and Pliny, in 77 AD, said of it: "the smoke of this plant, dried with the root and burnt, is said to cure if inhaled deeply though a reed, an inveterate cough." While I don't suggest you take up smoking coltsfoot, this wonderful herb is a relaxant, an expectorant, an antispasmodic, and a demulcent. It works even better when used with mullein and licorice, the latter acting as a sweetener also. Use equal parts of the herbs, steep for 15 minutes, and drink three times a day.

Mullein (*Verbascum thapsus*) is an expectorant and demulcent used to tone the mucus membranes and reduce inflammation. It is especially beneficial where there is a hard, dry cough; it helps ease the soreness of whooping cough, along with **white horehound** (*Marrubium vulgare*). Often bronchitis results in a nonproductive cough at first; white horehound relaxes the bronchial muscles and promotes gentle expectoration. It has an unpleasant taste; how well I remember the old-fashioned "cough candy" I was given as a child, so use it with licorice or aniseed.

Slippery elm bark (*Ulmus fulva*) is a wonderful demulcent that is used primarily to soothe inflamed membranes of the digestive system, and is also now available in lozenges for sore throats and irritated bronchi caused by coughing.

Pleurisy

Pleurisy is an inflammation of the pleura, the moist, double-layered membrane surrounding the lungs. Breathing is very painful and sometimes excess fluid will enter the area between the membrane layers. It is usually accompanied by a dry cough, fever, and weakness. You must look at the condition of the whole body as there are several causes of pleurisy; infection is the most common cause, and fever is usually a prevalent symptom. Several respiratory herbs that are also diaphoretic and promote perspiration, which reduces fever, should be combined with demulcents for a complete remedy. **Elder** (flowers) is a an effective remedy.

Boneset (*Eupatorium perfoliatum*) has a long history with North American Indians, who knew it as "ague weed," and is the best remedy for influenza. However, because of its effectiveness in breaking feverish conditions, it is perfect for pleurisy sufferers. Pour a cup of boiling water onto 2 teaspoons of boneset and steep for 10 minutes, drinking a cup every half hour until the fever breaks.

As its name suggests, **Pleurisy root** (*Asclepias tuberosa*) is particularly good for treating pleurisy, as well as influenza and chest complaints with catarrhal build-up. It promotes expectoration, soothes inflammation, and relieves the pain and difficult breathing that accompanies such illnesses. Combine it with angelica and sassafras to promote perspiration.

How many of us remember having a hot gooey mess placed on our chest when we were miserable with the flu or congestion? I certainly do; I don't recall what was in it, just the heaviness, spreading warmth, and unpleasant smell. To me, it always seemed singularly unfair that things that were supposed to make you feel better always smelled or tasted horrible. In spite of this, pleurisy is a perfect opportunity to make use of such a poultice.

Flaxseed (*Linum usitatissmum*), with its demulcent, antiseptic and anti-inflammatory properties, is an excellent herb for this purpose. To 3 ounces of seeds, add boiling water and stir until it becomes a thick paste. Spread this on a half piece of clean linen—the paste should be ½ inch thick—and make sure the edges of the linen are clear of paste. Fold over the linen to make an "envelope" and place onto the chest. The poultice should be tolerated as hot as possible and left on for two hours. Repeat a few hours later. For adults, you can add a little mustard powder or mustard seed, but make sure this does not come into direct contact with the skin.

Spasm-Related Conditions

Spasms in the respiratory system are caused by several factors, but all result in coughing and wheezing. The most common disease of this type is asthma. About 20 million people in the United States suffer from asthma, and it is the most common chronic condition among children. While 50 percent of asthma attacks are a result of allergic reactions, asthma also has a genetic factor. Regardless of the origin, asthma is characterized by inflammation and narrowing of the bronchial passages that subsequently causes breathing difficulties, coughing, and, often, frightening shortness of breath. At present, there is no cure, but a thorough awareness and reduction of those conditions that can trigger attacks, such as pollutants, anxiety, stress, or hyperactivity, can help manage the disease.

Antispasmodic herbs such as elecampane, eucalyptus, lobelia, and wild cherry will help ease breathing. Elderberry wine with a dash of cinnamon is an age-old remedy for soothing asthmatic coughing. Where there is an excess of mucus, use a gentle pectoral like **aniseed** (*Pimpinella anisum*), which is often found in cough medicines and lozenges. The liqueur, anisette, when mixed with hot water, is a simple, but effective, remedy to ease spasmodic asthma symptoms if you can tolerate alcohol. When attacks are severe and put strain on the heart, **motherwort** (*Leonurus cardiaca*) is a wonderful herb for cardiac support, as its Latin name denotes. Relaxing but strengthening, motherwort is invaluable in quieting anxiety and tension, so often both a cause and symptom of asthmatic attacks.

Nasal Catarrh

Nasal catarrh (also considered a congestive condition) is a very common but bothersome spasm-related respiratory complaint due to infection and allergies. Both the flowers and berries of **elder** (*Sambucus nigra*) have almost countless healing properties. Indeed, the veritable Mrs. Grieves in *A Modern Herbal* refers to it as "the medicine chest of the country people," while Nicholas Culpepper says: "The first shoots of the common Elder, boiled like Asparagus, and the young leaves and stalks boiled in fat broth, doth mightily carry forth phlegm and choler." The flowers are diaphoretic, anti-catarrhal, expectorant, and topically anti-inflammatory; the tiny berries act as a diuretic and diaphoretic, and can be made into a syrup for coughs. My grandmother made copious quantities of elderberry wine, which she swore by to treat winter colds and the feverish chills of influenza. Here is a recipe for Syrup of Elderberries, taken from *A Modern Herbal*:

> Pick the berries when ripe from the stalks and stew with a little water in a jar in the oven or pan. After straining, add ½ ounce of whole ginger and 18 cloves to each gallon. Boil the ingredients an hour, strain again, and bottle. The syrup is an excellent cure for a cold. To about a wine glass of elderberry syrup, add hot water, and sugar to desired taste.

When catarrh is accompanied by infection, antimicrobials such as echinacea or garlic are a good choice. A chest rub than I make every winter is made by gently melting 6 ounces of Vaseline and adding 5 milliliters each of peppermint, eucalyptus, and pine essential oils. The mixture is poured into a sealable glass jar when it has cooled (just before it sets) and used on the chest at night, or a little is placed under the nostril to help with restricted breathing. Steam inhalations can also be used for this purpose.

Colds and Influenza

Colds and influenza are the bane of human existence, it often seems. The best way to treat a cold is prevention. Once again, cut out mucus-forming foods in the diet, and work on boosting your immune system with garlic and echinacea. Increasing daily amounts of vitamin C is essential, and a good herbal source of this is rose hips and hibiscus. Another good tea to drink three times a day is made from equal parts of elderflower, peppermint, and yarrow. As mentioned, boneset should always be kept in the herbal medicine chest to help relieve body aches so typical of the flu. Add it to the above remedy in place of yarrow, and sweeten with licorice or honey.

Sinusitis

As a longtime sufferer of sinus infections, at the slightest hint of sinus "activity" I take echinacea and goldenseal capsules. An infusion of equal parts of echinacea, goldenrod, goldenseal, and marshmallow leaf can also be effective. **White willow bark** (*Salix alba*) can help relieve the pain that a sinus headache brings; use with caution if you are aspirin sensitive, as it contains salicylic acid. Use the chest rub (see above) and steam inhalation to bring short term relief.

Strengthening the Lungs with Breathing Exercises

Our breath is literally our life force and is also of enormous importance to our state of mind. Breathing exercises are paramount in the practice of yoga; proper breathing allows more oxygen to flow to the brain, which manifests in greater clarity of thought, peace, and prana or life energy. Both the respiratory and circulatory systems work together to supply the cells of the body with oxygen.

Conscious, correct breathing will improve lymph movement and blood oxygenation and circulation, help the digestive process, slow brain waves, and increase lung capacity. All of this can help maintain a healthy respiratory system, which in turn can ward off circulatory system problems such as heart palpitations and angina. A simple exercise follows:

Lie on your back, knees elevated, your feet on the ground. Put a paperback book on your abdomen over your navel. Place your hand on your chest. First, breathe normally, taking notice if your hand or the book rises. For proper breathing, the book should rise as your diaphragm expands. To do this, breathe through your nose for a five count while consciously and gently pushing the book up with your stomach. Hold the breath for a count of three. Slowly exhale through the nose in the same way while gently pushing down your abdomen. Repeat ten times. Go as slowly as possible; if you feel you have to breathe faster after a breath, you are going too slowly. As you get used to doing this exercise, you can gradually increase the amount of time for each stage, but always be mindful that there should be no tension or discomfort involved.

In the Eastern systems of Chinese and Ayurvedic medicine, the breath is regarded as the life force or vital energy. When we take in the breath of life, we share that air with all living things on our planet, creating a definitive connection with all of nature. By using our plant relations, we can heal diseases of our respiratory system and so bring our breath, and our lives, back into harmony.

Medicinal Herbs for All Seasons

❧ by Michelle Higgins ❧

Herbal medicine was not invented; it evolved, slowly. For many centuries, remedies came from local tree bark, flowers, roots, berries, and leaves. Real illness often brought death, so preventive medicine was absolutely imperative throughout the four seasons. Today we tend to look for the cure after an illness has begun, in part, because modern advancements have made common illnesses less fatal. However, with minimal planning, we may have herbal tonics for preventive and curative health care in the form of dried herbs, or plants grown and collected fresh from the garden.

Many people in the twenty-first century are now adopting the ways of our forebears, partially due to the virulent strength of the synthetic chemical compounds that may lower the immune system while curing a cough, and desire to be in charge of health care for themselves, their families, and the world immediately around them. In herbal medicine, general tonics abound in our own gardens and we may make our medicine into infused teas and honeys, vinegars, and tinctures, or eat the herbs raw.

Violets, for instance, are used to both prevent and dissolve cancers and tumors, and have great nutritive value for the digestive system. Mints are an antiseptic, preventing bacteria and viruses of all kinds from growing and causing colds and influenza. Herbal medicine combines the preventive with the curative; if the preventive is part of our daily routine, the curative may only be needed rarely, or never.

Most herbal wellness practices may be performed with fresh or dried material so our friends in cities and apartments may also benefit. Cities usually have farmers' markets or stores that sell fresh herbs. If you cannot find an herb, tell the salesperson or merchant so they know it is in demand. In rural areas, encourage your Community Supported Agriculture club to grow vegetables that are also medicinal, such as nettle, red clover, and the raspberry leaves in addition to the fruit.

Most herb merchants are happy to accommodate your requests because herbs, often considered a personal choice are grounded in community, creating a bond amongfamily, children, and friends. That caring side of a man or woman blends with the home and kitchen herb formulations discussed here. Nurturing has been a direct link between plants and man since the days we lived very simply. Stories here are about medicine for the soul as well as herbal dosage.

Most of the herbs listed below are perennials; they die back in the winter and go dormant in temperatures below 32 degrees Fahrenheit. In climates where there is little or no winter, the perennial may not slow down or die back. Many, like rosemary, sage, lavender, and rue, grow year-round. The annuals, such as basil, grow from spring to autumn and need to be replaced the following year, or may reseed, as the nasturtium does so successfully, appearing year after year from new seed discarded by the old plant.

My research, from the early Pagan, Celtic, and European times to about 1800, pertains to the northern peoples from lands with four seasons. All their folklore, herbal remedies, and community celebrations center around what plants are available at certain times of the year, or around the farming calendar of the region.

So, if you live outside the northern realms, please do not be insulted by this grouping, which may not work to the exact month in your area. The herbal result will be the same as long as the plants, flowers, or leaves are healthy and collected at the height of potency, before they begin to brown, slump, or tire.

Spring – April, May, June

Chickweed (Stellaria media)

Chickweed appears very early in spring and lasts through late summer. This hardy herb is used in weight-loss teas and pills while exuding nutrition, and is said to dissolve many meanies in the body, including, over time, some ovarian cysts. Most importantly, it is a coolant, great for reducing heat and inflammation anywhere in the body; I have used it very successfully as a damp poultice on sore and infected eyes. An herb vinegar featuring chickweed maintains and improves eye strength and health. The tincture is fast acting for bladder and urinary tract infections (it's the cooling), and the plant is palatable enough to eat straight from the garden or blended with other breakfast food herbs, such as violets or lemon balm mixed with a little molasses and hot water. Sit in your garden chair and enjoy. You will smile for the rest of the day!

The tiny white flowers that appear in mid-spring are star shaped. Chickweed is considered a vile and invasive weed by many lawn enthusiasts, so if you hear them cursing, do tell them about the plant's curative powers.

Nettle (Urtica dioica)

Many medicinal herbs may be grown in the garden, but some herbs just appear exactly where needed. I bought an old house with forty wooded acres at the back gate and within a year, I noticed beautiful, strong nettles appearing. An herb I use every day, nettle is a complete vitamin and mineral food—the perfect preventive medicine young and old alike. Stinging nettle softens when cooked or, as the case may be, boiled or steamed. As a vegetable, nettle is unparalleled in vitamin richness and, when in season, we add chopped leaves, a dab of butter, and raisins to the breakfast oats. The leaves, fresh or dried, make an excellent daily tea as preventive medicine for men and women. Nettle soothes nerves in midlife, builds strong bones and brains in children, and eases teenagers into their tough years. This medicinal herb is strong and can be eaten or drunk as tea in large doses, alone or with other herbs.

People who may take prescription medicines for asthma, anemia, diabetes, or rheumatism may like to try nettle and be surprised at the extra help and energy they get from this natural herb.

Add your favorite essential oil to nettle infusion, plus a cup of water and half a cup of vinegar, and use as a hair rinse for softness, shine, or to take out the gray. Nettle is wonderful for the skin, the body, and also for the spirit, giving one perseverance and determination.

Motherwort (Leonurus cardiaca)

Motherwort is a friend to all women—she balances the hormones to keep the personality on an even keel while toning the reproductive and digestive tracts. As the name implies, motherwort is helpful for all aspects of menopause, bringing sleep, sanity, and sense. As a tea, it has an acquired, then delicious, taste. She appears in the garden when needed and will seed easily, but will never become invasive. Motherwort is good to take between ovulation and menstruation.

Mugwort (Artemesia vulgaris)

Mugwort, an antidote to hysteria and jangled nerves, is particularly helpful with menopausal rage and winter stress. A bit heftier than motherwort, Mugwort helps you sleep beautifully and dream serenely. By morning, there is no more cranky woman. I use it when I need that sledgehammer to quieten me, as its bitterness takes away mine. You may want to infuse a little honey, as she is an acquired taste. It is easy to grow in the garden or may be found in the sunny part of woods a little later in spring than nettle. To bring your children home safely, put a small pouch of dried mugwort in their backpacks.

Lemon Balm (Melissa officinalis)

Here is an easy herb to grow (best in a large pot in or above ground to prevent spreading all over the county), and is also the best medicinal herb young children will take without much fuss. Lemon balm is a cure-all and daily tonic, a calmative, a pain reliever, and an anesthetic. As a tea for harsh, sore, and strep throats or infused in honey, it is almost unbeatable.

Sprinkle the sweetly aromatic leaves in the bath or in a baby's cot as a relaxant. It is also wonderful for any stomach cramp in men and women, as muscles relax and tension leaves the area. Iced or sun-infused tea cools the body in hot weather.

I often add lemon balm to strong-tasting teas as a natural sweetener, or it may be tossed in salads or eaten straight from the plant. Lemon balm is allied with love and the pursuit of romance.

Rose (Rosa, sp.)

This medicinal herb heals colds, sore throats, and most anything you can catch from a school-age child. Pick wild rose petals in late spring, leaving the hips on the bush until fall, and then add them to the best raw honey. Use an eight-ounce glass jar, fill it with petals and then with honey, tighten the lid, add a label and put in a cupboard until September. Then take a teaspoon a couple of times a week as preventive medicine. It may also be used to mend a broken heart, both the honey and the roses being medicinal, calming, and strengthening. Rose is an aphrodisiac, a general women's tonic, and a nerve relaxer.

Rose is the most enveloping, trust-inspiring herb to grow and to keep; it is in my top three favorites.

Summer

Basil (Ocimum basilicum)

What would tomatoes and mozzarella cheese be without basil in the summer? Plant basil late, after Memorial Day in the Northeast, so it is ready at the same time as the tomatoes. While we are familiar with basil as a culinary herb, adding to its fame are its medicinal powers as an antiseptic, expectorant, and digestive. Basil may be used as a tea, tincture, or vinegar, or infused in honey for coughs, chest colds, and flu. As a cleaning herb, chopped and added to water as a bathroom scrub, basil has a wonderful aroma and is safe to wash down the drain or toilet.

Rue (Ruta graveolens)

Plant rue near the front door and jealousy will not live in the house. Rue appears suddenly in early spring with its small round leaves and bright yellow flowers that bloom until late summer. An herb of protection, rue brings fortune to the house, metaphysically and literally, while also strengthening bones, calming nerves, and regulating menses. Rue is very strong, so I only use it in herb vinegars, much preferring to look at it in the garden where it inspires my respect. Make an infusion of rue leaves and jojoba or olive oil for heated topical massage and give to anyone with even severe muscular pain. Oils will last for many years in a tight-lidded jar.

Chicory (Cichorium intybus)

This is the wild chicory with the bright blue flowers seen on roadsides and in pastures in early summer. The roots make a coffee alternative and the fresh young leaves may be eaten in salads.

Chicory is a digestive, making the stomach work more efficiently to help to break down the excesses. Conversely, it can increase the appetite of those who do not eat well, even children! It builds the blood and helps the anemic and the nursing mother.

Southernwood (Artemesia abrotanum)

Southernwood is associated with attraction and sex appeal, particularly for men. It has a strong male smell when pinched between the fingers and the rough stalk bends over as it grows, appearing to protect its loved ones. Young men may want to put some southernwood in their pocket when venturing out with a love for the first time. I found this herb in a neglected kitchen garden originally planted in the 1950s—the southernwood was still glowing over forty years later! Strength and endurance are deservedly two of its attributes. Adding one tablespoon or a small sprig to a large glass of boiling water makes for an excellent general tonic (taken in small doses) for all women's ailments. It can cure bladder infections and, as a hair rinse, kill parasites or make you shine. We can also share the benefits with our four-legged friends. Small sprigs may be cut up and given to dogs and cats for worm prevention or expulsion. I use a weak apple cider vinegar or herb-vinegar rinse with a handful of chopped southernwood or wormwood as a dog or horse bath rinse for whatever makes them itch.

Rosemary (Rosmarinus officinalis)

One of the most important medicinal herbs in the world, rosemary stands alone as an all-purpose tonic for good health. It is great for the heart or as an internal and external antiseptic, and is a calmative oil for child and adult skin. And that's only the beginning. It is a lion among medicines and grows best in warm climates, hardy to Zone 7 only, and does not like being kept inside the house. Those in frost areas must make vinegar, tincture, and honey extract in the summer and hoard the booty for cold months. Like thyme and the artemesias, rosemary is an effective insecticide, either interplanted to protect dill or tomatoes or blended with water and soap to spritz on plants and fences to deter woodchuck, deer, and some insects and slugs. Rosemary is strong, but also gentle, in its curative powers and may be eaten raw in salads or taken as an infused tea. It is the one herb that is a complete "all 'rounder" for any occasion.

Lavender (Lavendula officinalis)

Who cannot admire this most gracious and useful herb? There are many different forms of lavender, so check with your local nursery for the best area variety.

Medicinally, lavender counteracts asthma when inhaled or taken as a tea and is well known as a nervine or relaxant, inducing sweet sleep. Our grandmothers made sachets of dried lavender for keeping under pillows or, less romantically, to keep clothes scented and moth free in drawers.

Lavender is often used in cosmetics, the essential oil being just that when added to our homemade shampoos or face and body moisturizers. It is one of the most wonderful herbs to work with, the scent filling the house as we tie it in bundles to dry in the cellar.

Autumn
Ginger (Zingiber officinale)

Since ancient times, ginger has been the herb of health. For robust health, keep ginger root in your drawer or medicine bag. For sore throats and any chest or nasal congestion, even in small babies, weak ginger tea given at room temperature will aid resistance and allow the patient to sleep. Ginger gets the blood circulating and may be taken as a general tonic, particularly in cold weather. We feel warmer when drinking ginger and it is very beneficial when used in the same way as garlic, chopped very fine for use as a culinary medicinal herb.

In warm and tropical climates, grow ginger and be totally blessed by its presence in your garden.

Sage (Salvia officinalis)

Sage is an herb of protection and love, an herb to use in the home to change, eliminate, or encourage energy, thereby keeping the family stress-free. The wisdom of this herb attracts our respect, so in my home there are small, tied bunches of sage where we sleep. If something unhappy has crossed your path or entered your life or home, light a bunch of sage and go around every room and every corner from the top of the house to the bottom until you finally walk out the back door. Bury the sage or throw it away—along with the bad energy. To merely freshen or encourage good energy, open all the windows and walk around the house burning the sage sticks or bunches, finishing at the front door.

In apartments, use a back or side window instead of a back door and put the sage bunch at the bottom of a houseplant. As a medicinal herb, sage is an antiseptic, cures constipation, curbs obesity, and dries the sniffles. As a tea, it even tastes clean. An easy-to-grow annual or perennial in much of the United States, sage is also an excellent antidote to sore throat or aching dry muscles and limbs. Coincidentally, sage grows in the driest gardens and climates. The gray-green leaves let us know it is drought tolerant.

Burdock (Arctium lappa)

Burdock leaves are nice and big by July when the bugs are biting ruthlessly. Infused in vinegar, even for one day, burdock will draw the sting or itch out of the skin, ease poison ivy and sunburn, or dissolve ringworm. I keep pickle jars throughout the year to house burdock leaves and roots for many medicinal and culinary purposes. Burdock moves slowly and gently enough to drink every day as a cancer preventative and to maintain healthy reproductive systems in men and women. The root is used for medicinal purposes and has a strong, nutty smell that inspires longevity and stoicism. European researchers have found burdock to kill bacteria, viruses, and fungi. If ringworm breaks out at your school, the tea, as well as the leaves, can rid the infestation for teachers and students.

Red Raspberry (Rubus idaeus)

The raspberry plant throws up long fuzzy stickers that wave around and do not twirl like a vine. The leaves are somewhat prickly, but may be picked without gloves. Sprouting in the spring, its leaves are collected in the summer and made into teas. The autumn brings the mature raspberry hips, which are added to the infused honey and flower petals. Raspberry is one of the best women's tonics and the leaf tea sipped during pregnancy prevents morning sickness and builds vitamins and minerals naturally in the changing body. So it is no surprise that raspberry is widely regarded to aid an easy birth and allow the complete expulsion of the afterbirth.

Raspberry is definitely an all-season herb, and so beautiful.

Lemon (Citrus limon)

Known to all, lemon is good for almost anything that ails us. Lemon and honey in hot water reduces a fever, clears a thick head or chest, and slows dysentery and diarrhea. In warm climates, lemon trees are beautiful to grow in gardens. Its fragrance is its strength and the leaves, bark, and flowers as well as the fruit are pungent, especially at night as the tree cools after a hot day.

Winter

Fresh herbs are hard to come by during the snow-laden or just plain bitter days of winter when our immune systems are tested most. Now we are happy to feel strong. From December to March take a teaspoon of honey-infused herbs for a great and nourishing start to the day. The warm feeling in the throat mentally pushes colds away.

Winter is the time to stay warm, dress from head to toe, exercise with a brisk walk, and enjoy indoor sports. Eat the winter foods such as soups with good quality organic meat and vegetables, warm (not hot) drinks, and lots of nourishing teas. As in past times, winter is an excellent catch-up time for making face moisturizers, hand creams, candles, and hair tonics, and performing all those hobbies for which you may have infused herbs in olive oil ready to go. There are few things more gratifying than having ingredients for a project on a snowy afternoon.

Author's Note

1. A tea comprises approximately a medium handful of herbs. A tincture dose is approximately 21 drops. Vinegar and honey infusions would be approximately one teaspoon to one tablespoon.

2. The author does not suggest the modern medicines be abandoned, and any holistic practitioner who fails to include modern intervention when necessary should be avoided.

For Further Reading

I list here the main resources for this particular article, bearing in mind they are constantly used references and there are many more that, over the years, I have learned from and lost or lent, yet carried the knowledge onwards.

Culpeper, Nicholas. *Culpeper's Complete Herbal*. Hertfordshire, UK: Wordsworth Editions Ltd., 1995.

De Bairacli Levy, Juliette. *Common Herbs for Natural Health*. Woodstock, NY: Ash Tree Publishing, 1997.

Edwards, Gail Faith. *Opening Our Wild Heart to the Healing Herbs*. Woodstock, NY: Ash Tree Publishing, 1999.

Falconi, Dina. *Earthly Bodies and Heavenly Hair*. Woodstock, NY: Ceres Press, 1997.

Perenyi, Eleanor. *Green Thoughts*. New York: Random House, 2002.

Spencer, Edwin Rollin, Ph.D. *Just Weeds*. New York: Charles Scribner's Sons, 1957.

Sturdivant, Lee, and Blakley, Tim. *Medicinal Herbs in the Garden, Field and Marketplace*. Friday Harbor, WA: San Juan Naturals, 1999.

Weed, Susun. *Healing Wise*. Woodstock, NY: Ash Tree Publishing, 1989.

Thanks for the Memories

⋙ by Lynn Smythe ⋘

"It is singular how soon we lose the impression of what ceases to be constantly before us. A year impairs, a luster obliterates. There is little distinct left without an effort of memory, then indeed the lights are rekindled for a moment—but who can be sure that the Imagination is not the torch-bearer?"
—Lord Byron (1788–1824)

I f you are having problems remembering the small details of your daily life or sometimes feel as though your brain is in a fog, then you could be suffering from minor memory-recall problems. As we age, circulation of blood in the brain decreases, which can eventually lead to mental confusion along with problems with short-term and long-term memory recall. While memory problems can occur as part of the normal aging process, herbal remedies—along with getting more

exercise and eating a healthy, low-fat diet with plenty of fresh fruit and vegetables—can help increase the flow of blood to your brain and can help maintain, and possibly improve, your memory functions. A popular herb magazine mentions a few herbs that are commonly used to enhance memory and help prevent mental confusion. That got me thinking about other herbs that are reputed memory enhancers. "These herbs work by increasing circulation, oxygen, sugar, and nutrients to the brain and by enhancing neurotransmitter activity and production, helping it to work more efficiently," says Christopher Hobbs, herbalist and author, in his book *Herbal Remedies for Dummies*.

Although herbal remedies will not reverse more severe memory problems, such as those associated with Alzheimer's disease, certain herbs may prevent your memory problems from getting any worse. Alzheimer's disease is a neurological disorder associated with disorientation, personality changes, and a progressive loss of mental capacity. Memory-enhancing herbs often work as a type of general nervous system tonic and are important for relieving blood stasis in the brain. Blood stasis, or a congestion of blood in the brain, may eventually cause problems such as senility and dementia. Along with helping improve blood flow to the brain, the following herbs, used alone or in combination, can help to improve concentration, focus, and clarity and otherwise boost your memory.

The Herbs

"The existence of forgetting has never been proved. We only know that some things don't come to mind when we want them."
—Friedrich Nietzsche (1844-1900)

Ashwagandha (Withania somnifera)

Also known as the winter cherry or Indian ginseng, Ashwagandha is a herb used in Ayurvedic medicine, the traditional Indian system of medicine, as a general tonic. Ashwagandha treats many symptoms related to senile dementia and memory weakness. This herb helps calm the mind and reduce stress, which can boost concentration.

Ashwagandha also helps to increase vitality, energy, endurance, and stamina along with nurturing the nervous system. The roots of the plant are used in herbal medicine regimens.

Bacopa (Bacopa monnieri)

Also known as smooth water hyssop, bacopa is a somewhat invasive plant commonly found growing in and around fresh and brackish waters in tropical and subtropical climates.

Bacopa is used as a traditional Ayurvedic brain tonic to bolster learning and academic performance, improve mental alertness, and sharpen both short-term and long-term memory. Various formulas of this herb can be found in capsule and pill form at health food stores.

An added benefit of bacopa is its ability to relieve anxiety symptoms, such as lack of concentration, irritability, and insomnia, which may contribute to memory problems. These anxiety-relieving properties make bacopa suitable for use, often in combination with gotu kola, in ADHD (attention deficit hyperactivity disorder) patients.

Basil (Ocimum basilicum)

Sweet basil essential oil can help calm and clear the mind. I like to use basil in my essential-oil diffuser at my home office while working on my latest writing project. It has a clean, fresh, green scent that helps relieve mental fatigue and the inability to concentrate. The calming, soothing, and mildly sedative essence of basil can be used at night and may even help you to fall asleep.

Others like to use rosemary essential oil in a similar manner to help them get out of a slump and give their creative process and memory recall a burst of needed energy. However, rosemary is a stimulating herb and should be avoided late at night as it may cause problems with insomnia.

Chinese Club Moss (Huperzia serrata)

This herb was formerly classified as *Lycopodium serrata*. In traditional Chinese medicine, the whole herb, known as Qian Ceng Ta, has been used for centuries as a folk remedy. In recent years, an extract of the Chinese club moss plant emerged as a possible remedy for Alzheimer's patients. The extract contains Huperzine A, also known as HUP-A. Huperzine is a potent inhibitor of acetylcholinesterase, the enzyme that breaks down acetylcholine, a neurotransmitter essential to memory and brain function. Using formulas containing HUP-A may help temporarily increase the acetylcholine in the brain and diminish the progression of dementia associated with Alzheimer's disease. Formulas that include HUP-A can also be used as a general brain tonic by healthy individuals to help improve memory, focus, and cognitive functions.

Chinese Foxglove (Rehmannia glutinosa)

Chinese foxglove is one of the most important herbs used in traditional Chinese medicine. The fresh or dried roots, which are known as sheng di huang, are the part of the plant that is used medicinally as a general tonic to help strengthen heart, liver, and kidney functions.

Chinese foxglove is one of several herbs that helps improve memory function by improving blood flow to the brain, relieving blood stasis. Blood stasis is one of the factors thought to lead to senility in the elderly. Chinese foxglove also helps remove toxins from the blood, which can help reduce blood pressure and cholesterol levels and may be helpful in cases of hypoglycemia.

Gingko (Ginkgo biloba)

The leaves of this plant, which is also known as maidenhair tree, are the part used medicinally in Western medicine. "If you feel a major brain strain from work and all of the myriad of details you have to take care of, an extract of the leaves of the ancient gingko tree can help," mentions Hobbs in his book.

Gingko acts by dilating the blood vessels, which in turn increases the flow of blood to the brain and helps alleviate symptoms such as memory loss, mental fatigue, senile dementia, and the inability to concentrate. My son was diagnosed with ADHD a number of years ago. He was having a hard time concentrating on anything for any amount of time, but now takes ginkgo every day to help improve his concentration, which is especially important when taking tests.

Gotu Kola (Centella asiatica)

In Ayurvedic medicine, gotu kola, also known as Indian pennywort, is one of the chief herbs for revitalizing the nerves and brain cells. Regarded as one of the most spiritual and rejuvenating herbs, it is often used with bacopa (see above). These two herbs used in combination may help prevent mental deterioration associated with aging.

Gotu kola is said to develop the crown chakra, the energy center at the top of the head, and to balance the right and left hemispheres of the brain, which the leaf is said to resemble.

According to Deni Bown in her book *The Herb Society of America New Encyclopedia of Herbs and Their Uses* (Dorling Kindersley, 2001), gotu kola helps to "improve performance in those suffering from learning difficulties and mental confusion." Gotu kola works to improve memory by increasing circulation to the brain.

Periwinkle (Vinca minor)

Vinpocetine, derived from an alkaloid found in the lesser periwinkle plant, helps dilate blood vessels, which increases circulation in the brain. Periwinkle acts similarly to gingko as it can help improve memory and enhance concentration. Vinpocetine has also been shown to improve short-term memory and lessen the severity of mild to moderate dementia. As an unrelated bonus, vinpocetine also exhibits antioxidant properties.

Great care should be taken when using this plant. While the leaves of this plant are used medicinally, they are toxic if ingested in their raw unprocessed form. Commercially prepared periwinkle is safe to use and generally available at most health food stores.

Rhodiola (Rhodiola rosea)

The rhodiola root, also known as golden root or artic root, is used for a variety of symptoms and has recently undergone close scrutiny. This herb can help increase mental work capacity during times of stress and may help prevent age-related memory problems. An adaptogenic tonic, rhodiola has been proven to enhance memory, attention, and learning functions along with improving your resistance to stress.

Rhodiola is also an antioxidant that can help shield the nervous system from damage by free radicals. When looking for supplements containing this herb, make sure the label specifically mentions Rhodiola rosea because other species of rhodiola do not exhibit the memory-enhancing properties.

Rosemary (Rosmarinus officinalis)

Whenever I think of this herb I recall Ophelia's famous lines in Shakespeare's play *Hamlet* (Act IV, Scene V): "There's rosemary, that's for remembrance; pray, love, remember: and there is pansies, that's for thoughts."

In *A Modern Herbal*, first published in 1931 by Mrs. M. Grieve, one of the comments made regarding rosemary is that "The ancients were well acquainted with the shrub, which had a reputation for strengthening the memory."

Supplements of rosemary contain antioxidants, help improve circulation, bring clarity to your thought process, and help support mental vitality. While staying sharp is a good outcome for anyone, students of all ages should know that inhaling a few drops of rosemary essential oil that have been applied to a tissue can help to stimulate the brain while taking exams.

Sage (Salvia officinalis)

In ancient times, sage was used as a mental stimulant and was credited with increasing brain power or mental capacity.

John Gerard attributes the following qualities to sage in *Herbal*, first published in 1597: "Sage is singularly good for the head and brain; it quickens the senses and memory . . ."

Sage is currently being studied to determine if it can help combat the symptoms of Alzheimer's disease, such as memory loss. Sage is one of the herbs that helps to improve circulation and as such can help to relieve blood stasis in the brain. The roots of Dan shen (*Salvia miltiorhiza*), also known as red sage or Chinese sage, are used in traditional Chinese medicine to stimulate the circulatory system.

Exercise caution when using this herb. Common sage contains thujone, which can be hallucinogenic, addictive, and toxic if used in excess or for extented periods.

Schisandra (Schisandra chinensis)

Schisandra, or Sandra berry vine and Chinese magnolia vine, is a premium brain tonic in traditional Chinese medicine. Current research has herbalists prescribing it along with herbs such as American ginseng and rehmannia to help relieve poor memory by improving blood flow to the brain. Schisandra stimulates the central nervous system, which can help improve short-term and long-term memory functions and sharpen concentration and mental alertness. The seeds, obtained from the dried berries of this plant, are also used medicinally for their antioxidant and stress-relieving properties.

Velvet Bean (Mucuna pruriens)

Velvet bean is a member of the legume family. Also known as cow-itch and itchy bean, the velvet bean is another important herb in Ayurvedic medicine. The seeds of this plant, the pods of which are covered with reddish-orange hairs that can cause extreme skin irritation, contain L-dopa, a precursor of the neurotransmitter dopamine. They are used to help treat some of the symptoms associated with Parkinson's disease. Used in combination with other memory-enhancing herbs, velvet bean improves mental alertness and concentration ability.

Velvet bean also exhibits stress-relieving, antioxidant, and cholesterol-lowering properties. The toasted and ground seeds are also used as a coffee substitute in some countries, giving rise to another one of its common names, Nescafe.

Additional Herbs

"Everybody needs his memories. They keep the wolf of insignificance from the door."

—Saul Bellow (1915-2005)

There are other herbal remedies that are currently being investigated to discover if they offer any memory-enhancing properties. Keep an eye on the following herbs, which might be used to treat problems such as Alzheimer's disease and senile dementia. Many of these herbs are used as either Native American healing herbs or as traditional herbs of Chinese medicine. They include:

Asian ginseng (*Panax ginseng*)

Bilberry (*Vaccinium myrtillus*)

Blessed thistle (*Cnicus benedictus*)

Cat's claw (*Uncaria tomentosa*)

Dandelion (*Taraxacum officinale*)

Evening primrose (*Oenothera biennis*)

Fo-ti (*Polygonum multiflorum*)

Ginseng (*Panax quinquefolius*)

Hawthorn (*Crataegus laevigata*)

Horsemint (*Monarda punctata*)

Lemon balm (*Melissa officinalis*)

Morning glory (*Evolvulus alsinoides*)

Musk root (*Nardostachys jatamansi*)

Peppermint (*Mentha piperita*)

Stinging nettle (*Urtica dioica*)

Sweet flag (*Acorus Calamus*)

Thyme (*Thymus spp.*)

Willow (*Salix spp.)*

In Conclusion

"The advantage of a bad memory is that one enjoys several times the same good things for the first time."
—Friedrich Nietzsche (1844-1900)

Alzheimer's disease patients often show nutritional deficiencies such as low levels of vitamin B12 and zinc and the antioxidant vitamins A and E. There are myriad herbs currently available to help increase or at least retain your memory skills. The effects of these memory-enhancing herbs can be greatly strengthened by taking certain antioxidants such as vitamins C and E, along with a comprehensive vitamin B supplement on a daily basis.

The herbs mentioned in this article should be available in either tincture or capsule form from your local health food store or pharmacy. Additionally, these herbs can be taken either singly or in formulas which combine two or more herbs that work in harmony. Ask the clerk at your local store to recommend specific memory-enhancing formulas, many of which come manufactured in tablet form. Taking a single multiherb formula is often more convenient and economical than trying to purchase several individual herbs.

Stress can also be a factor when you are having difficulty concentrating or focusing on common chores and activities. You may also want to investigate the stress-relieving herbs as a possible aid to improving memory. Stress-relieving herbs you may want to use along with your memory enhancing herbs include chamomile, catnip, hops, lavender, passionflower, and skullcap.

Safety First

"The leaves of memory seemed to make a mournful rustling in the dark."

—Henry Wadsworth Longfellow (1807–1882)

Herbal remedies are not a quick-fix solution. Unless otherwise noted, herbal formulas should be taken on a daily basis. It may take several weeks or even a few months before the effects are noticed. Never self-medicate because some herbs may cause an adverse reaction with certain types of prescription medications. Pregnant women and people taking prescription medications should first consult with a qualified medical practitioner before starting any herbal therapy regime.

For Further Reading

Bown, Deni. *The Herb Society of America New Encyclopedia of Herbs and Their Uses*. New York: DK Publishing, 2001.

Davidson, Jonathan R.T., MD. *Herbs for the Mind*. New York. The Guilford Press, 2000.

Gerard, John. *The Herbal; or General History of Plants*. New York: Dover Publications, Inc., 1975.

Grieve, Mrs. M. *A Modern Herbal*. New York: Dover Publications, Inc., 1982.

Harrar, Sari. *The Woman's Book of Healing Herbs*. Emmaus, PA: Rodale Press, 1999.

Mohammed, Gina. "Give Your Brain a Boost with Bacopa." *Herbs for Health* (October 2005): 52–53.

Men's Health

❧ by Sally McSweeney ❧

Two things struck me when I had my herb store: First, the female customers greatly out-numbered male, and second, the paltry amount of information available about herbal health for men. Perusing books offered in both wholesale sources and bookstores made our emphasis on health aids for women very apparent, while men were overlooked unless it was related to bodybuilding.

Then came spam e-mails and a bewildering number of advertisements for penis enlargers and libido enhancers on TV—and we were bombarded with ads for medications for erectile dysfunction. While erectile dysfunction and related complaints are certainly important, men face many other health issues. However, a big problem still seems to be getting men to admit they are not feeling good and need help. Meanwhile, the role of men in the United States has become more demanding and stressful than ever, which exacts a huge toll on their bodies and their psyches.

As with most health problems, prevention is the best medicine, starting with diet and exercise. Eating right, not smoking, keeping alcohol to a moderate level, and working out at least thirty minutes a day will improve your health. Exercise promotes cardiovascular efficiency, increases circulation, stimulates muscle strength and tone, keeps joints and bones strong, strengthens the immune system, reduces body fat and cholesterol levels, and relieves stress.

Nothing can replace regular exercise, but adding a few herbal remedies will help support the heart, the nervous system, and the excretion systems. In most instances, a combination of herbs synergize to work very effectively. Each herb enhances the others, targeting the underlying causes as well as the manifesting symptoms.

An example of such a combination is a tonic, an agent that restores or increases body tone. Such tonics stimulate and improve the gastric system, helping the body absorb essential nutrients that improve overall energy and strength. Other herbs have specific actions important for optimum male health:

Adaptogens: Siberian ginseng, schizandra, and ashwagandha are among agents that stimulate nonspecific resistance and help the body to cope with and adapt to various situations. They decrease hypothalamus, pituitary, and adrenal gland over-reactions to stress, and normalize blood pressure and blood sugar levels.

Alteratives: Burdock, red clover, and nettle restore health by aiding both assimilation and excretion, bringing balance to the body. This helps combat infection and prevents chronic degenerative conditions that men become more vulnerable to as they mature.

Antacids: Fennel, slippery elm, and dandelion help combat the ever-increasing problems of acid-reflux disease and heartburn, which are often due to poor diets and stress because of hyperactivity.

Anti-inflammatories: Very important in preventing arthritis and other joint-related disorders, they also help current painful conditions by facilitating tissue repair. Calendula, arnica, and wild yam are all available in salves at health food stores.

Aphrodisiacs: Ginseng, yohimbe, and horny-goat weed are among the ancient remedies that help with impotency by stimulating sexual arousal.

Hepatics: For strengthening and toning the liver, herbs such as Oregon grape root, milk thistle, and dandelion play an invaluable role by increasing the flow of bile and enhancing the health of the liver in cases of overdrinking. They are not a substitute for professional care or intervention if alcoholism is a factor.

Hypotensives: Hawthorn, cramp bark, and garlic reduce blood pressure, an essential for heart health.

Nervines: Beneficial effects on the central nervous system include strengthening and toning (oats), stimulating (yerba mate), and relaxing (chamomile).

Vasodilators: Gingko, ginger, and feverfew expand the blood vessels, which helps increase circulation.

Specific Male Health Problems
Heart Disease

According to the American Heart Association, an amazing 13,900,000 Americans suffer from coronary heart disease, making it the single leading cause of death today. Risk factors include high blood pressure and cholesterol, smoking, being overweight, and a sedentary lifestyle. Important, too, is the way men see themselves and enact their role in modern society. Stress, the innate adaptive fight or flee response to threatening or disturbing situations, and the response to it has an enormous effect on how men function—or not. Unlike with our ancestors, who either ran away from the charging mammoth or flung spears at it to catch dinner, stress itself has become the "enemy" that can literally destroy us. Our husbands, brothers, and sons still react to stress in the same way when faced with the modern equivalent of the mammoth—home and work responsibilities, corporate pressures, balancing finances, and planning for retirement to name but a few—but now this hypertension often manifests in heart-related diseases.

Drinking three cups of green tea (preferably decaf) a day is beneficial for hypertension. Avoid trans fatty acids like margarine, which can raise cholesterol levels. Also, limit red and processed meats, bacon and sausage, and salt. Eat a diet rich in high potassium foods such as vegetables and fruits, increase fiber intake, and supplement your diet with two tablespoons a day of flaxseed oil, 400 mg of magnesium, 2,000 mg vitamin C, and 50 mg of Coenzyme Q10. These all help lower blood pressure. Avoid ephedra and licorice, which can increase blood pressure.

Hawthorn (*Crataegus oxyacantha*) is the best tonic remedy for the heart—it tones cardiac muscle, improves circulation, and dilates the arteries. Both the berries and the blossoms can be used as a normalizer, which means they either stimulate or depress activity as the heart requires. While not producing fast results, its effect builds up over time and persists. Angina is reduced, hypertension is lowered, and, after a heart attack, hawthorn can help the recovery. A tincture is the best way to take hawthorn; twenty to forty drops, three times a day.

Ginkgo (*Ginkgo biloba*) relaxes blood vessels and is a circulatory stimulant; it increases the blood flow into oxygen-deficient tissue. Ginkgo will also prevent blood clotting and platelet build-up. Probably best known for its effect on the brain as a vasodilator, it has been used to treat dementia and is great for improving mental clarity, concentration, memory recall, and alertness. As an antioxidant, it prevents the production of free radicals that can damage cells, which in turn can accelerate the progression of cancer, cardiovascular disease, and age-related diseases.

Linden (*Tilia europea*) is a nervine, hypotensive, antispasmodic, and anti-inflammatory. Blood pressure will be lowered, so it is especially effective in treating arteriosclerosis. **Yarrow** (*Achillea millefolium*) has an ancient history and is a diaphoretic, hypotensive, and astringent. It is excellent for use in thrombosis. All four of the above herbs can be combined to make an infusion. Use two parts of hawthorn berries to one part each of linden flowers, ginkgo leaves, and yarrow flowers. Drink three times a day.

Garlic (*Allium sativum*) has an ancient reputation for lowering blood pressure and cholesterol levels. Among many other properties, garlic is an alterative, anticatarrhal, antimicrobial, diaphoretic, and expectorant, so it is an excellent herb for supporting the respiratory system. Eating two cloves of fresh garlic or taking garlic capsules (the number depends on the amount of garlic in them) might not help you make friends, but will help prevent arteriosclerosis, a condition in which plaque builds up in the arteries.

Panax Ginseng has a worldwide reputation as a "male" herb, used in China for over 5,000 years as a vitality tonic. It regulates blood sugar and cholesterol levels, stimulates the immune system, and is also used as an antidepressant (particularly effective when debility and exhaustion cause the depression). Also known for improving memory, extending endurance, fighting fatigue, strengthening the immune system, balancing the metabolism, overcoming insomnia, and improving male virility, ginseng root can be made into an infusion or administered in capsule or extract form.

Many herbs can help minimize the stress and anxiety that underlies many cardiac disorders, including chamomile, lemon balm or lavender for a mild remedy, and skullcap or valerian for a stronger one. All promote better sleep, soothe tension headaches, and help clear mild depression. Combine 1 milliliter each of chamomile and lavender essential oil in 25 milliliters almond oil and use as a massage oil for neck tension and headaches.

Diabetes

Diabetes is a disease in which the body does not produce or properly use insulin, a hormone necessary to convert sugar, starches, and other food into energy. According to the American Diabetes Association, 18.2 million people in the United States have diabetes. Type 1, or insulin-dependent, diabetes is the fairly uncommon condition in which the body fails to produce any insulin. Since type 2 diabetes, which is when either the body does not produce enough insulin or the cells ignore the insulin, is much more prevalent, I will address managing it here.

Diet is an extremely important factor for diabetes sufferers. While it seems like you must avoid all popular, enjoyable foods, such as cold cuts, sugar, pasta, and most carbohydrates, those with type 2 diabetes should take heart. There are many tasty foods and substitutes for diabetics available today, such as foods sweetened with Splenda and margarine that does not contain hydrogenated oils. Obesity is a contributing factor in diabetes, so it is vital to exercise daily and work to achieve or maintain an ideal body weight. Increasing daily vitamin C to at least 3,000 mg will support vascular health and taking 800 to 1,000 IU (International Units) of vitamin E will improve circulation and insulin action. Zinc deficiency is associated with diabetes, so take 50 to 80 mg daily.

Herbal remedies are bitters, which stimulate pancreatic action. **Gentian** (*Gentiana lutea*), a tonic that accelerates emptying the stomach, combined with **yarrow** support the pancreas, while hypoglycemic herbs help reduce blood sugar levels, thereby increasing insulin efficiency. **Fenugreek** (*Trigonella foenum-graecum*) was highly regarded by Hippocrates, and is a prime choice to help control glucose metabolism. Gentian is a root and fenugreek is a seed, so a decoction should be made by putting them in cold water, heating to a boil, and gently simmering for 15 minutes. Strain and cool.

Baldness

While there is no cure for baldness, herbal remedies can slow down the loss of hair. Testosterone levels, poor circulation, stress, and genetics are responsible for hair loss, but some medications for arthritis and high blood pressure also contribute. The scalp must be treated more than the hair itself, as this is where the hair roots are. For generations, people have massaged **rosemary** in olive oil into their scalps, which stimulates circulation and encourages hair to grow more thickly. Mix ½ teaspoon rosemary essential oil in ½ ounce jojoba oil and rub gently into the scalp in circular motions. Use twice a week and leave on for at least four hours before washing out.

Reproductive System

Men are reluctant to talk about problems with their reproductive systems, but simple logic dictates that the longer you remain physically fit and active, the longer you will remain sexually active. Hormone imbalances, while not as severe as for women, are experienced by men as testosterone levels drop, causing irritability and depression. A good combination of herbs that will restore balance is the same one that is suggested for female menopause: wild yam, black cohosh, damiana, oat, and raspberry leaf. To this, add saw palmetto, another reputed "male" herb. You do not need to take it every day, nor should it be taken for a lengthy amount of time—once or twice per day for three days a week is sufficient. Take it for a period of two months and then have a break for two months.

Prostate

Problems with the prostate gland have become a major concern for modern men. The gland is located within the pelvic cavity below the bladder and near the rectum, wrapped around the urethra, into which it empties its secretions. Most men over 55 will experience some congestion or growth of the prostate, which usually remains benign, but if it becomes inflamed, it will press on the urethra and cause urination difficulties. The worst-case scenario is prostate cancer, so, as unpleasant as the process might be, men must have regular examinations to ensure ongoing good health.

Saw palmetto (*Serenoa repens*) is an herb that has a positive influence on the entire reproductive system, but its most important role is maintaining a healthy prostate. It also increases the tone of the bladder, which will help if there is pain during urination. To combat an enlarged prostate gland, it combines well with hydrangea and sarsaparilla. For Prostititis, a gland infection, saw palmetto works in combination with with echinacea, Oregon grape, and buchu. Diuretics such as dandelion, gravel root, hawthorn, uva ursi, and yarrow will increase the secretion and elimination of urine. Drinking plenty of water is vital for overall health and will help prevent urinary and prostate problems.

Genital Health

Men should do testicle examinations every month to detect any changes. The testicle forms the sperm and also secretes hormones into the blood. Orchitis is when the testes become inflamed and results in a feverish condition and painful swelling. Confinement to bed is necessary, plus a support strap and—as shivery as it sounds—an ice pack to the testicles. The infection must be treated and **dong quai** (*Angelica sinensis*), usually considered a female herb, is of great benefit. Next to panax ginseng, the root of dong quai is the most respected herb in China. An analgesic, antibiotic, and tonic, dong quai also contains vitamins

A, E, and B12. Its antispasmodic and vasodilatory properties help ease painful spasms and relax blood vessels, thereby reducing swelling. As a blood purifier and toner, it will reduce fever. Combined with cramp bark and chamomile, it also acts as an anti-inflammatory and a relaxant. People taking blood-thinning agents should not use dong quai. A mixture of ¼ cup each of **comfrey** leaves and mullein, and ⅛ cup of **chamomile** can be steeped in 1 quart of boiling water for 15 minutes and then added to a warm bath. This will help with swelling.

Genital Rash, Infections, and Irritations

While there are many douches available for women, there is nothing comparable for men. Yet, male genital hygiene is equally important to prevent infection, particularly if the sexual partner has a problem, such as a yeast infection or genital warts. A mixture of 1 teaspoon each of **yarrow** (antimicrobial), **lavender** (antibacterial, antiseptic), **sage** (astringent, tonic), and **Oregon grape root** (tonic) in 2 cups of boiling water should be steeped for 20 minutes, strained, and cooled. Pour into a glass or bowl and submerge the genitals, soaking for between 5 and 10 minutes, three times a day. An oil that will soothe the irritation of infection is made by mixing ⅛ teaspoon each of lavender and tea tree essential oils in 1 cup of almond oil and applying twice a day. Capsules or tinctures of **echinacea** and **goldenseal** combined will help combat infection.

Genital Warts

Genital warts resulting from a sexually transmitted virus can be very serious—possibly developing into cancer of the penis. They form on the tip of the penis or on the scrotum and are very tiny in the beginning, but when developed form a hard, raised wart. An herbal formula taken internally to combat the virus, boost the immune system, and aid in liver support consists of three parts **milk thistle** (see below), two parts **calendula**, and one part **wild oat**. It should be made into an infusion and drunk three times a day. **Calendula** (*Calendula officinalis*) is an anti-inflammatory, astringent, vulnerary, antifungal, and antiseptic. To use externally, soak a pad in an infusion and apply to the infected area. **Wild oat** (*Avena sativa*) is a tonic, nervine, nutritive, demulcent, and vulnerary; oat straw contains silica and calcium, which is excellent for skin conditions. It is also wise to increase your vitamin C and zinc intake.

Genital Herpes

An infection caused by the herpes simplex virus can be transmitted during sex. It produces painful sores and is not curable; the virus remains in the body, causing episodes throughout life. According to the U.S. Centers for Disease Control and Prevention, forty-five million people in the United States are infected with the virus. In the past thirty years, occurrence has increased by 30 percent, mostly in teenagers. James Green, in his book *The Male Herbal*, recommends this preparation for the relief of symptoms in an outbreak:

Calendula flower tincture	3 parts
Oregon grape root tincture	1 part
Gumweed bud & flower tincture	1 part
Cleavers tincture	1 part
Burdock root tincture	1 part
Black haw tincture	1 part

Thirty drops should be taken two or three times a day. It can also be applied externally at the first sign of symptoms.

Impotence and Libido

Low sexual energy can result from poor diet, heart disease, diabetes, neurological disorders, stress, fatigue, and the use of drugs and stimulants. Drugs such as Viagra can have serious side effects; consequently, there have been many herbal products advertised as an alternative. Aphrodisiacs have been around for millennia, but there is little scientific data about their efficacy.

The most popular herbs are ginseng and yohimbe, which stimulate the release of nitric oxide in the body, increasing peripheral blood flow to the genitals. However, **yohimbe** (*Pausinystalia yohimbe*) also has side effects such as elevated blood pressure, anxiety, and nausea, so it should not be used by people with liver or kidney disease or those with inflammation of the prostate. The aptly named **horny goat weed** (*Epimedium sagittatum*) is used in traditional Chinese medicine and is called Ying Yang Huo. It acts like testosterone, stimulating sexual activity and desire, and increasing sperm production. **Oats** (*Avena sativa*) are one of the best remedies for "feeding" the nervous system and can be taken when lack of libido is due to nervous exhaustion. **Damiana** (*Turnera diffusa*) also helps strengthen the nervous system, specifically in anxiety and depression where there is a sexual factor. An herbal remedy as follows can be taken 30 drops, three times a day for three months to improve libido:

Ginseng root tincture	½ ounce
Ginkgo leaves tincture	½ ounce
Yohimbe bark tincture	½ ounce
Fresh oats tincture	½ ounce
Damiana leaves tincture	½ ounce

In today's fast-paced life, men are expected to be Superman—physically strong and "macho," and mentally strong in relationships, from romantic to professional. They are expected not to cave under pressure, but most do not provide the body with the elements needed to remain strong under such pressure. Doing so means making it a habit, so it is of vital importance for men to teach their sons about their bodies from an early age. Boys should be encouraged to talk about what ails them without feeling that they are not being "manly," and told that appropriately releasing emotion is important to the overall health of the body, spirit, and mind.

Teach them about diet and exercise—and, as hard as it may be, lead by example. Take them for a hike and stop for a healthy snack instead of driving through the nearest fast food restaurant. Most important for all men, should you develop any of the previous disorders, consider herbal remedies instead of just popping a pill. Wherever possible, work with a naturopath or find a doctor who is open to discussing herbs and combining them with allopathic medicines where appropriate. At the center of naturopathy lies the belief in the individual for self-healing, which gives us a sense of personal empowerment and control over the health of our bodies. Herbal knowledge can offer this to men.

Remedies for Domestic Animals

Using echinacea to ward off an oncoming cold, arnica for bruises, and chamomile to help heal the skin has become so commonplace that pharmacies now sell herbs in capsule and liquid form right next to over-the-counter pharmaceuticals. Chances are you've tried at least one herbal remedy to improve your health, avoid a prescription drug, or complement a more traditional treatment. But have you considered the natural, balancing effects herbs can have for your pets?

Statistics show that pet health has declined in recent decades, most likely due to environmental factors and inadequate commercial diets. Overuse of vaccinations and antibiotics may also be contributing to the illnesses and allergies our animals suffer. Pets also experience anxiety and exhibit behavioral problems that can't be traced to drugs or chemicals, but may be common to their breed or a result of trauma. Even the healthiest animals have the occasional minor injury or upset stomach, and herbal remedies can help.

I began using supplements for my own pets after adopting a border collie pup, Sully, with a seizure disorder. My older dog was going on his second knee replacement and the vet visits and bills were piling up. We were also concerned that the most frequently prescribed medications and treatment for epilepsy might negatively affect the growing pup's development. So our family decided to investigate some alternative therapies.

We were fortunate enough to find a veterinarian experienced in natural methods, including herbs and homeopathy. For the border collie's seizures, she recommended Rescue Remedy, a flower essence, which relieved some trauma and shortened his recovery periods. Homeopathic remedies including arnica and belladonna were added to the postseizure regimen, and we fed this pup a raw food diet to eliminate toxins or unnecessary additives that might trigger these episodes. Even when we finally opted for traditional medications to help control his seizures, we continued these herbs and natural remedies to complement the potassium bromide and Phenobarbital. Sully's seizures were hard on his body, but he was an incredibly athletic and otherwise healthy animal with a gorgeous thick coat and split-second responses. His liver never suffered from the medications and his blood counts were always perfect.

Seeing the results of natural treatment influenced us to extend remedies and supplements to our older dog's diet, and at ten years old he is active, strong, and drug free! The seasonal skin problems he typically developed are all but gone, and any arthritis from his knee surgeries is minimal. We credit improved diet, herbs, and homeopathic solutions.

While not a replacement for modern medicine, natural, plant-based remedies can prevent some health problems, help treat others, mitigate the side effects of some medications, and complement traditional medical care. However, before beginning an herbal regimen for your pet, consult a professional.

A veterinarian who specializes in natural care is your best source of information and a quality pet shop that sells healthy supplements is another. Remedies typically come in pill, capsule, and tincture form. The form best administered varies by pet. For example, cats are more sensitive to certain substances, like alcohol, the base of some blends. Supplements found in human health food stores are typically suitable for animals too, so there's no need to find special formulas. It's more important to explore appropriate dosages based on your pet's size. Children's doses often work for smaller animals. Herbs can interact with medications or can be toxic if overadministered, so give the health professional your pet's complete medical history. The short- and long-term benefits are worth your time and energy.

Anxiety and Trauma

Rescue Remedy and other flower essences by Bach can enhance your pet's emotional well-being. Rescue Remedy is commonly used during thunderstorms, vet visits, and any other experience that triggers anxiety. After a traumatic incident, such as a fight with another animal, you and your pet can both take a few drops to restore balance. Other flower essences help animals cope with jealousy, loss, lethargy, and new situations. Made with spring water and wild flowers, these essences are 100 percent safe.

Skin

Animals with skin conditions can suffer chronic itch, pain, and sores, but there are several possible treatments. Aloe has amazing skin-healing properties and can be administered externally in gel or spray form or ingested in capsule form. Birds and other pets with skin issues may benefit from a spray of one part aloe vera juice to three parts distilled water. Chamomile soothes irritated skin and helps prevent infection. Chamomile gel or cream can be safely applied to "hot" spots your dog develops.

For best results, look for formulas that contain at least 3 percent of the herb. To prevent skin conditions and speed the healing in existing cases, omega-3 fatty acids may be the most effective. Flaxseed oil contains omega-3s, which also promote a healthy coat, protect against cancer, and ease digestion. Both dogs and cats can take this supplement for general health. Flaxseed in oil form is probably best, but it has a limited shelf life and requires refrigeration.

Fungal infections and warts can also be treated naturally. We used garlic to clear up the warts one of my dogs developed on his mouth. The juice or oil of garlic can be directly applied to the affected area and powder, liquid, or soft gel forms may be ingested. For birds with fungal infections, fresh slices of garlic work or drops can be added to the pet's water for short periods of treatment. Garlic also boosts the immune system and may help prevent cancers, especially those of the digestive system.

Healthy Organs

Many illnesses can be traced to poor liver function. Dog, cat, and bird ailments that can't be traced or easily cured may respond to milk thistle, which supports and cleanses the liver. This member of the sunflower family prevents the liver from being depleted of glutathione, an amino-acidlike compound required in the detoxification process. In capsule, oil, or tincture form, milk thistle helps regenerate new liver cells, repair damage, and treat viral infections. It is generally used for short periods of time such as during an illness, recovery, or change of season. Though it can have a slight laxative effect, milk thistle is considered very safe for both humans and their animals.

Aloe can be used with other herbs to detoxify the liver. This is most helpful for animals in generally poor health who need daily medications that the liver must process. Aloe Detox (by Naturade) is a formula that includes milk thistle, echinacea, green tea, and other herbs. Parrot owners boast of its effectiveness.

Arthritis

Injury and age leave pets vulnerable to joint pain, and adding foods rich in omega-3 fatty acids like salmon or supplements like flax oil to their diets can ease arthritis symptoms. Vitamins C and E, as well as glucosamine chondroitin, may also help. Herbs that can prevent and treat degenerative disease include turmeric root, considered a natural prednisone, which both dogs and cats may take in capsule form. For dogs only, meadowsweet and white willow bark are worth investigating as alternatives to rimadyl.

Digestion

All animals suffer bouts of indigestion and several herbs can help. Slippery elm powder, made from the plant's inner bark, soothes the stomach, bowels, and kidneys; reduces inflammation; and heals the entire digestive tract. Dogs and cats (it's safe for both) readily accept this sweet powder when mixed with water and a bit of honey. A teaspoon of slippery elm powder mixed with water and given three times a day can restore the appetite of a pet who refuses to eat during cancer treatments or while recovering from an illness. Your pet's ulcers, gastritis, and vomiting can be treated with slippery elm.

Peppermint and ginger also support digestion and are generally safe for your pet. Ginger, available for pets in tablet form, helps with flatulence and motion sickness. Peppermint is also used for motion sickness and can stimulate the appetite of an ailing dog. While these herbal extracts can help and heal, remember that chronic digestive problems should be explored with your veterinarian. Do your homework: Some herbs are not advised for certain ailments, pregnant or lactating animals, those preparing to undergo surgery, and the very old or young.

Cancer

Herbs can help prevent cancer and support our animals during cancer treatment. Like humans, our pets benefit from antioxidants found in foods and supplements. While a healthy diet without additives could be the most important thing you do for your animal, strengthening the immune system is another key to keeping your pet cancer free. Some herbal remedies recommended for other conditions also fight cancer by supporting the immune system's ability to sense and destroy free radicals that cause cell damage. Flaxseed oil, helpful for healthy skin, joints, and digestion, also contains many cancer-fighting compounds and may be part of a regular diet. Garlic and ginger have anticancer properties, and green tea and grape seed extracts are preventatives found in herbal tonics that support general pet health.

Sea plants are also wonderful sources of protection. Spirulina and kelp, two types of aquatic algae, may boost the immune system, aid in chemical and environmental detoxification, and help prevent certain types of cancer. Seaweeds can be found in capsule, tincture, or liquid form, but one easy way to add them to your animal's diet is by sprinkling the flakes (for example, kelp granules) in your pet's regular food. As with other herbs, seaweeds can interact with certain drugs such as thyroid medications, so get advice from a professional if you have any questions.

If your animal has already been diagnosed with cancer, astragalus is an herb worth looking into regardless of how you've decided to treat the disease. Astragalus is used to balance the chi, or life force, and effectively prevents and treats many illnesses. An herbal tonic used to promote general well-being, astragalus enhances immune functions and should partially make up for an immune system weakened by radiation and chemotherapy. Holistic veterinarians have recommended this tonic, which may be combined with herbs such as ginseng or echinacea, for pets either undergoing or forgoing cancer treatments. It improves resistance and resilience, is safe, and seems to have no side effects.

Finally, as you begin or continue your journey into herbal remedies, remember that not all are created equal! Quality counts, so consult an expert or look for standardized extracts with guaranteed potency to make sure you are providing the most consistent and beneficial herbal product for your pet's health.

Herbs
for
Beauty

Chamomile for Beauty Inside and Out

❧ by S.Y. Zenith ❧

Chamomile is a well-known commodity worldwide, but uses for this herb go well beyond its calming, cozying effect as a tea.

Whether used as an atmospheric to induce rest or in a concoction directly applied to the skin as a facial treatment or body cream, chamomile can keep you looking and feeling your best. The uses as a cosmetic beauty aid are rooted in its substantive qualities. Chamomile is known to promote healing, digestion, peace, positivity, understanding, relaxation, stability, and the release of past emotions. It also helps improve communication and spirituality. When emotions go troppo, chamomile helps you regain emotional balance. Known for alleviating stress, insomnia, nervous tension, and depression, chamomile

also soothes scattered nerves, hysteria, oversensitivity, hypersensitivity, and resentment.

In medical terms, chamomile is known to be anodyne, antiseptic, anti-inflammatory, antispasmodic, and antiallergenic. It is also regarded as a suitable herb for infants and young children prone to colic, vomiting, loss of appetite, restlessness, nightmares, teething troubles, and skin rashes. All that is required is for one or two teaspoons of mild to normal strength chamomile tea to be administered directly for a maximum of three times a day. Alternatively, the chamomile tea may be mixed with beverages or food.

A Word of Caution

Many health practitioners do not recommend using chamomile during the first three months of pregnancy. If in doubt about any herbal uses, consult a health practitioner. Those suffering from hypertension, cardiac-related ailments, and allergies should consult qualified medical professionals such as the family doctor. Others with miscellaneous health problems not described herein are encouraged to approach a qualified herbalist, naturopath, aromatherapist, or alternative health-care counselor.

Relaxing Nerves and Inducing Sleep

For inducing sound sleep during restless nights, breathe in the scent of fresh or dried chamomile flowers. Alternatively, chamomile essential oil can be sniffed for similar effects. On the day when you are extremely stressed, put two or more drops of chamomile essential oil on a handkerchief. Take several deep breaths, exhale, and then sniff the scent of chamomile to settle rattled nerves and thoughts. For folks who have difficulty entering a meditative state as a means to relax overworked mental energies, get an oil burner going in the room with a few drops of chamomile essential oil.

Chamomile Floral Spray

Practitioners of alternative healing modalities will find that scenting the healing room with chamomile is conducive to peaceful remedial sessions, especially useful when handling cranky clients. A simple room spray can be prepared using:

20 to 25 drops chamomile essential oil

⅙ ounce vodka

16 ounces distilled water

Using a sterilized and dry glass bottle, dissolve chamomile essential oil in the vodka, then thoroughly blend it with the distilled water. When ready, store the concoction in a dark-glass pump-spray bottle with a "fine-mist" setting. Use for spraying around the healing room whenever required. This recipe can also be used in the home, shop, or office—anywhere there is relentless daily stress. You can also spritz some in the car before a long drive!

Tea Bags for Eyes

Being one of the most versatile herbs, chamomile can be applied in many cosmetic contexts apart from being just commonly consumed as sedative tea. Actually, used chamomile tea bags have further uses. From those who are prone to dark rings and "saggy bags" under the eyes after a big night out or from sheer lack of sleep, to sufferers of chronic eye irritations such as swollen, sore, and red peepers, many can find relief from two cool chamomile tea bags. Much like cucumber slices, you can place used, cooled-but-still-moist chamomile tea bags on each closed eyelid to ease eye discomfort.

Facial Sauna

Give the face a good pampering with a chamomile facial sauna or steam treatment at home that cleanses, soothes, tightens, smoothens, and refreshes. Recommended use of this beauty treatment is only once a week. Grab a handful of chamomile and boil in spring water in a saucepan for five or ten minutes. Remove the saucepan from heat and place on the table. Drape a towel over the head and sit on a chair, positioning the face over the saucepan's rising steam. Allow the vapor to play over the face. When the steam stops rising, return the saucepan to the stove for a second boil. Repeat the facial steam treatment before washing in cold water, wiping dry, and applying moisturizer.

Chamomile Compresses

As an alternative to facial steam treatments, bring one cup of spring water with two tablespoons of chamomile flowers to a boil. Then strain the container. Dip a piece of clean linen or white cotton cloth in the chamomile solution and let the surplus drip off. Place the cloth over the entire face while still warm. Lay back and relax. When the facial compress turns cold, repeat the process by boiling the solution a second time and applying the cloth again. Afterward, rinse the face in cold water, pat dry, and apply moisturizer. A weekly facial compress is usually sufficient for most skin types. (Note: A chamomile compress is also useful for headaches and migraines, in which case a warm or cold cotton towel is placed on the forehead while resting.)

Whitening Chamomile Cream

This homemade recipe for chamomile cream was given to me by a fabulous elderly lady in Australia who uses it to soften and whiten her facial complexion, neck, and hands. It requires making a strong chamomile infusion by pouring boiling water over a quarter cup of organic chamomile flowers. Let the flowers steep in the cup until cool, then strain into a clean, dry, good-sized glass jar. While the infusion is steeping, get the following ingredients ready:

1 tablespoon cocoa butter

¼ cup vitamin E cream

3 tablespoons strong chamomile infusion

Proceed with melting cocoa butter in a small saucepan on low heat. After melting, remove the pan from the stove and allow the cocoa butter to cool down slightly. Put both the vitamin E cream and chamomile infusion into the saucepan and start whisking. Continue whisking until the mixture cools further and shows signs of thickening. Pour into a sterilized, dry glass jar, and seal. This recipe makes about a quarter cup of chamomile cream.

Floral Water

A chamomile floral water decoction stored in a pump-spray bottle makes a pleasant pick-me-up when applied as a facial spritz or revitalizing body spray. In making floral water, put four tablespoons of fresh chamomile flowers, a wee sprinkle of dried rosemary herb, and a few rose petals along with twelve ounces of water into a steel saucepan. Cover the saucepan and bring it to a simmer for 30 minutes. Remove from heat, let the mixture cool, and then strain. If you prefer a stronger scent, add more chamomile to the liquid. Top off the water if necessary.

Chamomile Body Lotion

This is good to use in summer after spending time on the beach or a day outdoors under the sun. The recipe requires:

⅓ cup chamomile floral water

2 tablespoons glycerine

Whisk chamomile floral water and glycerine together in a small glass bowl and pour into a small bottle, seal the bottle, and shake thoroughly before using. Experiment with this recipe before making a large batch of chamomile lotion to store in bottles to carry around when outdoors for long periods.

Body Cream

For use on dry or dehydrated skin, prepare as follows:

- ⅓ ounce beeswax
- ¼ cup avocado oil
- 3 drops chamomile essential oil
- 3 drops jasmine essential oil
- 2 tablespoons chamomile floral water
- ¼ teaspoon Borax

Find a double saucepan, fill the bottom pan with water, place on the stove, and set it to simmer. In the upper saucepan, put the beeswax, avocado oil, chamomile essential oil, and jasmine essential oil. Place the upper pan containing the ingredients on top of the simmering lower saucepan. Heat the ingredients gently and stir until the beeswax melts and the mixture forms a smooth texture. Remove both saucepans from heat. Blend chamomile floral water together with borax in a bowl before stirring into the beeswax mixture. Keep stirring until the mixture in the saucepan cools completely. Using a dry, sterilized spoon, scoop the cream into an appropriate jar with a secure lid and label. This recipe makes approximately a quarter cup of body cream.

Blond Hair Rinse

A useful rinse for enhancing and conditioning blond tresses while bathing can be made at home by combining a strong infusion of fresh or dried chamomile flowers with virgin olive oil, or baby oil of personal choice in a glass jar with a secure lid. Crush the flowers and steep in the oil for three weeks. Place the glass container in a warm place and be sure to shake it at least once a day. After three weeks, strain the chamomile concoction using coffee filter paper, a piece of clean linen, or a fine muslin cloth into a decorative, dark glass bottle. Label and store the dark glass bottle in a cool corner of the bathroom cabinet.

Body Bath Bliss

After a stressful day, kick off those shoes, let everything hang loose, and reward yourself with a calming chamomile bath. This not only washes off the day's grime, but also provides a nurturing effect. There are two methods for using chamomile for bathing.

The first is an infusion created by gathering a handful of chamomile flowers—fresh or dried—and putting them in a muslin, cotton, or linen pouch. Secure the pouch and tie it to the bath tap. Make sure that when the taps are turned on, the water will run through the pouch, thus wetting the chamomile flowers. The resulting infusion will be part and parcel of the bathwater. Sprinkle Epsom salts into the tub while the water is running. When the desired water level is reached, disrobe and hop into the bath. Nourish as much skin as possible by immersing yourself up to the neck—an often-neglected area in many beauty regimens.

The second method utilizes chamomile essential oil and Epsom salts. Run a bath with warm water at your preferred temperature. Add Epsom salts and two drops of chamomile essential oil while the water is gushing into the bathtub. For an extra "oomph" to delight the senses, throw in a cupful of fresh rose petals. Whole roses with stems snipped off can also be added. When ready, plop yourself into the bath for a blissful wash.

Chamomile Therapeutic Foot Bath

Exhausted feet will be relieved with a foot bath before drying, moisturizing, and putting them up for well-deserved rest. Plonk a large basin on the floor and fill it ankle-high with warm water. Plop several used chamomile tea bags or a handful of chamomile flowers into the water. Three drops of chamomile essential oil may be used instead of the tea bags. A few drops of solubalizer for essential oils can also be added. Stir the water around with a wooden or stainless steel implement until the mixture is well blended. Sit comfortably on a chair and soak both feet in the basin for up to twenty-five minutes. If the mind is restless while sitting down for a foot bath, read a book or magazine. Or have the foot bath while watching television.

Aromatic Chamomile Shower

Busy folks with frantic lifestyles who haven't time for baths can also reap the benefits of chamomile while showering. Simply stuff a handful of fresh or dried chamomile into a cotton pouch and tie it up with string. Affix the pouch to the shower head with another piece of string. Allow the pouch to dangle so that when the water runs, it whooshes past the chamomile pouch downward as you wash. Remember to smell the gentle aroma of chamomile. Those who love a good body scrub can make a second chamomile pouch. After applying soap or shower gel on the wet body, hold the pouch in your hand like you would use a loofah for scrubbing, toning, and rejuvenating. This method, although simple and quick, is nevertheless effective.

Chamomile Jacuzzi

Why not be the first to start a chamomile Jacuzzi for unwinding and reviving drained physical energies? If you have a Jacuzzi, this is a perfect haven for maintaining beauty and health. The whirl-pool jets of a Jacuzzi combined with five drops of chamomile essential oil is one of the best solutions for toning the decollette region (under the neckline) and relieving sore muscles, aching limbs, overworked bodies, and mental tension. For those who enjoy flowers swishing about during a Jacuzzi session, in place of chamomile essential oil chuck in a handful of fresh chamomile flowers with some roses.

Health note: Jacuzzis may pose a health risk for people with heart conditions and blood pressure problems. Remember that heart problems may perhaps be affected by temperature changes from cold to hot or vice versa. With each temperature change, the heartbeat can increase approximately 60 percent or more, depending on an individual's condition. This increment is not much different than when performing moderate exercise.

Please also be mindful that when one's body acclimatizes to the highest temperatures (for those who like it more than warm, verging on the hot), blood pressure may decrease. This is a definite risk, especially for folks who've made the half century milestone (i.e., over fifty years old) and/or are predisposed to arteriosclerosis. People with dysfunctional or poor heart functions must be mindful and cautious about using Jacuzzis, just in case a decline in heart function can set off a mild stroke.

Body Massage Oil

Massage therapy is an essential part of a beauty and health regimen that maintains skin firmness and reduces cellulite. It also revitalizes skin cells, relieves certain ailments, loosens tense muscles, and perhaps also assists the release of unresolved personal traumas stored in the body. A body massage oil can be made using the following ingredients:

3   ounces cold-pressed almond oil

1   ounce cold-pressed hazelnut oil

1   ounce cold-pressed jojoba oil

⅙   ounce chamomile essential oil

Sterilize a dry, dark glass bottle (amber or cobalt blue). Pour the oils into the bottle and give it a hearty shake so the combination of oils is well blended before use. Get your partner, best buddy, or family member to exchange massages with you at least once a week. If there isn't anyone you're comfortable with nor would allow to massage you, it is fine to massage yourself.

Pour a teaspoon of chamomile massage oil onto your palm. Rub both hands together to warm them up and begin massaging the neck very, very gently with upward sweeping motions.

Health note: Do not massage the neck if you have cardiac conditions such as high blood pressure or angina, have previously experienced strokes or undergone bypass surgery, or are taking any medication for heart ailments. Certain glands in the neck are highly sensitive and could trigger heart attacks or associated complications when the neck is massaged.

Neck aside, pour another teaspoon of massage oil onto one palm and rub both hands together again. Apply to breast, torso, belly, and buttocks with circular motions. This helps condition the skin and tone muscles. Those who suffer anxiety attacks will find it soothing to specifically massage the solar plexus in a counterclockwise direction at least nine times.

Massage both shoulders with one hand on each side. If able to reach behind to touch the shoulder blades, then rub them too. If you are not able to reach them, use a longish piece of cotton cloth dabbed with massage oil. Hold the cloth with both hands and swing the cloth over the head, to the shoulders. Glide the cloth right and left and back again until satisfied. The same methods can be applied to the back of the body.

For the arms, use another teaspoon of oil and massage upwards with long, firm strokes from the hands to the shoulders. Next, gently knead each arm upwards with the fingertips. It is also beneficial to rub tired, dry feet and soles with one teaspoon of massage oil. A little more oil is required for the legs and thighs. Begin from the ankles with firm strokes, working up the legs to the top of the thighs.

A Bauble Bath of Herbal Body Goodies

⬿ by Laurel Reufner ⬾

Few things beat the feeling of giving gifts from the heart that you have made yourself. With a little money, a little effort, and some usually inexpensive ingredients you can create something truly stunning. Just as important, playing kitchen chemist and crafting lovely herbal bath gifts is great fun. The fun continues after the chemistry as you place your lotions, potions, and powders in beautiful containers and assemble gift baskets, boxes, and bags. (You know, baubles.) I've raided my stash of beauty recipes to share these delightful bath and body treats with you.

There are a few things to keep in mind when beginning to make your own bath and body delights. Rule No. 1: Have fun. Rule No. 2: Always use clean utensils, bowls, and other equipment. Avoid using metal because some oils and salts react with it unfavorably. Glass mixing bowls are best. Plastic will do in a pinch.

Scents are another consideration. Some, like vanilla and lavender, have universal appeal, but other scents are more personalized. Make sure you really know the recipient and which scents they like before getting too creative. For instance, if you know your gift recipient's favorite perfume or cologne, use some of it to scent their bath gifts.

For everyone else, here's a quick primer on the five basic scent categories:

Floral scents—lavender, lilac, jasmine, rose, etc.— are self-explanatory and generally considered feminine scents.

Green scents include chamomile, rosemary, and eucalyptus. While some green scents are traditional feminine scents, others are used for either sex.

The other categories are primarily gender neutral, appropriate for masculine or feminine items.

Woodsy/earthy scents include smells like patchouli, sandalwood, rosewood, cedarwood, musk, and other resins.

Citrus scents give a clean, invigorating scent. These include bergamot, orange blossom, lemon, and lemongrass.

Spicy scents are myrrh, frankincense, ginger, cinnamon, and other such smells.

Keep in mind that some essential oils, such as pennyroyal and cinnamon, should not be used directly on the skin. If you need to err on the side of caution, use a fragrance oil instead of the essential oil.

One final note on ingredients: Several recipes call for liquid or grated soap, preferably castile soap. Castile soap is usually made from 100 percent olive oil and is very mild, scentless, and even moisturizing. It tends to be eco-friendly and biodegradable. One of the mildest, most cleansing bar soaps around, castile soap is also the least likely to annoy anyone with allergies.

Bath Salts

Let's start our kitchen creations with one of the easiest to make: bath salts. At the absolute simplest, you simply take some salt and add it to the bath water. However, since we are talking gifts here, let's get a little fancier. Table salt is the simplest and easiest to obtain, but chunkier salts, such as kosher salt or the rock salt used for pickling and ice cream making, are even better. I like to use sea salt, although it can be expensive depending on where you live. Epsom salts are lovely to use in the bath as they not only soften the water but soothe tired muscles as well. Baking soda is another option.

Basic Recipe

My favorite basic recipe uses equal amounts of sea salt, Epsom salts, and baking soda. You need to pulverize both salts so they blend better with the finer grained baking soda. Some people like to add a tablespoon or two of liquid glycerin to their bath salts, which works as an added moisturizer and helps eliminate clumping, a hazard in humid areas.

You can use this mixture "as is" or have some fun with it. Food coloring is one of the easiest ways to alter your bath salts. Place your bath salts into a jar, leaving some room between the bath salts and the lid. Add your food coloring, screw on the lid, and shake until the color is mixed through. Another way to mix colors is to place the salts in a plastic zipper-type storage bag, add some drops of food coloring, zipper the bag shut and shake, shake, shake.

You can scent bath salts using the same methods. Add no more than 10 to 15 drops of essential or fragrance oil to the salts and mix. (I like a lot of scent to my bath goodies. You might want to adjust accordingly.) Allow it to sit for a few days before giving as a gift. This allows the scents to mingle and permeate throughout the salts.

You can have a lot of fun playing around and experimenting with this basic recipe, which is what I usually do. However, some folks are more comfortable with more definite directions to follow. With that in mind, here are some scentfully delicious recipes to enjoy.

Vanilla Milk Shake Bath Salts

1   cup sea salt, kosher salt, or rock salt

1   cup Epsom salts

1   cup baking soda

1   cup powdered milk

1   tsp. vanilla extract

Combine the salts together and then add in the vanilla and powdered milk. Mix very well. Store in an airtight container. To use, sprinkle ¼ to ½ cup under running water.

Candy Stripes Bath Salts

2½   cups basic bath salts

     red food coloring

     Peppermint oil

Mix half of the bath salts with the peppermint oil (about 8 drops) and red food coloring (about 10 to 12 drops).

Mix about 8 drops of oil with the uncolored bath salts. In a pretty container, alternate layers of colored and uncolored bath salts for a striking effect.

This particular project is quite versatile. By simply changing the scent and color, you create a brand new theme. How about blue food coloring with a blueberry fragrance oil? Yellow/orange coloring and a citrus fragrance to re-energize. Another idea is to use the recipient's favorite scent and then color the stripes to match their bathroom.

Herbal Bath Scrub

     Wide-mouth glass container

     Sea salt or rock salt

Fresh herbs (Lavender and rosemary are a good combination.)

Place a layer of salt in the bottom of your container. Roughly chop or tear the herbs and place some on top of the salt layer. Lay down another layer of salt, followed by another layer of herbs. For the best effect, try to make the layers ½ to 1 inch thick. Continue in this fashion until the jar is full. If your jar has a metal screw top, add a piece of plastic wrap to the top before screwing on the lid. Let set for two weeks to give the scents time to permeate the salts. Strain the herbs out and package for gift giving.

Cleo's Beauty Milk Bath

- ¼ cup oatmeal, finely ground
- ⅓ cup almond meal (use blanched or slivered almonds)
- 3 cups powdered milk
- ¼ cup orrisroot (adds a soft violet scent)
- 1 capsule vitamin E
- ⅓ cup cornstarch

Use a blender or food processor to grind the oatmeal into a powder, as well as to make almond meal. Then place ingredients in a glass bowl and mix them completely. Store in an airtight container. To use, simply scoop some of the mixture out and place it in a small muslin bag or tie in a washcloth. Hang it on the faucet where the running water can flow over it.

Here how you can make a great little gift set. Place your container of milk bath into a pretty basket and then adding a small scoop and either some muslin bags or pretty washcloths. Be sure to add a tag to your container with the directions on it.

Bubble Baths

Is there any better luxury than a nice soak in a bubble-filled tub of hot water? Your own customized bubble baths are deceptively simple to make. The hardest part will be finding a pretty bottle to store them in.

The basic recipe for making bubble bath is quite simple: mix 1 quart distilled or spring water with 1 bar grated castile soap. Add in 3 ounces of liquid glycerin, which will not only soften your skin, but also make the bubbles last longer. Add anywhere from 3 to 10 drops of your desired scent, and you're done. If you can't find castile soap or don't want to do all that grating, substitute 1 cup of unscented shampoo or extra mild baby shampoo.

Have fun playing around with this base recipe. Try combining scents, like vanilla and raspberry or strawberry, lavender and rose, or sandalwood and orange. Take a walk down the bath aisle of your local store for even more ideas.

The only other recipe I'm including in this section is for a fun jellylike bubble bath. It's a great idea for kids, but don't forget the young-at-heart as well. They'll love it too.

Jelly Giggle Bubble Bath

1   package unflavored gelatin

¾   cup water

½   cup clear liquid soap or bubble bath

    Chosen fragrance or essential oil

    Food coloring (optional but fun)

    Small objects (silk flowers, toys, pretty stones,
        etc., … also optional)

Heat water until just boiling. Remove immediately from the heat and pour into a glass bowl containing the gelatin. Mix gently until the gelatin is completely dissolved.

Slowly stir soap into the gelatin water. Add one or two drops of food coloring and a 5-10 drops of your scent of choice. Stir very gently or you risk making your bubble bath very frothy.

Pour your bubble bath into the desired storage container and gently nest your little object into the jelly. Refrigerate until the gelatin sets (about 4 hours).

To use, simply scoop up a small amount in your hand and hold it under the running water. That's where the giggles come into play, especially if the kids get to do it.

Bath Oils

Bath oils help sooth and soften dry skin, make for a very aromatic bath experience, and really just make for a pleasant experience for those not into bubbles in their tub. A wide variety of oils can be used for these particular products. I like light oils, like extra virgin olive oil, walnut, grapeseed, jojoba, or almond oil, which has its own delightfully light scent. Some recipes that you might come across suggest using mineral oil or baby oil. It really comes down to a matter of preference, availability, and maybe cost. Baby oil is definitely less expensive than olive oil.

The basic recipe for bath oil is almost as simple as the one for bath salts. At its simplest, just add a teaspoonful or two to your tub, settle in, and enjoy. Of course, it's much more fun to play around, adding fragrance or essential oils to your bath oil. They're also nicer to give as gifts when they smell nice.

Lava Lamp Bath Oil

½   cup light oil

½   cup rose water, lavender water,
     or spring water (for scentless oil)

2   colors of food coloring of your choice

You will also need a bottle that holds at least 1 cup of liquid and has a tight-fitting lid. Add one of the food colors (about 3 drops) to the oil and pour into the bottle. Add the other color to the water and pour that into the bottle. If you wish, add some scent to the bottle as well.

The two liquids will separate into pretty bands of color that can be mixed by gently shaking before use. To use, add a teaspoon to the tub and enjoy.

Soaps

What would a bath and body gift set be without some soap tucked in there somewhere? Many wonderful results can be obtained using a simple melt-and-pour technique. Actual soap bases can be found in many craft stores and crafting departments. The directions for melting them are usually on the packaging, but basically all you do is cut it into chunks and then melt it in a double boiler or the microwave. All sorts of things can then be added to the soap base, including small toys for children to "liberate" over time.

Another way of doing melt and pour is to use castile soap or beauty bars such as Dove, Ivory, or Olay. Chunk or grate the soap and then melt in a double boiler or carefully in the microwave. Glycerin soap bars could also be used this way.

Experimenting is easy and part of the fun in making soap. You can do small amounts of soap at a time, so you aren't out lots of time, supplies, or money if you don't like the end result. I've given a couple of fun recipes here, but there are so many books and websites out there to go explore. Check out the websites listed at the end of this article for some good places to start.

Oatmeal Scrubbie Soap

1   cup melt-and-pour soap or grated beauty bar
¼   cup coarsely ground oatmeal

Melt the soap base using whichever method you prefer. Add in scent if desired. Stir in the oatmeal and pour into the molds of your choice. Allow to cool completely before unmolding.

Lavender Soap Balls

⅓   cup boiling water
1   tablespoon dried lavender buds
3¼   cups grated castile soap

Make a lavender tea by steeping the lavender buds in the boiling water for 15 minutes. Reheat after steeping and add 4 drops of lavender oil. Pour the lavender "tea" over the grated soap and knead together. Form the mixture into balls, place them on a piece of wax paper, and allow to air-dry for about a week. Store them unwrapped.

Either of these would be lovely tuck-ins for a gift set for someone close to you. Wrap them up in some tulle or organza and tie with a pretty ribbon.

Miscellaneous Bath Recipes

There are always those wonderful sounding recipes that defy categorization. Here you will find a barrage of recipes that just sounded too delightful to leave out, yet didn't really fit in any other category.

Chamomile Relaxation

    4   cups powdered milk
    ½   cup chamomile or 5 chamomile tea bags

Draw about three inches of H-O-T water into the tub. Place the chamomile into a muslin bag, large do-it-yourself tea bag, or washcloth and toss into the water. Let steep for 20 minutes. Add powdered milk and gently swirl to dissolve. Finish drawing your bath and enjoy.

Another way to do this would be to steep the chamomile in 1 cup of boiling water. Let the tea steep for 20 minutes and then add it to the milk. Add to the bath water.

This could easily make a lovely mini-gift set for someone. Package the chamomile in large tea bags or tie it up in a lovely washcloth in a color the recipient likes. Tuck in the powdered milk, perhaps having packaged it in special envelopes that can easily be found online. Check the end of this article for some useful websites.

Green Tea Salt Scrub

1   cup sea salt

1   cup sugar

½   cup baking soda

2-3   tablespoons green tea

⅛   teaspoon vitamin E (or one capsule)

½   cup almond oil

Combine all of the dry ingredients together, mixing thoroughly. Place in container of choice. Mix the vitamin E and almond oil. Pour over dry ingredients. To use, take a small amount in your hand and gently rub on the desired area with a circular motion.

If you've never used a salt or sugar scrub, you are really missing out. They invigorate blood flow to the skin's surface, exfoliate the dead skin cells, and soften all at the same time.

Rose Petals Hand Cream

⅓   cup glycerin

⅔   cup rosewater

Pour the ingredients into a pretty bottle. Shake gently to combine them before use.

Soothing Foot Lotion Recipe

1   tablespoon almond oil

1   tablespoon olive oil

1   teaspoon wheat germ oil

12   drops eucalyptus essential oil

This is another recipe where you simply combine the ingredients in a bottle and shake gently to combine. Massage into feet and heels daily.

Bathtub Finger Paints

⅓ cup liquid soap (mild)

½ tablespoon cornstarch

Food coloring of choice

Small containers

Mix all of the ingredients together in your chosen container, stirring or shaking gently until they are all mixed together. Make sure you store it with the lids tightly capped.

Packaging

There are as many ways to package up your homemade goodies as there are folks out there making homemade goodies. Thankfully, nowadays, you can find wonderful jars and bottles just about anywhere, including the local dollar store. Dress them up with ribbon, raffia, glass paints, glass etchings and even stickers. There are also some wonderful websites listed at the end of this article that provide labels and tags if you don't feel up to making your own.

Baskets can also be had cheaply at dollar stores, the Salvation Army, or various thrift stores. Many craft departments also have inexpensive baskets (and bottles). Dress them up with some spray paint, and add some ribbon and dried or silk flowers. Let yourself be as creative as you want. If you need some inspiration, stroll through a craft store or visit websites for businesses such as Michaels or JoAnns. Above all, have fun and enjoy yourself. It really does come through in the final product.

For More Information

Many wonderful bath and body recipes can be found online at the following websites. Have fun browsing through them!

Pioneer Thinking. http://www.pioneerthinking.com/mbs.html

Crafter's Touch. http://www.crafterstouch.com/craft.aspx?categoryid=14

Craftbits.com. http://www.craftbits.com/viewCategory.do?categoryID=BAB

There are also many sites out there with templates for gift tags, labels, envelopes, and boxes. Here are a few that I like:

Mirkwood Designs. http://www.ruthannzaroff.com/mirkwood-designs/index.htm

Alenka's Printables. http://www.alenkasprintables.com/free_printables.shtml

Mardar's Stuff. http://www.mardar.us/misc.htm

Delve into Rich Coconut Goodness

≈ by Stephanie Rose Bird ≈

The food of the motherland has been an important part of my heritage as an African American. One of the most important plants for sustenance, as well as trade and commerce, in Africa and the Caribbean is the coconut. From this single nut, we can condition our hair, cleanse the body, detoxify the system, make crafts, build homes, and, of course, use the delicious white flesh to prepare many wholesome meals.

The coconut tree is not to be confused with similar-looking cousins. While there are about 2,650 species of palm tree, the coconut is one of the few nut-producing trees from this family that is widely used. Today, the coconut crop remains a major economic force for Ghana, the Ivory Coast, Kenya, Nigeria, Mozambique, Togo, Somalia, Tanzania, and other African countries.

Value of Coconut Stands Test of Time

New markets for coconut products have emerged worldwide due to simple population growth, as well as the cosmetic industry's response to the increased demand for more natural products. However, the products are not some new discovery or brainchild of some marketing guru. The multiple uses were established long ago.

During early African American history, black people had many uses for coconut. The shell was pulverized and consumed with wine as a systemic tonic to accelerate movement of the blood, which made it a favorite among the elderly. Like the calabash, the shell was transformed into numerous household tools such as cups, measuring containers, liquids, spoons, and small plates.

Going back a bit farther, the multiple uses of the coconut are well-documented as part of the Swahili lexicon—the most widely spoken language in Africa. Like the numerous terms eskimos have for different types of snow, language reflects the value of a culture. Here are a few terms that help define the important historical perception of the nut.

Joya: the soft, spongelike substance inside coconut shell.

Mbata: the dried endosperm that is an edible cooking oil and is also used cosmetically.

Kidaka: coconut's first stage of growth on stem.

Kisamli: the Pemba coconut palm nuts used for drinking.

Kitale: second stage of coconut growth.

Shata: leftovers from making coconut oil.

Ununu: the fiber from inner skin of coconut leaf stalk.

Usumba: soaked coconut fibers, used to make string.

Utangule: strips of the fan-palm leaf, used for braiding.

A Kitchen Staple

With modern conveniences, you can enjoy pure white coconut flesh in a form prepared and packaged in advance, but when it comes to consuming the freshest possible coconut, many may look at the stubborn brown hull and wonder how to get inside. Here are tips for selecting, opening, and creating basic milk from the coconut.

Selection: Choose coconuts with a chestnut brown hull that is smooth and has no apparent holes or mold. Shake and listen for water. If it still contains water, it will be moist and tasty.

Opening the Nut: Bore two holes in the eyes (the dark brown spots at either end of the coconut) using an ice pick or sharp knife. Pour the coconut water into a bowl. You can add this coconut water to your bath and beauty recipes or use it in a ritual. Hit the hull on a hard surface sharply a few times—it should crack open. You can also hit the nut with a mallet or hammer. Once cracked open, scoop out flesh—also called coconut meat—to use in recipes.

Making Coconut Milk: Heat 1½ cups water in a kettle on medium-high heat. Meanwhile, grate the coconut flesh and put it in a sieve over a large bowl. Just before the water comes to boil, slowly pour the water over the grated coconut in the sieve. Press the coconut meat with the back of a wooden spoon. Remove sieve. Pour this liquid into a measuring cup with a pouring spout (for convenience). Repeat this step 3–4 times. This will make 1¼ cups of rich coconut milk, which makes an excellent addition to curry dishes, Caribbean soups, and African stews.

Coconut Cream: To make coconut cream, bring 1½ cups whole milk almost to the boil. Go through steps above (for making coconut milk). Coconut cream is a bit denser, with a full-bodied, sweeter taste that is just right for desserts and drinks.

Toasted Coconut: Remove coconut meat from the hull with sharp knife. Shred the coconut. Add 1 tablespoon of olive oil to a cast-iron skillet. Add a pinch of sea salt if desired. Toss until medium brown. Toasted coconut is a great low-carb snack. I like to toast almonds and sunflower seeds with shredded coconut and use this as a snack food when watching movies. You can also use toasted coconut as a topping for fruit salads, yogurt, or cereal.

Using Coconut Oil

Coconut oil can be a polarizing substance in the herbal community—some love it while others despise it. It is said to be drying to the skin, particularly if used as a large part of a soap oil base. For those who feel that many African body butters—which contain emollients that might overwhelm normal or combination skin—are thick and oily, coconut oil is a welcome alternative. Coconut soaps are very useful for cleansing oily skin, as they make a frothy cleansing lather. This ability to form a thick lather—even in saltwater—made coconut oil soaps popular with seafaring people for hundreds of years. For those who enjoy a light moisturizer, coconut cream or other coconut products may well do the trick. Coconut oil can be combined with cocoa butter or shea butter to create a balanced soap that is neither too astringent nor excessively emollient.

Another product gaining popularity as a botanical for skin and hair care is coconut cream—but not the type in the food aisle. Coconut cream is available from Togo, where female villagers hand press the coconuts to extract creamy oil. This virgin coconut oil is pressed from fresh coconut milk and meat rather than copra. Coconut cream works well as massage therapy oil because of its silky texture.

In Africa, coconut cream has been used traditionally as hair conditioner, strengthener, and growth aid. The oil is rubbed into the scalp and may also be applied to the ends. Melted oil, cooled slightly and then applied to the scalp and ends as a hot oil treatment (followed by a shampoo), is preferable for those with an oily scalp.

Face Value: Communicating Beauty

✷ by Kaaren Christ ✷

Faces are truly wondrous. Faces provide us with our very own personalized calling card in the world. Aside from some identical twins, no two faces through all of history have ever been the same. No one has a face like yours. Not only do our faces make us unique and allow us to recognize one another, they are absolutely key to human communication, interaction, connection, and attraction. Our faces, and the intriguing beauty about them, are more than skin deep!

Beauty at Birth

It starts when we are born. Human connection and attraction begins with lots of face-to-face contact and eye gazing between babies and parents. One of the first things we learn shortly after birth is to recognize the person

(or people) who care for us. Our ability to tell our parents apart from other people, and then communicate with them using sounds and facial expressions, helps us get the nurturing and loving care we need to survive.

As babies, our eyes would "light up" at the sight of a familiar parent, and this would make them feel warmth and love toward us. In turn, this increased the likelihood that our parent would interact with us in a loving way. This is a fundamental, beautiful, and intricate dance in which both baby and parent feel that the other is uniquely beautiful and special—a kind of "first love" for the baby and a new love for the parent. It is the first time we associate a specific face with a specific feeling of love and warmth. We take these early experiences of warm feelings and faces with us into all of our other human relationships. How beautiful that our faces help us survive!

Our faces also give clues to other people about our ancestors and parentage. A quick glance into our face will tell others plenty about our mood, and give them clues as to what actions we are planning to take next. Imagine for a moment the facial expression and eye movement that accompanies a plan to throw something in anger. This can be very helpful for others to recognize. A person's face can also tell us about values and lifestyle and offer clues about what they have experienced. Faces can also provide information about our overall health and wellness.

The Beauty Myth

It's a shame that we don't think of all of these wondrous things when we think about our faces. Many fascinating qualities are just not recognized or appreciated. In these youth-obsessed times we tend to have a very narrow way of looking at the face and thinking about its value. We just want to know—is it "beautiful"?

When it comes to the question of beauty, we can be pretty hard on ourselves. In fact, even with the knowledge that we have a completely unique and special face, we can be downright unappreciative and nasty. Although there may be aspects of our faces we like, positive thoughts about them are often followed by more negative or critical ones. We may feel blessed to have received our mother's straight teeth, but cursed to have inherited our father's wide nose. We may feel lucky that we got Grandpa's rich auburn hair, but bemoan the fact we also got Aunt Edith's wild and unruly curls.

Of course, we can always try to change our appearance in a number of nonstructural ways. And there is a booming cosmetic industry that makes sure of that. We can try hair straighteners, perms, colors, and curling irons. We can shape eyebrows or tint eyelashes, but ultimately we don't change their fundamental nature or structure. It can be quite a never-ending cycle of purchasing and primping with expensive products in order to capture this elusive "beauty" that our culture says is so desirable.

Our Ideas About Beauty Are Only Skin Deep!

Most of us probably sense that the idea of beauty that is "sold" to us in the media is not "true" beauty. We may sense this deception in our bones, but it's a difficult message to fight and we don't always win. We may tell our children that "beauty is in the eye of the beholder" and that every person is beautiful in their own way. Sadly, at the end of the day, many of us find ourselves standing in front of mirrors, looking into our faces, and speaking to ourselves with disappointment. My skin tone is uneven. My teeth look yellow. My eyes are too far apart. My neck is saggy. Where did those wrinkles come from? I wish I had my sister's nose.

Interestingly, this is not how we see beauty in other people. When we talk about beauty in others, we tend to comment on the more mysterious or expressive qualities about their face. When we find another person attractive, we typically think things like "There was a sparkle in his eye," or "She was just glowing," or "He had a smile that lit up an entire room." When we notice beauty, most often we are noticing something about a person's character or spirit—not simply their physical characteristics.

How often have you heard someone describe their

seemingly "ordinary" looking lover as "the most beautiful person they have ever seen"? This likely has little to do with the physical construction of their lover's face or the color of their hair. The allure is more akin to the connection between a little baby and her parent. Attraction is often about our human need for nurturing and care, and the joy of experiencing connection and trust. Our sense of beauty is closely related to the way the object of our desires uses facial expressions to communicate emotions and thoughts to us.

Beauty & The Beholder

When someone's eyes sparkle, there is energy and life force that we associate with growth, emotional health, and vitality. We sense this life energy and respond to it positively because it feels good to be around them. When we feel good, this affects how we feel about the person who inspires this feeling. All of this adds to our sense of whether someone is, in fact, "beautiful." Beauty can't really exist without a Beholder—it's an inherently interactive experience.

When we notice that someone is "glowing," we sense an aura of peace or joy coming from them. Most of us recognize that this is not because they discovered a new skin cream. Typically, this kind of beauty comes from a state of mind that other people find irresistible and want to share. We feel better about ourselves and others when "glowing" people are near and are more likely to feel attracted to them and find them beautiful.

On the contrary, think of what happens when a "conventionally" beautiful woman has a harsh or critical personality instead of an open and warm way of looking at the world and others. People may notice that she is beautiful, but are more likely to think things like, "She seemed beautiful until I got to know her," or "looks sure can be deceiving." It seems that when physical beauty is not matched with inner qualities that make the face appear open and warm, people are more likely to discount the value of physical beauty.

Our faces give messages to others about our nature. The better we feel on the inside, the more likely we are to make good eye contact and make facial expressions that invite, rather than warn people away.

Time to Face Facts
Face Fact #1

When we make a facial expression, we are speaking a universal language that we didn't have to learn. Unlike spoken languages, facial expressions share the same meanings around the globe. Researchers have found that a number of major emotions are expressed identically in matching facial expressions across all cultures. Whether you are in Tibet or New York City, you will find people expressing happiness, fear, disgust, surprise, disapproval, and sadness using the same basic groups of facial muscles in the same way. This suggests that facial expressions are neurologically wired as opposed to entirely learned. Isn't that beautiful?

Face Fact #2

You can't fake a heartfelt smile. Sure, you can lift the corners of your mouth, but you won't fool the experts. That's because it's not just the muscles around your mouth that craft your smile, it's also the muscles around your eyes. Some people (including Darwin) thought that it was the squeezing of the eyeball when the eye muscles contracted that caused the sparkle. When someone's eyes sparkle, you just know they mean it!

Face Fact #3

Our faces have more than forty muscles. That's a lot of muscles!

The main smile muscle is called the zygomaticus, and it is responsible for "lifting" your smile. Think of this muscle as the "main ingredient" in your smile with the rest being "spices" that make your smile special and unique. If you want to appear really beautiful to a "certain someone," add those orbicularis oculi muscles to your smile recipe—those are the ones around your eyes—and this will make it easier to connect with them. When you really think about it, what's the sense of being beautiful if you don't connect with anyone?

Face Fact #4

"Making faces" can change your mood! Some therapists working with depressed patients report having success improving their patient's emotional state by practicing "smile therapy." This can be very effective helping those who have lost touch with their emotions, or who are afraid of expressing emotion because of bad experiences, to consciously relearn expression. These researchers believe that after long bouts of depression, people actually lose smile muscle "memory" and benefit from exercising regularly. They find that with daily exercise, even a "fake" or "forced" smile can eventually clear the way for a genuine one. Researchers have also found that intense facial expressions such as grimacing can actually increase hand strength.

Beauty—Free for All

When we think about beauty as something that isn't "fixed" or "constant" in our face but something that is expressed through our faces, there are suddenly many ways we can express and enhance our unique beauty. Most require no money, are physically pleasant or fun, and all have benefits that go deeper than the skin.

About Face: Change Your Thinking!

The first thing you can do is change the way you talk and think about your face. If you find yourself feeling negative about the word "wrinkle" because you struggle to accept your body's natural aging process—forbid yourself from calling them wrinkles for a while. Remind yourself that most lines in your face are there because of repeated use. So, when you find yourself grimacing at the lines at the corners of your eyes, imagine how many smiles you must have given others for them to become visible. Count each one a blessing, and recall happy memories. Call them smile lines.

When you notice tiny lines above your lip, count the kisses you have been blessed to give and receive in your lifetime. Relive your last kiss. While you're at it, blow yourself one in the mirror. You'll see. You will appreciate them in a whole new way. If you find it hard to do, make a little note and post it on your mirror. All it needs to say is "smiles and kisses." It should help turn around some of that negative self-talk! And for goodness sake, if you haven't smiled at or kissed anyone lately . . . get out there and do it!

Smile Therapy

Although you won't fool the "smile reading" experts with a "fake" smile, it's good to feel the difference. Get to know your own smile. Take a few minutes and practice smiling in front of a mirror. First, try a fake smile. Some people have a hard time doing this, but it's easier if you think of it as a simple muscle exercise and don't think about anything happy. Simply lift the corners of your mouth. While you are doing this, take mental notes about the way your face appears. What lines change? Do you notice any difference in your eyes?

Then think of something that makes you feel genuinely happy. If you need a little prompt, put on your favorite CD or look at a picture of someone you love. Maybe open your favorite essential oil and breathe the scent in deeply. Most people will notice very clear differences between their genuine smiles and their "fake" smile, particularly in their eyes. Watch for the sparkle.

Massage

Become aware of your facial muscles using gentle massage. There are more than forty of them to become acquainted with, and each one affects your ability to connect with others.

One easy way to do this is when you wash your face in the morning. Slow down this process a bit. Take time to make the water just the right temperature. If you have a favorite face cleanser, take an extra minute to massage it into the skin of your face with gentle circular motions. Make sure you attend to the muscles along your jaw line and in the joint. Breathe deeply while you do this. Let your jaw rest and hang loosely.

Scents, Sounds & Beauty

Few purchased products are as effective in bringing you to a state of relaxation and inner peace as natural scents and sounds. Many people don't consider having flowers or music in their bathrooms or at their dressing table. But why not? We spend important time in these little sanctuaries every day, preparing our bodies and minds to greet the world. It's a wonderful opportunity to attend to our outer beauty by caring for our inner worlds of thoughts and feelings.

Consider putting potted lavender or a lemon-scented geranium beside the basin where you can lean over and smell it while you wash your face and brush your hair. Cut lilacs in the spring and put them in a vase near the tub and enjoy the scent that fills the room. Use essential oils with votive candles that help you find your happy place.

A favorite recording that uses the sound of water or other sounds from nature can also do wonders for the spirit. I have a friend who loves to hear the gentle ticking of a favorite clock in her bathroom. She finds the sound soothing.

It doesn't really matter how you do it. The important thing is to take a little bit of time to think about how you can foster a gentle and relaxed mind so your own beauty can be seen clearly on your face.

Beauty isn't something we can buy. We aren't born with it either. It's something we each have inside of us. It's something we share with others when we face them, eye to eye, and connect with them in an accepting way. The path to expressing our personal and unique beauty is always there for us to take. And it may be as simple as opening the window to hear the birds singing that will paint a glow on our cheeks or put the sparkle in our smile.

Herb
Crafts

Herbally Enhanced Gifts

～ by S.Y. Zenith ～

The most memorable gifts to someone special are not necessarily the most expensive. Often, the thought, effort, and personal touches are appreciated much more. Since getting started is often the hardest part, here is a collection of delightful gift ideas that are sure to please and easy to make. Herbs and flowers can transform a simple spontaneous gift into a special present any time of the year. Another convenience of homemade gifts is that you can make many items as a hobby during your free time and store them for special occasions.

With a treasure trove of herbal-enhanced gifts, the frantic, last-second shopping trip for someone's birthday or anniversary can become a thing of the past. These gifts are also useful for impromptu invitations to luncheons, tea parties, celebratory get-togethers or reunions, holidays, and other festivities. Get those creative herbal juices flowing and enjoy swathing the gifts in paper, fabric, and lengths of ribbon.

Herbal Craft Toolbox

Gather herbs such as lavender, marigold, rose, jasmine, basil, bay leaves, parsley, and others that tickle your fancy. Leaves, tiny stems, and other very small parts of an herb or flower may be used. Place them on a drying rack for a few weeks to ensure they are thoroughly dry before using. A flower presser available at craft stores may be used for flattening and drying the herbs. If there is a large amount of herbs stuffed in the flower presser, put several heavy books on top of it.

If you have a stash of dried herbs in packets or containers in the kitchen, these can be used on their own or in conjunction with pressed herbs and flowers. These include mint, chamomile, rosemary, dandelion, and even spice bits that emit exotic aromas such as cumin, coriander, cloves, flaked ginger, lemongrass, and even a whiff of dried chili. Some spices will make certain people sneeze, but this is a great way to clear blocked sinuses as well.

Besides herbs, you'll need an array of miscellaneous tools to fashion these homemade gifts. Necessary tools to have on hand are thick drawing or art paper, wrapping paper, tissue paper, paintbrushes, water-based acrylic paints, watercolor paint, craft glue, glitter-glue, sticky tape, a pair of good scissors, penknife, pencil, colored pencils, felt-tip pens or markers in different colors, several sea sponges, gold and silver dust, sequins, tiny glass seed beads, and glitter. Also keep some fabric off-cuts, ribbons, colored threads, and an assortment of ribbons and natural-fiber strings for tying gifts. This is only a general list that can be used time and again for crafting herbal gifts. As we progress through the following gift topics, miscellaneous items may gradually be needed, with the leftovers bolstering your toolkit. Keep all tools together in a box so they are easy to find when you need them.

Greeting Cards

Several times a year, most of us send greeting cards for various reasons. Personally decorating a sizable stack of different greeting cards is ideal for those who are economically conscious.

The cards can be kept in a stationery drawer or wooden box with potpourri sachets for scenting them during storage. Depending on the potpourri used, it might stain white and pastel cards. If staining is inevitable, place the potpourri sachets in two separate corners of the drawer or box. Fasten the potpourri sachets into fixed positions with sticky tape or stuff two cloths of natural fiber in between. Natural fibers allow the sachets and the contents in the drawer or box to breathe so the fragrance can be easily emitted and circulated.

Find some sheets of thick art paper of good quality, preferably acid-free. Make sure that the size of the paper when folded in half will fit into standard envelopes sold in your country of residence. If time permits, you may also wish to decorate envelopes to match the motif or essence of each card. Put all tools and materials on a clean table with dried herbs, spices, and flowers. Use a pencil to mark the parts of the card where you wish to glue the herbs. Ponder a variety of designs, make a simple sketch of how you would like the card to look, or trace a design from a favorite source.

If you feel white cards are too common and boring for backgrounds, create some batches in different colors. Lightly color the front and back of the cards with colored pencils or paints. Outline with a black pen or use felt-tip pens. Create a border if desired. If you are really ambitions, here is a more elaborate method for setting backgrounds. Start by squeezing blobs of different color paint into separate small glass bowls. General colors suggested are green, blue, red, orange, pink, magenta, deep purple, yellow, gold, and silver. You can add other hues of your choice or experiment with blending colors on scratch paper before making up your mind. Mix each blob with a little water in its own bowl to a consistency of your liking. Using one sponge per color, dip a sea sponge into each bowl and squeeze off excess water. Apply the colored sponged to the card using your own initiative or go with whatever unfolds with the movements of your hand.

Someone else may prefer to dab various sponge colors all over the card for an abstract multicolored effect. Another may like the idea of a midnight blue sky splattered with silver stars. For pastel backgrounds, make sure a bit more water is added to a particular paint. Use a wide paintbrush to gently glide or brush across the card. Allow the cards to dry thoroughly before proceeding further. Place a few containers of clean water for rinsing sponges and paintbrushes.

Design Ideas

Ideas are fairly easy to come by if you think about it. Common sense often has its rewards. If the card is for a girl and if she adores flowers, create a bouquet with various bits of herbs, leaves, and flowers, then glue onto the card. A tiny bow can be made with straw or cotton string for gluing onto the bouquet. Leave enough space for writing the appropriate words such as Happy Birthday, Thank You, Happy Anniversary, I Love You, Bon Voyage, Have Fun, or Thinking Of You.

Embellish the card's border with colored pencils, paints, and other materials as much as you want. If heart-shaped items are her thing, use red or pink flower petals to make plenty of layered hearts and, for good measure, sprinkle some gold or silver glitter over them. Sequins, shimmering bugle, and tiny glass seed beads can also be glued onto herbal card designs.

Years ago, I received an extraordinary card decorated with lilac tissue paper cut into the shape of a handbag. The design utilized tiny lavender bits, a few leaves, and rose petals painted in different colors. These were glued onto a gold card along with sequins and quite an assortment of glittery stuff. The overall effect was stunning. This special card is deeply treasured and preserved in memory of the wonderful friend who made it with her own hands—and a lot of thought.

Male Motifs

If a guy is crazy about cars, cinnamon sticks can be trimmed with scissors to form the shape of a vehicle and glued to the card. Dab a few dots of ground turmeric to form headlights or taillights. Use other herbs and spices for the windshield and relevant vehicle parts. Thinly sliced, dried, and flattened citrus peels will do fine too. Lightly paint over the "herbal vehicle" with the intended recipient's favorite colors. Golf clubs, tennis rackets, baseball bats, boats, footballs, and other male paraphernalia can be made with similar materials—and they smell good too!

Whether someone is besotted with images of sun, moon, stars, dawn, dusk, animals, waterfalls, tribal stuff, kings, queens, soup tureens, or clowns on sawdust rings, just about everything can be craft-implemented on a personalized greeting card. The inside of the card can be decorated with more herbs or left blank for writing a personal message.

Gift Tags

When making herb-enhanced gift tags, use small cards. They can measure around two to three inches in size. Shapes can be square, round, oval, or rectangular. For round and oval shapes, use a small cup or dish to trace, in pencil, the desired shape on the thick art paper. Simple gift tags utilize one piece of thick paper with a hole punched in the middle of the top section so ribbons, straws, strings, or colored threads can be inserted and later tied to a wrapped present.

Gift tags resembling mini-greeting cards are cut in squares of 6 or 8 inches and folded in half so a message can be handwritten inside. Punch a hole in the top left corner of the folded card for tying to the gift later. Let your imagination run wild with designs, or follow the same tips as mentioned above for making greeting cards.

Bookmarks

Cut several strips of thick drawing paper into 6 x 2-inch rectangles. If larger bookmarks are preferred, cut larger sizes after tracing the desired measurements onto the paper with a pencil and ruler. Punch a hole midway across the top of each bookmark. Decorate with herbs and flowers using methods described above for greeting cards. When the bookmarks are ready, secure an attractive ribbon in the punched hole.

Fragrant Herb Stationery

If time is a luxury you don't have for making personalized stationery and compendiums, these can be bought at a store, taken home, and scented with herbal fragrance before using. Dedicate a special drawer just for storing and scenting stationery supplies. Those passionate about wooden boxes can use an appropriately sized one for storing.

Scented Lining Paper

Lend a special herbal touch to shelves and drawers for storing linen, towels, underwear, and clothes by using scented lining paper. Find a good-sized box with a lid. Perfume sheets of lining paper by spreading dry potpourri over the bottom of the box. Place sheets of lining paper in the box and gently sprinkle potpourri in between. Cover the box and leave it alone for a month. Every few days, turn the sheets of paper over to absorb the scent.

Perfumed Wrapping Paper

Botanical and floral gift-wraps in numerous varieties and tissue paper in all sorts of colors can be perfumed with small bags of herbs to match each theme or color. Make several different herbal bags in cotton fabric. Insert dried jasmine flowers into a bag for scenting jasmine floral paper, rose petals for rose-themed paper, and a combination of dried flowers for wrapping paper that features bouquets. An example of matching scent to colored tissue paper is using dried violets or lilac to match lavender shades. Pink hues will become enticing when scented with rose petals. Match the smell of gardenia to white paper. Select a personal signature fragrance of one special flower or use multicolored freesias for all perfumed papers in the household.

Table Mats

Table mats also make attractive personal gifts for birthdays or seasonal festivities. A single but beautifully decorated mat, inscribed with a special verse meaningful to someone dear, will speak volumes. Sets of two can be made for a romantic couple. Matching sets for entertaining can be designed to order with the backing, herbs, and flowers chosen in accordance with the room's theme or color scheme. Or simply match the table mats with china, tablecloth, or the recipient's taste.

Thin wood should be used for the backing while a layer of untreated cork should be pasted on top of it. The top can be painted or carefully glued with fine fabric or art paper. Use a pair of tweezers to arrange sprigs of herbs or pretty posies as the centerpiece of a table mat. Pat tiny drops of transparent adhesive to toothpicks for fixing the design into place. When the herbs and flowers are satisfactorily positioned, use a clean piece of cardboard to press firmly down on the table mat. This sets the design in place, but remember to let the glued herbs on the table mat dry completely. Cover the design with custom-cut, high-quality heatproof glass or Perspex. Anchor with strong adhesive or clips. Then cover the edges with appealing edging braid from craft stores, or leave it plain.

Oven Gloves

Oven gloves are easy to make in rectangular, square, or mitten shapes with a hole large enough to fit a hand. Two thick layers of closely woven material with padding in between can be sewn up with dried citrus peels, rosemary, mint, thyme, and basil. Another option is to unstitch a few sections of newly bought oven gloves and tuck dried herbs in before sewing up the openings.

Coat Hangers

Lilac, honeysuckle, rose, lily of the valley, lavender, jasmine, hyacinth, and tuberose emit strong scents that are ideal for insertion into homemade coat hangers. Other plants to use are jasmine, rosemary, and even lemon peels. Dry them before using. Select the scent you favor most and intersperse the relevant dried flower with the padding for wrapping around a coat hanger. Stick several dried flowers on the outside of the padding and tuck, pin, and sew a floral covering into place. Decorate the neck of the coat hanger with ribbon. Making a number of different scented coat hangers will provide a good choice when inclined to give one or two as presents.

Lingerie Bag

Set aside some assorted silk ribbons and dressmaking chalk. Cut a piece of silk or cotton fabric into a 12 x 12-inch square and sew up the sides and bottom. Draw or trace a pretty flower on the front with dressmaking chalk. Scent the middle of the bag by using thread and needle to sew some dried rosemary, rose petals, and jasmine into the fabric's flower pattern. Weave two or three more layers of thread over the secured dried floral contents and iron the bag to set its contents properly. Cut ribbons into two lengths of eight inches. Hem the top part of the lingerie bag and cut a hole in the middle for inserting the ribbon for tying the bag. The ribbon should enter and exit the same hole and be tied in a bow.

Garters

Though frivolous and perhaps even cheeky, herbal or flower garters may work wonders for inducing a sense of romance, confidence, daring, and passion. Select dried herbs and flowers that you know will appeal to the recipient. If you are trying to encourage a very shy girl or give hope to a woman caught in love stakes, use almond blossoms or hawthorn blossoms. Cut two appropriate lengths of wide elastic, taking the recipient's measurements into consideration along with the fact that garters are supposed to be decorative rather than too logically functional or tight fitting. Heart-shaped patterns in hot red, gold, or silver can be cut and sewn onto the garter along with sequins and shiny crystals.

Cut two identical pieces of feminine material such as voile, silk organza, or fine linen into two strips that are at least two times wider and twice as long as the elastic. Sew the long sides together with the reverse side out. Turn the fabric the right way out. Make several stitches within the two long sides. Thread in the elastic and secure one end of the "garter tube" with a couple of pins. From the open end of the tube, push the selection of herbs or flowers in as much as possible. Sew both ends of the tube together and, voila!

Hops Pillows

Hops are renowned as a natural sleep-inducing agent for insomniacs although many would initially complain about not being crash hot with the smell. If one is prepared to "suffer the smell" over a period of time, like any good thing it becomes an "acquired taste." If you really can't stand hops, then combine it with other herbs that also contain calming properties such as lavender, chamomile, rose, and woodruff.

Sleep pillows around 10 by 8 inches are sufficient for stuffing a choice combination of herbs. Cut a piece of cotton cloth and sew up three sides of the material. Fill the opening with herbs and sew it up. With a piece of decorative material, make a pillowcase slightly larger than the pillow containing herbs. Insert the herb pillow into the pretty casing, then slip it all inside your usual pillow. The scent will calm whirly thoughts and lull the overworked brain to a relaxed state, enabling restful sleep.

Herb Pots

An herb pot makes a great gift for someone who lacks a green thumb, but craves having a certain culinary herb or two at home. Fill one or more terra cotta pots with potting mix and plant a variety of herb seedlings. Keep the pots regularly watered and apply suitable fertilizer. When the herbs begin to grow, pinch off the tips to encourage bushier growth until you have a well-established plant. When the time comes to present an herbal pot, wrap the bottom with cellophane and tie a ribbon around the pot with a gift tag.

Naturally Fun Crafts for Kids

❧ by Sally Cragin ❧

Encouraging your child to take an active interest in nature and being outdoors is the greatest gift you can provide as a parent. Even if you live in an urban environment or are otherwise removed from what you define as "nature," there are plenty of natural craft materials available, herbal and otherwise.

These crafts are suitable for most children older than seven, although some could be done by very young children. My son has just turned two, and he has had enormous fun with all kinds of natural and herbal products.

One-Two-Three Blow!

Ingredients: Dandelions!

It's an enormous accomplishment when a child is finally old enough to puff out their cheeks and blow! Now they can make bubbles, blow out birthday candles, and blow the seed puff off a dandelion. It's one of nature's best design tricks—seemingly overnight, the bright yellow sun-face of the dandelion transforms into a ghostly silver-feathered orb. What a treasure to come across a seed-head intact—and what a delight for a little one to disperse the seeds (bearing in mind that when you blow a dandelion seed pod, you're very likely to get more little dandelions next season!).

Picking Flowers with a Purpose
Clover Clothes Closet Potpourri

Ingredients: Clover flowers, embroidery floss, scissors.

Our great-great-great grandmothers knew how to use clover flowers to make a simple potpourri clover closet pick-me-up. Simply gather a bunch of blossoms (nine, or multiples of three is good). Try to keep the stems as long as you can. Small children should be able to slide their fingers down the stem to where it emerges from the earth. Let the flowers wilt for a little bit (but not to the point where the stems are completely limp). Then tie a bit of embroidery floss around the bunch just beneath the blossoms, braid the stems, and tie the end with a narrow ribbon. Hang in a clothes closet to help relieve stuffiness.

Lavender/Sage Magic Fragrant Wand

Ingredients: Lavender flowers with long stems, fresh sage leaves, ¼-inch ribbon.

You can do the same with lavender buds and sage leaves, but you'll need at least a dozen. Make sure the blossoms are staggered, but keep the stems all pointing in the same direction so that you have a wand, rather than a bunch. Use thin (¼ inch) ribbon in a color that harmonizes with the lavender. White or pale violet is pretty. You'll need about a yard of ribbon, which you'll tie at the base of the last flower in your wand, so that the two ends of ribbon are of equal length. Then weave the two ends in and around the flowers and stems, so that flowers and leaves peep between bits of ribbon. There is definitely room to improvise here as long as you leave enough ribbon to tie a pretty bow when you are finished.

Shakespeare's Roses

Shakespeare used rose imagery to accentuate many sonnets and plays, and here is one of my favorite crafts with rosebuds. Making a necklace.

For extra credit, share a sonnet with a flower theme. Here's No. 55, which is pretty self-explanatory. Shakespeare is talking about how we judge things (people, objects) by their appearance and how the most memorable personalities can achieve a bit of immortality if we appreciate (or write about) them. Most children age seven and up will have no difficulty getting these verses.

O, how much more doth beauty beauteous seem
By that sweet ornament which truth doth give!
The rose looks fair, but fairer we it deem
For that sweet odour which doth in it live.

The canker-blooms have full as deep a dye
As the perfumed tincture of the roses,
Hang on such thorns and play as wantonly
When summer's breath their masked buds discloses:

But, for their virtue only is their show,
They live unwoo'd and unrespected fade,
Die to themselves. Sweet roses do not so;
Of their sweet deaths are sweetest odours made:

And so of you, beauteous and lovely youth,
When that shall fade, my verse distills your truth.

The Rosebud Necklace

Ingredients: Rosebuds, needle, thread, pearl beads of various sizes.

Gather rosebuds before they flower. (Yes, you need a very healthy rosebush to afford to do this!) Dry on a screen. When they are mostly dry, but not yet crumbly, thread a needle with pink, red, or white thread so that the double loop of thread is at least 18 inches. To make sure the rosebuds in the necklace are in the middle, thread numerous pearl beads first. Then alternate buds with beads, making sure you push the needle into the very base of the bud where it meets the stem. You'll want this necklace to go over your head or have a simple clasp attachment because it is very fragile when finished. But beautiful!

The Joys of Birch Bark

Birch bark is one of the most fabulous materials out there. Native Americans stripped bark from whole trees to make canoes. This gives you an idea of how enormous the trees were in the North American forest prior to European settlements. You can peel off the papery white outer bark to reveal a rich beige inner bark, flecked with what look like black dashes. I never tire of devising projects to make using this material.

Birch Bark Votive Candle Holder

Ingredients: Several long strips of birchbark at least 2 inches wide, tuna fish or cat-food can, glue gun (or white glue and a rubber band and clothespins), raffia or twine, tea lights.

Since wood is flammable, you definitely want a large, but short, can to make this project. A tuna fish or cat-food can works well. Make sure you have a big enough piece of bark to go all the way around the can and then overlap, so no can shows through. Fit this before gluing. If your piece is too big, you can tear the strip so that it's not taller than the can. Use a glue gun to fasten —white glue will work for a while, but not quite as long. If you use the white glue, use a rubber band and clothespin to fasten. When this project is dry, tie a bit of twine around the birch bark for decoration, or leave plain. Put a tea light in the middle. If you put tape on the metal cup holding this small votive candle, it will stay centered.

Birch Bark Bookmarks

Ingredients: Birch bark, pen. Optional: hole-punch, raffia, twine or embroidery floss.

So easy to do. Here, you'll want to use the beige inner bark. Make sure you don't peel too much of the bark so you are left with a flimsy sheet. Tear or cut (using scissors for a neater look) a rectangle about 1½ x 6 (to 8) inches. You can cut a short fringe on one or both ends, but the problem with making small cuts is that bark is is prone to tear from use. Use a hole-puncher to put a small hole in the top and then thread a bit of raffia, or green or yellow yarn or floss. If you want to decorate further, think simply. Glitter is highly disrespectful to the essential nature of bark because it's a very austere material.

I made a set of bookmarks and used a child's printing set (one that has tiny letters you can set into a frame) to make two stamps that I printed with black ink. On one side, the bookmark read: IF A TREE FALLS . . . and on the other side, I stamped . . . WILL ANYONE HEAR? You can also stamp someone's name if these are a present.

Vine Wreath or Orb

Ingredients: Vines, large juice can, and/or balloon.

Is there any climate that lacks a tree-stressing vine? In the northeast we have Virginia creeper, farther south you'll find kudzu, and many climates have honeysuckle and wisteria. You can actually have fun eradicating these vines from your woods and make an amusing decoration as well. You'll need lots of vines (with the leaves removed), some twisty ties, and a large coffee can for the wreath or a balloon for the orb. Begin by wrapping a long vine around the can, and then start weaving the end in and out of the layers. When you have completed one length of vine, gingerly remove your vine (use twisty ties to keep it together). Next, take another piece of vine and start weaving it in and out of the one you just made. Stop when you like how it looks. The orb is slightly more challenging, but is basically the same idea where you're crisscrossing vines around a balloon. You'll need piles of vines for this, and don't blow the balloon up too far. You'll know when you're finished because you'll have a dense, interwoven wreath or orb. Let it dry.

Spice Garland

Ingredients: Star anise, popcorn, dried cranberries, cinnamon sticks, stout thread and needle.

Star anise threaded with popcorn, berries, and even cinnamon sticks makes a fragrant yuletide garland. Choose cinnamon sticks that are completely cylindrical so you can drop the needle down the middle. To prevent minor injuries (which are never fun), a thimble is also helpful.

Seed Packets

Ingredients: Paper or envelopes, seeds, pens and crayons.

If you have a bumper crop from your garden (or remembered to save the seeds from your pumpkin), you'll have a super craft that makes a great stocking stuffer. You can use an old seed packet to make a template, which you can copy. Or you could try using small gift-envelopes or a regular-size envelope cut in half. Here, the fun is in the decorating. Who wouldn't want to receive a packet that says "Super Orange Jack O'Lantern Seeds" or "Marigold Seeds—plant on your borders to keep the bugs away"? You can glue your extra seeds onto the packets for decoration.

Flower Power Pounding

Ingredients: Clean white muslin or white T-shirt, tape, hammer, white bond paper or opened-up brown paper grocery bag, folded newspaper, leaves and flowers.

What child wouldn't love to use a hammer? This project requires adult supervision, but the trick is not to "check" before you should. Tape flowers and leaves colorful side down onto your fabric or shirt (clear tape works fine). Put fabric or shirt on newspaper pad with a layer of white bond paper or a grocery bag between shirt and newspaper. Pound those leaves or flowers, making sure you cover every area. You could do this on paper rather than cloth, but chances are good the paper will tear with the pounding unless you're using cloth-based paper.

Sycamore Seed Case Ornaments

Ingredients: Sycamore seed cases, glitter, glue, beads.

Do you live in a temperate climate? Chances are there is a sycamore tree in a park or green space near you. These trees have fabulous seed cases, which can be an excellent base for all kinds of craft. They're a little prickly, but easy to work with. These look like tiny mines, ranging from less than an inch to nearly 2 inches across. Since the sycamore is very brittle in high winds, lots of seed cases get knocked off, and if you find one, you'll find two dozen. Decorating these is easy, and even a very small child can daub white glue onto a seed case. You can then help the child sprinkle glitter or artificial "snow," or mix ¼ cup salt with ½ cup water. Mix salt solution and paint on seed case. This won't stay on for long when dry, but at least is a natural substance.

Orange Peel Critters

Ingredients: Orange peels, toothpicks, cloves.

It will probably take a grown-up to get the peel going, but see if your little one can make an animal shape when they peel their orange. A blob with a smaller blob can be any kind of animal. Take toothpicks and stick on for legs. Cloves make eyes. If these dry in the sun, the peel gets hard and the "critter" changes shape. A fragrant, low-impact craft.

Herb, Seed Legume Mosaic

Ingredients: Crushed dry herbs and seeds, birdseed, lentils, beans. Glue or glue-stick.

Start with a simple shape—perhaps a bird—or a divided circle drawn onto a piece of stiff cardstock. Use a bold marker so the outline is very visible. Apply glue to one section of your picture, then have your child sprinkle an herb or seed onto that area. Lift card and tap to remove excess. Make sure you've covered that area sufficiently before gluing the next area.

Helpful hint: Go from lightest objects (herbs) to heavier and heaviest objects (seeds, then beans) so fewer bits fall off as you go.

Catnip Glove Fish

Ingredients: Dry catnip, last winter's odd woolen glove, yarn, cotton.

What could be sweeter than making something special for the family kitty cat? These fish are quick and easy. Simply cut the fingers off the gloves. Take a pinch of catnip and stuff into the tip of the finger until you have the finger about one-third filled. Use cotton to fill up the remainder of the finger, then tie securely with yarn. At Yuletide, green yarn on a red glove fish (or vice-versa) makes for a cheerful toy. **Warning**: these make cats completely crazy, so tie that yarn on tightly. Variants: a tiny bell at the tip of the "fish."

Milkweed or Okra Pod Boat

Ingredients: Milkweed or okra pod.

Pods are a terrific material for crafts, and if you have milkweed, you'll have plenty of the magical fluff attached to the seeds. Simply separate the pod, clean it out, and set sail. If you're ambitious and it's late summer, you can add a miniature cornhusk dollie.

Cornhusk Dollie

Ingredients: Corn husks, strong sewing thread or embroidery floss, scissors.

These can be large or small, and you can split husks with your thumbnail. Take three to six cornhusks and put them in a stack. Fold them in the middle against the grain so that all the ends are together and you have a "book" of husks. Tie a thread about an inch or less from the fold for the "head." You can make arms by rolling up a husk and tying a thread at the "wrist." Tuck the "arm" into the body of the dollie and tie another thread for a waist. Trim the odd bits. If you want hair, you can glue corn silk on top of the head, or put a hank of it crossways to the first husk pile before you make that initial fold.

Easy Mint Tea

Ingredients: Fresh mint leaves, glass carafe or glass quart measuring cup.

Every little one wants to cook with mum and dad and there are plenty of dishes to make that don't require knives or an oven. Fresh mint tea is delicious and easy. Add a fistful of washed mint leaves to your container, fill with water, and put in sun until mint is golden yellow. Refrigerate, and drink in next couple of days. You can also use this mint tea as the liquid added to homemade lemonade to guarantee your guests come back for seconds.

Easiest Herbal Iced Tea

Every child likes to cook, and this simple and inexpensive recipe is also a good illustration of how we can use solar power. Put two chamomile tea bags and one peppermint tea bag into a quart container of water. Put in sun and let steep until tea is a bright yellow (two hours or more). Remove tea bags, refrigerate.

Hobbit Hotel:
Create a Faery House

❧ by Michelle Santos ❧

I f you're looking for a fun, inexpensive activity the whole family can enjoy, try your hand at decorating a faery house using dried herbs. Faery houses can be made in many different ways. Some people pile up stones and create little "rock houses" for their garden faeries. Others craft elaborate dwellings, complete with daybeds and a courtyard fountain, using flexible sticks and branches.

The herbal faery house is neither as easy as the rock house nor as difficult as the twig house—it falls somewhere in between. It can easily be completed by an eight-year-old child (with some adult supervision) or by a craft-challenged adult who has a childlike enthusiasm for life. All of the herbs are of the common, everyday variety, so they should not be too difficult to find.

Some will be available at your local grocery store, but others may take a special trip to the herb shop or your trusty Internet herb supplier. For the actual house, you have the option of building your own bird/faery house out of wood or purchasing a ready-made (but unfinished) structure at your local craft supply store. The choice is yours and largely depends on the amount of time and skill you possess. Once you've collected your faery house, herbs, glitter, and glue, you're ready to spread out the newspaper and commune with the faeries.

Items Needed

An unfinished wooden bird/faery house; a hot glue gun and glue sticks; popsicle sticks, paint stirrers, or plastic knives; ultra-fine glitter; polyurethane; a small to medium-size paintbrush; colored permanent markers (optional); an ounce or more of the following herbs: lavender, rose petals, oak moss, white sage leaves (whole), cinnamon sticks, star anise, acorns, and small pinecones. (Note: Craft and hardware stores are inundated with advertisements for a glue called Gorilla Glue. This glue is very strong and can hold anything together. Should you choose to use this glue instead of the hot glue, be aware that it is not appropriate for children, even with adult supervision. Once it gets on your hands, it cannot be washed off with water. Paint thinner must be used as a cleaning agent. Also, Gorilla Glue expands as its dries so a small amount goes a long way!)

Prepare your faery house by spreading a light coat of polyurethane with the paint brush on all wooden surfaces. While it is still wet, sprinkle your glitter (i.e., faery dust) over the entire house. Use as much or as little as you like. The more glitter you use, the more it will resemble snow or frost, reminiscent of the winter. If you are creating a winter house for your garden faeries to snuggle in during the cold months, you may like the snowlike effect. Once you have applied the glitter by throwing it at the house in wide, swooping motions (sound effects optional), allow the polyurethane to dry. Depending on the thickness of your polyurethane, this can take twenty minutes, two hours, or even half a day. Wait until the house is completely dry before applying the herbs.

If you have very young children, allow them to decorate the faery house with the permanent colored markers before you apply the polyurethane. They will dry almost instantly, but do a test patch of polyurethane to be sure the markers won't run. You wouldn't want to ruin your child's faery artwork! Very small children also enjoy throwing the glitter onto the faery house. Just be prepared to find glitter in rather unexpected places for the next month or two.

The Roof

Starting with the roof, apply the glue in small sections, no more than two inches square, and press your herbs into the glue. You may have to hold them in place for a moment or two to allow the glue to dry. (Use the Popsicle stick, plastic knife, or paint stirrer to push the herbs into the glue. It will save your hands from getting burnt or covered with glue.) You can use any of the herbs on the roof but oak moss, acorn tops, and lavender work especially well. Since faeries are known to inhabit and frolic around oak trees, the oak moss and acorn tops are especially potent herbs to use. The oak tree is one of the three trees that make up the Faery Triad, "oak, ash, and thorn." When these three trees grow together, the Path to Faerie is revealed. (See the article on "The Faery Triad" in this Almanac for more information.)

Oak moss (*Evernia prunastri*) is a lichen (a symbiotic combination of an algae and a fungus) that grows exclusively on oak trees. It is used in perfumery and aromatherapy as it helps to prolong the life of other scents. When dried, it has a soft white or light green-gray color and a fragile appearance that resembles deer antlers. Oak moss will give your faery house a wild, untamed appearance, reminiscent of faery tale cottages in the woods.

Acorn tops (*Quercus robur*—English Oak) are the fruit of the oak tree and full crops are only produced from trees that are at least sixty years old. Traditionally, the bark is the most medicinally potent part of the oak tree. However, some herbalists use acorns with the bark in a decoction to counteract the side effects of harsh medicines. In a pinch, you can eat acorns as food although they have an unpleasant, bitter flavor. The acorn tops will give your faery house a neat and orderly appearance, similar to a tiled or shingled roof. Cut the tops in half or in quarters and place them in an overlapping pattern. You will need to use a lot of glue because the acorn tops are not flat. Fill up the inside, rounded section of the cap with glue before placing it onto the two-inch section of glue on the roof.

Lavender (*Lavandula vera*—English lavender) is a beautiful, fragrant herb that can be placed in sachets or potpourri to freshen up any space. Also known as elf leaf, lavender has a wonderful calming quality and has been known to treat anxiety and insomnia, as well as skin ailments (eczema, psoriasis), headaches, nausea, and other digestive issues. With its small, compact "petals," lavender will give your faery house the look of a neatly thatched English cottage. You'll need to stick a large quantity of the dainty herb to your sections of glue to achieve the right look.

The Walls

Once you have covered the roof with the herb (or herbs) of your choice and allowed them to dry completely, it is time to decorate the walls of your faery house. You may need to place the house on its side while you are gluing the herbs in order to get enough leverage. Don't worry about the herbs from the roof falling off when you tip the house. Most of the herbs will stay on and a few bare patches will allow the glitter to shine through more prominently. The herbs that look best for the walls of your house are cinnamon and white sage. (Acorn caps will also look very nice as long as you did not use them for the roof.)

Cinnamon (*Cinnamomum cassia*) is a common spice often used in baking for its heady aroma and sweet yet musky taste. Widely used as a digestive aid, it can help minimize indigestion and the formation of ulcers. Cinnamon is also suggested by herbalists for healing menstrual problems and fibroids, and for treating yeast infections.

For your faery house, cinnamon (in stick form) can be used to create a log cabin effect. You will need a sharp knife to cut the sticks into appropriate lengths for your house. Try to create an interlocking pattern so the ends of the sticks do not always line up with each other (similar to bricklaying). Use a good amount of glue for each cinnamon stick, placing the glue on the stick itself instead of the house. Hold the stick in place until the glue dries or be sure to level off the wall of your house (by placing the house on its side) so the stick will not slide.

White sage (*Salvia apiana*) is an herb often used to flavor food dishes, largely due to its sharp, yet slightly minty, taste. It is also sometimes used as incense. Medicinally, sage is a wonderful mouthwash used in healing mouth, gum, and throat disorders. It will help to heal sore throats, bleeding gums, and an overabundance of saliva. It has also been used as a treatment for fevers and colds, to stimulate the stomach, and as a cleanser and purifier of the blood.

Adding white sage to your faery house creates a clapboard appearance that goes well with an acorn or lavender roof. (Since white sage and oak moss are almost the same color, the combination of the two makes for a drab and boring house.) Attach the whole pieces of white sage horizontally to imitate pieces of wood. Again, you will need to hold the sage pieces in place while they dry or tip your house onto its side. If you lean your house on its side, you will be able to apply several pieces of sage at one time. Since they are lighter than the cinnamon sticks, you will not need to use as much glue or as much pressure.

Decorations

Creating a faery house is an intuitive experience and it is important to follow your instincts. Faeries don't need everything to be perfect and orderly, so don't strive too hard—this is supposed to be fun! (And the reason why this craft is perfect for children!) As you decorate your roof and your walls, you may want to add other herbs for color or texture. These herbs can be added anywhere and do not need to be symmetrical. They will help create a more beautiful, more inviting home for your faery friends.

Star anise (*Illicuim verum*) is a plant that produces small, starlike fruit, from which it derives its name. The fruit is about an inch in diameter, has a deep red or burgundy color, and a licorice aroma. Besides being wonderful additions to sachets and potpourri, chewing the fruit sweetens the breath and promotes digestion after a meal. In the East, they are used as a remedy for colic and rheumatism. Due to the irregular shape and texture of star anise, you'll need a lot of glue to affix them to your faery house and hold them in place until the glue dries. The glue will probably leak out around the edges of the star anise, so either add some glitter or small herbs (such as lavender or honeysuckle) to cover it up.

Rose petals (*Rosaceae* family) are closely aligned to the world of faerie and can add any number of colors to your faerie house, from deep red to light pink to brilliant purple. Essence of rose is often added to perfumes because of its lovely fragrance, and petals can be used to create rose water for use in cooking and baking. Roses can be added to sweeten herbal teas and rose hips are an excellent source of vitamin C.

When adding rose petals to your faery house, use only whole petals. Because whole petals are difficult to purchase from an herb shop (usually they are broken up and mixed with the rose greenery), plan ahead and purchase a rose or two from your local flower shop. Two weeks before you begin your faery house, dry the roses by hanging them upside-down in a relatively cool, dark place. Once they are thoroughly dry, take them down and pull the flowers apart very gently. Store them in airtight containers until you plan on creating your faery house. Rose petals attach very easily to either the roof or walls of your house. They make excellent shutters if your house has windows, and smell wonderful.

Pine cones (*Pinaceae* family) come in all different shapes and sizes. For your faery house, try to find the smallest pine cones possible—no more than one inch in diameter. (You probably will have to purchase them at a craft store after scouring your property.) Pine cones are usually used for decorations or for starting fires, not for medicine. However, pine needles are a wonderful source of vitamin C, and pine bark and roots are useful as antiseptics and for curing chronic cough, especially in animals. Since pine cones are irregular in shape, you will need to utilize a lot of glue. Apply the glue directly to the pine cone, just as you would for the star anise and cinnamon. Then hold the pine cone in place until the glue dries. Pine cones have a rustic appearance and add natural beauty to the faery house. Their unusual shape allows the glitter to shine through, adding an extra flash of faery glamour.

Once all your herbs are glued in place, set aside your faery house for a day or two, allowing the glue to set and harden. If you'd like to add more glitter, do so at this time, sprinkling it over the completed house. (The glitter will catch onto the herbs and stay there.) On the next sunny day, place your faery house in your garden or in a special place in your yard or your house. If you set it outside, don't expect your house to last for years and years. Remember, Faeryland is a transitory place, continually shifting and moving. Your faery house, as a physical reminder of the Realm of Faery, should also change with time and exposure to the elements. Visit your faery house whenever you like, leaving gifts of food, poems, or prayers, and know that you have strengthened your ties to the denizens of faery and the natural world.

For Further Reading

Balch, Phyllis A. *Prescription for Herbal Healing*. New York: Penguin Putnam, Inc., 2002.

Cunningham, Scott. *Cunningham's Encyclopedia of Magical Herbs*. St. Paul, MN: Llewellyn Publications, 1998.

Grieve, Maud. *A Modern Herbal, Volumes 1 and 2*. New York: Dover Publications, 1971.

Hopman, Ellen Evert. *Tree Medicine, Tree Magic*. Blaine, WA: Phoenix Publishing, 1991.

Liqueurs, Brandies & Syrups

≈ by S.Y. Zenith ≈

Herbal liqueurs, brandies, syrups, and cordials are simple to make at home without too much fuss. Liqueurs and brandies can be drunk neat from a shot glass, whipped with cocktails, or used as a mixer with vodka, rum, gin, vermouth, and dry white wine. While potent nightcaps pbefore retiring to bed, they can also serve as lifting "perk-ups" for dulled senses during late afternoons. Pour some over cakes, ice creams, puddings, fruit pies, and other desserts for an astoundingly refreshing taste.

Brandied fruits are sure crowd-pleasers when hosting a party or entertaining visitors who are fond of elegant and scrumptiously chunky liqueur fruits. Many can be kept for long periods if stored correctly. If intended as a gift, add a trailing ribbon to the jars and bottles with an inspired message

on a gift tag. Generally, herbal additions of liqueurs, syrups, or cordials are great in both hot or cold beverages consumed for medicinal properties or simply for pleasure. Herbal syrups diluted in warm water during cold winters provide an overall cozy feeling while soothing sore throats and easing hacking coughs. In summer, when diluted with cold water with ice added, herbal syrups are fantastic thirst quenchers. Experiment by mixing with flat spring water, sparkling mineral water, soda water, tonic water, and milk.

Coloring may be added if it tickles your fancy. Most natural fruit or flower liqueurs and brandies are not colored nor sweet. Those fond of sweet stuff may add sugar or sugar syrup during the making process as this helps boost the flavor. Some recipes herein contain sugar, though it may be omitted if you are on a sugar-free diet because of a diabetic condition or another dietary restriction or limitation.

Ready? For starters, begin a collection of decorative and unusual glass jars, bottles, and decanters in various sizes and shapes with secure lids, caps, and tops. Folks who adore the bygone "olde worlde charm" may wish to get corks and wax for sealing. All equipment and implements can be bought new, used, at flea markets, or at garage sales. You will be surprised at what can show up when on the prowl for something out of the norm. All this adds an extra personal touch or creative flair to the entire works. Be sure that all jars, bottles, lids, tops, and miscellaneous containers and paraphernalia are thoroughly washed, sterilized, and dried before using.

Enjoy in Moderation

The difference between a remedy and a "negative substance" that is detrimental to health is a matter of dosage. Anything taken in moderation is generally fine. Compulsive, frequent high dosages and prolonged consumption are not encouraged. The rule of thumb for herbal spirits or alcohol intake is "We drink the drink, but do not let the drink, drink us." (Plain English translation: "We drink the spirit or alcohol, but bear in mind never to let the substance 'consume' us or overwhelm our senses to the point of unhealthy intoxication.") Persons who are pregnant or breast-feeding, or who suffer chronic, severe, or serious health conditions must consult their doctors, herbalists, health therapists, or other appropriately qualified health practitioners before consuming the recipes below.

Sugar Syrup

Most recipes require sugar syrup for sweetening and enhancing flavors. Of course, it is optional if preparing for someone who does not take sugar. For those who like it sweet, try this quick and easy method for preparing sugar syrup:

1   pound sugar

4   cups spring water

Pour water and sugar into a saucepan. Heat and bring to boil while stirring regularly to dissolve the sugar. Upon reaching a syrupy consistency, remove the saucepan from heat and let it cool down completely before using. This should yield approximately 7 cups of sugar syrup.

Aniseed Liqueur

Aniseed (*Pimpinella anisum*) contains a warming flavor, assists assimilation of food as an excellent digestive, and is a good remedy for flatulence. With both a calming and stimulating effect on lungs, aniseed is generally beneficial for conditions pertaining to asthma, bronchial spasm, coughs, and wheezes.

It is also said that chewing aniseed at night helps induce sleep. In ancient times, Romans ate spicy cakes baked with aniseed after rich meals. Produce approximately 16 fluid ounces of aniseed liqueur with:

2   tablespoons crushed aniseed

2   inches cinnamon quill, crushed

1   nutmeg, crushed (optional)

2   tablespoons honey

7   ounces good quality brandy

1   cup spring water

Put all ingredients in a glass jar, seal, and let the contents macerate for six weeks. Shake the jar at least once a week. After six weeks, filter the mixture through cheesecloth and bottle. Seal and label the bottle. After meals, 1 or 2 fluid ounces can be taken as a carminative digestive. For the rompy person, try ¼ cup before bedtime as an aphrodisiac.

Honeysuckle Liqueur

The *Lonicera periclymenum* honeysuckle produces one of the best and unusual floral liqueurs. Ingredients include:

6   ounces honeysuckle flowers

8   ounces sugar

1   cup spring water

1   pint vodka or other spirit of personal choice

Lightly bruise honeysuckle flowers and pack into a jar. Gently warm the vodka or other spirit on very low heat. Pour the spirit into the honeysuckle jar, seal it, and place in a warm part of the home for two months.

Shake the jar a few times each day. After two months, put sugar in a jug, fill it with 8 ounces of spring water, and dissolve sugar into a syrup. Strain the alcohol while pressing down firmly on the flowers. Add sugar syrup to the alcohol, mix thoroughly, and pour into a decorative bottle (adding fresh honeysuckle flowers if it's clear). Seal and label the bottle.

Pineapple Malibu

Juicy pineapple slices in Malibu rum are a real treat whether in cold or warm climates. Gather the following ingredients:

1   cup sugar

½   cup spring water

1   pineapple, peeled, cored, and sliced

½   cup Malibu rum

Combine sugar and spring water in a saucepan and bring to boil, stirring constantly. Then let it cook without stirring. Wait until the mixture becomes a thin, clear syrup. Pack slices of pineapple into warm, sterilized jars. Stir Malibu rum into sugar syrup for pouring over the pineapple slices. Seal and allow the jars to cool to room temperature, then store in the refrigerator.

Hazelnut Liqueur

Hazelnuts are not only yummy when chewed, or eaten in chocolate bars, cakes, or bread-spreads, but also are fabulous in liqueur form as an aperitif. The hazelnut liqueur is also heavenly when drizzled over ice cream and custard puddings. Coffee fans will find that adding a drop or two of hazelnut liqueur gives that morning cuppa joe some extra "oomph"! To make 1 pint of hazelnut liqueur, gather:

6   ounces hazelnuts

1   vanilla bean (1 inch long)

1   teaspoon allspice

1½   cups vodka

⅓   cup sugar syrup

Combine vodka, vanilla bean, and allspice in a jar. Finely chop the hazelnuts to release flavor. Add chopped hazelnuts to the jar and cap tightly. Let the contents age for two weeks, shaking the jar once a day.

After two weeks, have a taste to determine if a stronger flavor is desired. If so, add more hazelnuts to the jar and re-steep for another ten days. Strain and filter the mixture. When it is clear, add sugar syrup and stir well. Pour liqueur into a dark bottle and let it sit for another three weeks before serving.

Orange Blossom Brandy

Downunder in Australia, bottled orange blossom water is found at ethnic Greek, Lebanese, and Middle Eastern grocers. Orange blossom water may be added to cakes and desserts or simply drunk diluted with fresh water. This recipe for orange blossom brandy can be utilized similarly and requires:

    4   ounces orange blossom flowers

    2   tablespoons castor sugar

    ¾   pints good quality brandy

Put orange blossoms loosely into a dry and sterilized bottle. Pour the brandy into a jug, add castor sugar, and stir until fully dissolved. Pour the jug's contents into the bottle of orange blossom flowers. Seal the bottle and store in a warm place for at least four months.

At least once a week, shake the bottle. After four months, have a sip of the liqueur. If it is too weak for your liking, re-seal the bottle and let sit for another three weeks. Once the liqueur is satisfying to your tastebuds, strain it with coffee filter paper into a clean decanter or an attractive bottle.

Pear Mascarpone Gratin with Brandy

Mascarpone is a super-rich, double to triple-cream cheese with an Italian pedigree. Made from cow's milk, it has ivory or cream shades. The flavor is slightly sweet, yet sour. The texture ranges from soft to slightly firm. Mascarpone is traditionally served with bread for breakfast, but is also used in desserts. Mascarpone blends well with various fresh fruits such as pears, prunes, plums, figs, and berries.

    4   fully ripened pears, peeled, cored, and quartered

    9   ounces mascarpone cheese

    1   shot glass filled with brandy

    2   teaspoons sugar syrup

        Melted dark chocolate to taste

Arrange the pears with rounded side down in a greased gratin dish. Gently whip, then dollop mascarpone cheese onto the pears. Place the gratin dish under a moderate grill until the cheese begins to melt over the pears. Remove the dish from grill. Lightly pour brandy and sugar syrup over the pears. Drizzle some dark chocolate across the dish.

Serve and enjoy immediately!

Brandied Fruits

A dried fruit salad mix is more suitable for this recipe as it will keep longer and won't deteriorate in rich brandy syrup. In Australia, this is an all-time favorite as a Christmas gift or served during festive meals with loved ones and friends. The ingredients below make about 8 cups:

6	cups spring water
2	cups orange juice
12	fine strips orange rind
6	fine strips lemon rind
8	whole cloves
1	cinnamon quill (2 inches long)
1½	lbs. dried fruit salad mix (slightly more is OK)
1½	cups sugar
2½	cups brandy

In a saucepan, combine spring water, orange juice, orange and lemon rinds, cloves, and cinnamon quill. Put dried fruit salad mixture into a stainless steel container or large glass bowl. When the ingredients in the saucepan begin to boil, remove from heat to pour over the fruit salad. Let stand for five hours. Pour the fruit and liquid back into the saucepan, add sugar, cover, and cook until it comes to a boil.

Turn heat off and pour contents into a strong glass bowl. Leave to cool completely. Add brandy and stir thoroughly with a spoon. Ladle the brandied fruits into wide-mouthed jars, pushing the fruit down into the syrup. Seal the jars and refrigerate for three days before using. As brandied fruits are regarded as rather rich for some palates, ensure that only a small amount is served when poured over plain ice cream, custards, and puddings. Those who love eating it straight out of the jar should only gobble moderately. Another use for brandied fruits is to dice and blend them through a plain cake mix for baking.

Thyme Syrup

Although thyme is mainly used for culinary purposes, it also makes a great syrup for thinning mucus, opening the bronchi, easing coughs, and soothing various lung conditions. Thyme syrup, an expectorant, antiseptic, and antibiotic, is used as a base for many cough syrups during times of chesty coughs and humungously sore throats.

½	ounce dried thyme
¼	ounce dried sage
¼	ounce dried chamomile
2	teaspoons fennel seeds
1	teaspoon aniseed
15	whole cloves
2	garlic cloves
	pinch of cayenne pepper
1½	pints spring water
1	pound honey

Finely chop the thyme, sage, chamomile, fennel seeds, aniseed, cloves, and garlic, then place in a saucepan with water. Add a pinch of cayenne pepper. Cover pan, bring to a boil, and then lower the heat. Simmer for approximately 25 minutes.

Remove from heat and let cool down to lukewarm. Strain into a glass measuring jug while firmly pressing the herbs down with a stainless steel spoon. Chuck the herbs out. Rinse the saucepan and pour the herbal liquid back into it.

Return to heat and simmer uncovered. Wait until the liquid is reduced to about 7 fluid ounces. Try to follow the traditional Chinese herbal method: "The slower the reduction rate, the more the herbal goodness is retained in a decoction."

Add honey to the saucepan and set it to simmer. Allow honey to dissolve slowly while stirring constantly until it turns into a syrup texture. Let contents in the saucepan bubble for a about a minute more. Be careful not to overheat or it will thicken into a caramel herbal toffee! Pour syrup into clean bottles, label, and write the date.

The suggested amount for children should not exceed 1 teaspoon per dose, three to six doses a day. For adults, administer no more than 2 to 3 teaspoons at a time, between three and six times a day.

Violet Syrup

Obtain 2 pounds violet flowers, 3 pints spring water, and about 3 pounds sugar. Experiment a few times to get the right strength and sweetness before deciding on how much sugar to use.

Soak violet flowers for a day in a stainless steel container of spring water—overnight is fine. Using muslin or fine linen, strain the liquid into another clean container. When ready to use, measure the liquid.

For every pint of violet syrup poured into a saucepan, add about 1 pound of sugar. Stir thoroughly with a wooden spoon and then heat gently until the sugar dissolves. Gradually bring contents to a slow boil. When it begins to boil, turn the heat off and let the saucepan cool down. Pour syrup into bottles. Seal with corks and wax for an old-fashioned look.

Fig Syrup

Figs are nutritious, soothing to the lungs, easily digestible, and known to have gentle laxative effects due to their natural combination of fruit sugars and fiber.

Originally found in western Asia, the plant is now cultivated around the globe. Renowned Roman writer Pliny, in *Natural History* (circa 77 AD), mentioned more than twenty-nine types of figs. During the days of yore, athletes of Sparta regarded figs as an aid to strength and swiftness.

In modern times, figs are sometimes utilized as a base for stronger laxatives, such as senna. Fig syrup is tasty and also helps treat constipation.

8   dried figs without stones or seeds

1   cup spring water

1   cup molasses or dark brown sugar

    juice of half a lemon

1   teaspoon ground ginger

Thinly slice the figs and put them in a saucepan with spring water. Simmer for about 25 minutes or until figs become soft. Put softened figs in a bowl and pour the liquid into a cup. Fill up the cup with fresh water and pour into the saucepan again. Add molasses or dark brown sugar.

Gently heat while constantly stirring until molasses or sugar is dissolved. In a blender or food processor, add lemon juice, ginger and figs. Blend well and pour into a jar, label, seal and store in a cool place.

Daily dosage for children must not exceed 1½ to 3 teaspoons. No more than 4½ to 6 teaspoons should be consumed by adults each day. The recommended dosages of fig syrup may be diluted in a glass of water for drinking.

Blueberry Cordial

Fruity blueberry cordials can be made with or without alcohol such as gin or vodka. (If making for children, do not add alcohol at all.) Substitute cups of alcohol in the recipe for spring water. This cordial is marvelous for cooling the body during hot, sweaty summers. The ingredients below make approximately 1 quart of blueberry cordial:

4   cups blueberries

3   cups vodka or gin (optional and not for kids)

1   cup spring water

8   whole cloves

½   teaspoon coriander seeds

2   cups sugar

Wash and drain blueberries before crushing them in a bowl. A food blender may also be used for the crushing process. When done, scrape into a clean, wide-mouth, 2-quart jar. Pour spring water into the jar. If using alcohol, pour this in as well. Add cloves and coriander, then stir the jar's contents.

Cover the jar and let stand for ten days in a cool, dark corner of the larder. Shake the jar once a day. The contents will gradually turn a deep bluish-black color. After ten days, strain through coffee filter paper into a large jug. Add sugar to the jug and stir with a long spoon until dissolved. Pour the cordial into a bottle and seal.

Store the bottle in a cool, dark place for five weeks before using. Once opened for consumption, store the bottle in the refrigerator.

Vanilla Cordial

As with all cordials, this recipe can be made with or without alcohol. When purchasing vanilla beans, make sure they are fresh, soft, and fragrant. When making this cordial for children, use four cups spring water instead of vodka.

5   vanilla beans (5 or 6 inches long)

4   cups vodka or spring water

1   cup granulated sugar

½   cup spring water

1   vanilla bean left whole and intact

Cut the vanilla beans into five pieces. Using a sharp knife, carefully split each vanilla piece lengthwise. Insert the split beans into a clean bottle, add 4 cups spring water or vodka, seal the bottle, and shake it firmly.

Place the bottle in a cool, dark place for three weeks before removing the seal for a sip. If the taste is to your liking, filter the cordial into a dry, clean bottle and discard the vanilla pieces.

Combine sugar with half a cup of water in a saucepan and bring to a boil for 2 or 3 minutes. Let the saucepan cool completely before pouring the sugary liquid into the bottle containing vanilla. Put 1 whole vanilla bean into the bottle. Seal tightly and shake well.

Allow the bottle of vanilla cordial to "age" another five weeks before using or diluting.

Herb History, Myth, and Lore

Natural Wonders: Wild Plant Mysteries

by Nancy Bennett

What flower would you use to welcome the dead home in Mexico? Can a common lawn weed be used to send a message to your loved one? What do the four leaves on a clover mean? What trees did the First Nations make part of their special culture? Why do wild roses grow? Weeds to some, wisdom to others. Before you yank out or cut down these wild things, learn about their place in history, lore, and legend.

The Common Plant of Love from a Lion's Tooth

Dandelions, that aggressive lawn squatter, are widely used to make wine, salads, and even coffee substitutes. But they can also tell where you stand with a loved one. According to legend, the more seeds that remain on the stalk

after you blow on a seeding dandelion, the more you are being thought of by someone else.

If you want to let a loved one know you are thinking of them, point in the direction where they live and blow a seeded dandelion. Your love will travel with the wind.

The word "dandelion" is from the Greek or French, depending which side of the linguistic fence you are on (there has been much debate!). But luckily, the meaning is the same in both languages: "lion's tooth."

A Flower Welcomes the Dead

Marigolds in Mexico are used in part of a ceremony honoring the dead on November 1 and 2. Flowers are made into garlands, wreaths, and crosses to decorate the altar and the grave. In Aztec times, it was called the cempasuchil, the flower of 400 lives. It is said that the scent will lead the dead home, so a pathway of flowers is laid from the front door to the altar during the Days of the Dead. As the spirit approaches the altar, he steps across a cross of marigold leaves to expel any guilt he has carried with him, thus freeing him to enjoy this time with his relations.

Legend says that Tenoch, one of the nine great Aztec leaders, was saddened by all the death during the conquest of Tenochtitlan. He asked Tonatiuh (the Sun God) to help him remember and honor those who had died. The next morning, the fields were covered with bright orange flowers, which we know as marigolds.

Our own custom of having flowers for funerals has practical roots. Before the advent of preserving the body, corpses were not always fresh. Hence, the sweet smell of flowers was needed to mask the odor and make the ceremony less offensive.

A Wolf in a Blue Bonnet?

Native American lore tells of a young girl who burned her most valued possession, a doll with a bright blue feather headdress, as a sacrifice to the Great Spirit. After the girl blew the ashes in all directions, she came back the next day. The Great Spirit had smiled upon her sacrifice and covered the land with a blanket of beautiful blue flowers.

The Spanish called the flowers "el conejo" meaning jackrabbit. Old World botanists called bluebonnets "wolf flower" because they thought it robbed the soil of nutrients, the way wolves robbed shepherds of their sheep. Actually, bluebonnets enrich the soil by adding nitrogen.

Where the Weapons Lay Buried

The Tree of Peace is a tall white pine that has been planted by the Onondaga, representing the great binding law, or Gayanahsagowa, which unified the five nations of the Northeast tribes.

The points for north, south, east, and west are represented by four white roots growing from the Tree of Peace. An eagle sits atop the Tree of Peace, watching over the five nations, ready to cry out at the first sign of danger.

According to Haudenosaunee lore, the Creator, tired of the warring tribes, sent a peacemaker. The peacemaker made the Iroquois chiefs gather around a large hole, forming a circle by holding hands, in order to keep the peace. All the weapons of destruction were thrown into the great hole and the Tree of Peace was planted upon them. As long as the tree stands, peace will unite the tribes.

Why Some Trees Stay Green

According to a Cherokee legend, before making humans, Someone Powerful created the plants and animals. He told them to stay awake and keep watch for seven days and seven nights. But most of the plants and animals couldn't do it. Despite fearing Someone Powerful, some fell asleep after one day, some after two days, some after three.

When Someone Powerful returned on the eighth morning, only the cedar, pine, holly, and laurel were still awake. Someone Powerful said to them, "because you watched and kept awake as you had been told, you will not lose your hair in the winter." So these plants stay green (and warm) all the time. All the other plants lose their leaves and shiver in the wind for falling asleep on the job.

The Mighty Cedars
or, How Good Can Come From Evil

Long ago, the Haida believed, there were no big cedar trees. The people were created and set on the most beautiful place on earth, Queen Charlotte Island. But the people were ungrateful and began fighting among themselves. The Creator came down from the sky and warned them. They pleaded to try again and the Creator relented.

But again, the evil rose in some and they began to quarrel. The Creator darkened the skies and said, "now you will receive the punishment you deserve." It was dark for many days. When the skies cleared, all the evil people had been changed to cedar trees. The Creator spoke to the people who remained and said "here is the red cedar. With the planks of wood you will build your lodges. With the trunks you will build strong canoes. The roots will make your baskets and mats, and the fiber of the inner bark will make your food and your clothing." Thus, from evil came great good, and the Haida people had most everything they needed in life.

Corn Legends and Ceremonies

Before domestication by the people of Mexico, corn was found wild throughout areas of the Northeast. For the First Nations people of the Northeast, corn was a valuable crop and they made use of every part. Along with squash and beans, it later made up the "three sisters" crop, which not only sustained the people but helped one another grow.

Corn was planted first and became a support for the climbing beans. The beans gave nitrogen to the soil for the corn. The squash's leaves kept down the weeds and its prickles repelled raccoons and other pests. Using all three plants, the people created the first cooperative garden!

Such care should always be taken in a garden, as this next legend suggests.

The Voice in the Corn Field

An Arikara woman was gathering corn from the field to store away for winter. After she had gathered all she could see, she started to go. Then she heard a faint voice weeping and calling: "Oh, do not leave me! Do not go away without me."

The woman was astonished. "What can that be?" she asked herself. It sounded almost like a child, and her heart beat fast. "What babe can be lost in the cornfield?" She dropped her corn and went back to search, but found nothing.

"Perhaps it was the wind," she thought. She shrugged her shoulders and gathered up her corn when suddenly she heard again: "Oh, do not leave me! Do not go away without me."

She searched for a long time. At last, in one corner of the field, hidden under the leaves of the empty corn stalks, she found one little ear of corn.

This is what had been crying!

This is why all women have since gathered their corn crop very carefully, so that the food would never be neglected or wasted, and thus displease the Great Spirit.

The Arikara had a special reverence for "Mother Corn" and gave an elaborate ceremony honoring her. Throughout the ceremony, a stalk of corn stood before the altar representing her. At sunset, this stalk would be dressed as a woman and carried to the brink of the river where it would be floated downstream as a symbol of their affection for Mother Corn.

The Green Corn Ceremony was an annual community celebration among the Northeast native people in July or August. Also among the ceremonies dedicated to corn were the blessing of the seeds (in May or June) to assure a bountiful harvest, and the harvest ceremony in late October to celebrate the successful reaping of crops.

If There be Thorns
—Why the Wild Rose Grows

There once was a village on Lake Winnebago, where lived Witch Man and his daughter Hîtcoga ("Blue Fur"). A large wolf began appearing near the village, but none of the hunters could kill it. Witch Man realized that the wolf would appear only when his daughter was out. One day she went to gather water from the spring and her father followed her. There he watched as the wolf changed into a man. The father remained hidden but the wolf-man could see him and told him, "I claim your daughter for my wife and we shall live among my race."

Hîtcoga moved far away and lived among the wolves with her new husband. The wolf people did not trust her as she was the daughter of a witch. The mistrust grew when disease spread through the village, and the wolf people blamed her. When her husband became ill, she asked him for something to protect herself with in case he died. He gave her a white deerskin bag and told her that if she was ever in danger, she need only take what was in the bag and throw it behind her. Soon after, her husband died.

Hîtcoga fled, but the wolves were angry and gave chase. She remembered her husband's gift, and when she opened the bag, she found nothing but thorns. She threw a handful behind her and when the thorns touched the ground, tall hedges with sharp spines immediately sprang up. Yet the wolves continued to chase her, so for a second and a third time she threw the thorns, and hedges again sprang up to slow them down. She had but one remaining thorn.

She cried aloud to Earthmaker, who took pity on her. A voice spoke: "Hîtcoga, prick your finger with the last thorn and let the ruby drop fall into the white purse." So she did this, and as soon as the drop of blood touched the deerskin, the bag immediately filled again with thorns. She threw these and she was able to escape to her home. These hedges, filled with thorns and wild roses, still exist today.

The Dakota-Sioux people tell of how the Prairie Rose came to their lands. Mother Earth looked at her robe and thought she was rather dull. Brown was her color, and grass was her only decoration. Wind Demon did not like flowers—every time one would grow on the prairie, he would blow it away.

A sweet pink flower said to Mother Earth, "do not worry, for I will decorate you and make your robe beautiful." Mother Earth worried that Wind Demon would take this flower, but so sweet was its nature and scent, so gentle was its spirit, that Wind Demon was tamed and did not blow the wild rose away. Other flowers soon crept up through the earth and joined the rose in making the robe of Mother Earth beautiful.

The Four-Leaf Clover and Other Lucky Plants

Spend a day out on a lawn and you will inevitably find yourself looking for a four-leaf clover. Because it is much rarer than the prolific three-leaf variety, it has a special significance. According to legend, the first leaf is for hope, the second leaf is for faith, the third leaf is for love, and the fourth leaf is for luck.

Four-leaf clovers are different from shamrocks, though most people think they are the same plant. The word "shamrock" comes from the Irish word "seamrog," which means "little clover." Thus, a shamrock can be any type of clover an Irishman chooses to call his own. Ideally, a three-leaf shamrock is preferred, especially by the Christian Irish as this plant is said to represent the holy trinity.

You have all probably seen "lucky bamboo" at the plant store. These plants are supposed to bring good fortune, happiness, and balance, according to Chinese Feng Shui tradition. Ideally, five canes create a wall of "Chi" energy. It is also associated with bringing good luck for new business ventures, so you will find it at many office or restaurant openings in China. But buyer beware—as we have seen in the shamrock/four-leaf clover caper, not all plants are what they seem.

The stalks you normally find via mail order, in gift shops, and in Chinatown are not bamboo at all. They are actually a plant known as *Dracaena sanderiana*. Indigenous to West Africa, it now grows in tropical climates around the globe, including parts of China.

But it is not real bamboo. So if you're looking for Eastern luck, why not just go to a gardening shop and buy the real thing?

The Native Plant Witches' Garden

Plant lavender at your gate for luck, that is what the old ones say. (I have one on either side of my garden entrance.) But what else would be found in a wild Witches' garden? A hawthorn hedge would ring around it, for Witches were said to hide themselves in thick hedges. Also needed is a hazel or elm tree from which to make magic wands. (The Saxons used these trees for their temples. Groves of them were often called Witch Hazel or Witch Elm by the fearing folk.)

Of course, the nasty old hags were supposed to keep poisonous plants like foxgloves to cause heart attacks, horned poppy to cause hallucinations in the country population, and the ever-popular mandrake to stimulate or to kill young lovers. But realistically, some of the plants your run-of-the-mill healer Witch would cultivate from the wild would not be so sinister.

Meadowsweet, which has the same properties as aspirin, would be used for headaches. Swampwood or American valerian would be used for hysteria or stomach problems, or as a poultice for treating wounds. Black cohosh or black snakeroot would be used to help with menstruation and menopause (hence the common name "squaw root"). Dogwood bark would be used for colic and fevers, a remedy early settlers learned from native people. Highbush cranberry was used for stomach complaints. (The bark was used to make a sedative that was recognized by the medical profession as early as 1894.) Juniper was used for sore throats and stubborn sores. The list goes on.

The Witch of the wilding woods would find many plants to use for cures. She would also know which ones to avoid—camas lily with blue flowers, good; camas lily with white flowers, deadly—or even which dangerous plants could be used in small dosages for certain conditions. Foxgloves, for example, are now used to treat heart disease. Her tradition continues in gardens, health stores, and laboratories. Today wild plants are used in at least 25 percent of our "modern" miracle medicines.

What Natural Wonders Happen Now?

Many plants in the wild are making interesting contributions to our health and world. For instance, spiderwort, *Tradescantia virginiana*, a common North American native wildflower with three-petaled purple flowers, was once considered a cure for spider bites, but during modern times has become an effective watchdog for the environment.

Botanists noticed that the plant is extremely sensitive to pollution and radiation, which cause its blossoms to rapidly change color from blue to pink. Where dangerous pollution is expected, spiderworts are planted and their flower color is closely monitored for changes.

You can find evening primrose at your local drugstore. American Indians used this plant, with its vivid yellow flowers, for many medical purposes including treating obesity and sore muscles. Today, we know evening primrose oil is a natural source of gamma-linolenic acid and rich in vitamin E. In England, the oil is approved for use with eczema and high cholesterol. In women, it can especially be helpful for relieving breast pain and menstrual pains.

Saint John's wort, a lowly weedy flower that seems to grow everywhere, is now being called "Nature's Prozac" because of its calming nature. Red clover is used as a tonic for the blood and is said to help with health problems including jaundice, bronchitis, spasmodic coughing, asthma, and joint pain.

As with all medicines or herbs, you should always consult your healer before using. Though you might know which plants to take and some recommended dosages, only an expert knows the potential side effects and reactions to your other medications and treatments.

I am reminded of a dear old lady who lived on our mountain and fancied herself a do-it-yourselfer. She had heard about some native cures and without doing any training, used to boil birch bark for her headaches. (It contains a natural pain reliever). Sometimes it would work; sometimes it would not. Sometimes I would end up driving her to the emergency ward because she had swallowed too much bark juice!

If you get a chance, take some wild-crafting workshops and learn to identify the plants in your area. Spending an afternoon wilding (gathering and identifying wild plants) can be a fun, rewarding experience. But don't neglect to look for the legends and lore behind that bit of green you hold.

Who knows what will grow on you?!

Folklore and the Use of Kitchen Spices

❧ by Sorita D'Este ❧

We use the spices in our kitchen for culinary purposes all the time, but rarely consider their rich heritage. Herbs such as turmeric, pepper, chili, caraway, mustard, coriander, and nutmeg have been used around the world for thousands of years in folk remedies and charms.

Caraway

Caraway may be the first herb that man used, as we know from fossilized seeds found at old campsites dating back at least 8,000 years. Its name comes from the Arabic word "karawya," meaning seed, and it was so revered in the ancient world that Persians in the sixth century AD used to pay their taxes with bags of seeds, which were considered to be worth more than their weight in gold. Caraway is also mentioned in the Bible.

Caraway seeds were said to inspire loyalty, which might be why in the Middle Ages it was customary to give farm laborers caraway cakes or bread after they had sown the wheat. Similarly, caraway was also used in love potions to ensure fidelity in the object of your affections.

Caraway was also thought to prevent theft and stop animals from wandering. The seeds were fed to livestock and poultry—and even woven into collars to ensure this. Caraway cakes were also placed in dovecotes and pigeon lofts to encourage the birds to return. Seeds were placed throughout the house—everywhere from shirt hems to cupboards—to safeguard the domicile. In Germany, a bowl of caraway seeds would be placed under a child's cot as protection from witches.

Although caraway seeds are the most commonly used part, the entire plant is edible. The roots were also boiled and eaten as a vegetable and the leaves were used in broths, salads, and soups. The seeds were also used in breads, cakes, cheeses, and sweets as well as infused in cordials and teas—practices that continue today. They were even added to the German brandy called Kummel. This cordial, thought to tone muscles and smooth out skin, was very popular with women of the Middle Ages as a result.

Caraway seeds have been used medically to treat a wide range of conditions, particularly digestive complaints. As an antispasmodic, it helps soothe the digestive tract and ease cramping. Being carminative, it can stimulate appetite and reduce bloating.

A teaspoon of caraway seeds simmered for five minutes in a cup of boiling water and left to infuse another five minutes has many useful purposes. When cool, it can be drank or gargled to ease a cough or sore throat. The caraway concoction can also be consumed to soothe indigestion, ease tension, or relieve menstrual cramps.

Coriander

Coriander takes its name from the Greek word "koris," meaning bug. This is because coriander was thought to give off a smell reminiscent of insects. Though originally found in North Africa, it quickly spread through the ancient world.

Coriander has been used for at least 3,000 years. It was one of the richly aromatic plants grown in the Hanging Gardens of Babylon to fragrance the facility. Pliny the Elder wrote that Egyptian coriander was of the best quality, and it was certainly used very widely there. The Egyptians used coriander in remedies for bandaging broken bones, burns, cholera, expelling intestinal parasites, and increasing lactation, as well as for treating snakebites, sores, and stomach complaints.

The Hebrews used coriander leaves, which are also called cilantro, as the bitter herb in the Passover meal. In Exodus 16:31, manna is described as being like coriander seed, white.

Roman soldiers often carried coriander to flavor their food and to preserve meat. Through their conquests, they brought coriander to northern Europe, where it remains widely used today to add flavor to breads, cakes, and a range of liqueurs including chartreuse, gin, and vermouth. The Greeks mixed coriander with roast barley and flaxseed to make porridge. The Chinese used to believe that eating coriander when pregnant would encourage a baby to be more intelligent, and that it was one of several herbs to eat to gain immortality.

In the Middle Ages, coriander was used as an ingredient in love spells, often being carried in sachets or added to wine; it is also mentioned in this aphrodisiac context in the "1001 Arabian Nights." Coriander picked during the last quarter of the moon, mixed with dill, and drunk in wine was said to induce desire. Because it was also worn for healing, Culpeper declared it a martial herb. Coriander used to be called "dizzycorn" because of its effect on grazing animals—eating larger quantities has a slightly narcotic effect.

Fourteenth century nuns used coriander and other herbs and spices in making Carmelite water, which was used as a perfume and treatment for clear and smooth complexions. It was made by adding one ounce each of coriander seed, cloves, nutmeg, and angelica root; two ounces of lemon peel; and one pound of lemon balm leaves to two pints of water infused with elderflower and four pints of alcohol.

In Ayurveda, honey, coriander, and warm milk are mixed to make an aphrodisiac. Toasting the seeds dry with fennel seeds and a pinch of salt provides an after-dinner snack to aid digestion (remembering to spit out the shells). Sugar-coated coriander seeds are eaten as candy in the Middle East, which helps reduce cavities because of its antibacterial and antifungal qualities.

Coriander is a good antioxidant, and both the seeds and leaves can be used to help counter high blood pressure, regulate heart action, and combat the formation of the free radicals believed to trigger cancers. The seeds and leaves are both also used to strengthen the urinary tract and treat infections of that area. Coriander oil can be used in massage to treat rheumatism and swollen joints. As an herb, coriander also aids digestion, and eases colic and flatulence.

Turmeric

Turmeric has been used since at least 600 BC as a dye, flavoring, and medicine. As Marco Polo described the spice in 1290 AD from his travels in China, "it has the properties of true saffron, yet is not really saffron." Known as "Indian saffron" in Europe, turmeric was used as an inexpensive saffron substitute.

Widely used throughout Asia to treat liver and stomach problems and for healing sores, turmeric was also used cosmetically. In Indonesia, newlywed couples used it to dye their bodies as part of their wedding ceremony. A curious Fijian custom called for men who had killed others in war to be smeared from head to toe with turmeric by their chief and remain so for three days. This process reportedly transformed their appearance so the ghosts of their victims would not recognize them.

In India, turmeric is known as the "internal healer" and used in remedies for becoming pregnant. Indeed, in Ayurveda, it is considered the best spice to use for problems with women's reproductive organs. With tumeric being sacred to the elephant god Ganesha, remover of obstacles, it is easy to see why it should be used this way. Turmeric is used as a purificatory herb in Hawaii by mixing it with salt and water, then sprinkling the solution on the ground.

A teaspoon of turmeric in a glass of warm water is an old remedy for dealing with loose stools and gas. The same quantity in a glass of warm milk is used to relieve joint and bodily pain. In the Far East, turmeric poultices are often applied to relieve inflammation and pain, one recipe being to mix turmeric with lime juice to make a paste to apply to sores, herpes, and other external inflammations. Burning turmeric is a good remedy for clearing a stuffy nose.

With its anticoagulant, anti-inflammatory, antioxidant, and antitumor properties, turmeric is a very useful herb—current research suggests it may even be beneficial in the fight against cancer. Turmeric extract or ointment is used to treat abscesses, gingivitis, inflammations, rheumatism, and ulcers. Also because it dissolves blood clots and promotes circulation, it is being used to treat irregular menstruation.

Mustard

The healing qualities of mustard were written about in the sixth century BC, though it was probably used for many centuries before. The Egyptians and Assyrians used mustard seeds in remedies for coughs, jaundice, toothache, swelling, and stomach ailments. The Bible connected mustard with spirituality when Jesus said that with faith no larger than a mustard seed, mountains could be moved.

The name mustard is said to come from a paste used as a condiment, called "must," that the Greeks made by mixing the crushed seeds with wine vinegar. Sacred to their god of healing, Asclepius, mustard was very popular with the Greeks as well as the Romans, who took it with them across Europe. Pythagoras suggested it as a remedy for scorpion bites, a theme continued by the famous herbalist Culpeper, who also recommended it as a poison remedy. The Greek physician Dioscorides, who traveled with the Roman army, recommended chewing mustard or using it as snuff to purge the sinuses.

As a purgative and condiment, mustard became very popular and was widely grown in monasteries. Some monasteries even had a role of mustardarius, a monk who made sure that mustard was served with the meals.

Hot mustard baths and mustard plasters applied to the chest are used as remedies to alleviate the congestion associated with bronchitis. It has also been used to treat colds, fevers, rheumatism, and sciatica. A gargle of mustard-seed tea is an old remedy for sore throats.

In Italy, mustard seeds were sprinkled on the doorstep (or buried underneath it) to protect the home from supernatural creatures. Carrying mustard seeds in a red cloth sachet is an old remedy to protect against colds and to increase mental clarity. A possible old wives' tale suggests that if a bride sewed mustard seeds into her wedding dress, she would always have the upper hand in her marriage.

Nutmeg

Nutmeg has been used since ancient Egypt, when nutmegs were stuffed into mummies as preservatives. The dried outer covering of nutmeg is ground and better known as mace. Saint Theodore was famous for allowing his monks to sprinkle powdered nutmeg onto their pease pudding to make it more palatable. An old Arabic use was as a cure for bad breath, making the breath smell sweet and attractive.

In Europe, nutmegs were carried as lucky charms and were incredibly valuable. They were thought in Elizabethan England to protect the bearer from the plague, and with a few nutmegs, a man could be set up with a house and income for life. The famous magician, Dr. John Dee, wore a bracelet containing a whole nutmeg and a range of other talismans. Nutmegs became so popular that some people even carried portable nutmeg grinders for scraping off small amounts of nutmeg to add to food or drink.

Since the Renaissance, nutmeg has been a popular ingredient for wealth and business spells, and is also sometimes used as a substitute for High John root. Similarly, Creole folklore recommends sprinkling powdered nutmeg in a woman's left shoe at midnight every night to make her fall madly in love with the man doing the sprinkling. In China, nutmeg was also considered an aphrodisiac, and sprinkling it in food was a common practice to obtain a desired man.

Today nutmeg is particularly popular at Yule and Christmas when added to mulled wine and spiced beer or cider. The American state of Connecticut is also known as the nutmeg state due to the old practice of confidence tricksters selling carved wooden nutmegs in place of the actual spice to unsuspecting housewives.

Small amounts of powdered nutmeg sprinkled in milk can aid digestion and ease stomach complaints, though pregnant women should avoid it because it could induce miscarriages. Powdered nutmeg has been used as an ingredient in remedies to treat boils, neuralgia, rheumatism, and sores. Other remedies using nutmeg include adding nutmeg and flour to hot water and drinking it for an upset stomach, or rubbing nutmeg-laced mutton fat on the chest for bronchitis.

Chili Peppers

Chili peppers have been used since at least 7000 BC, and cultivated since 3000 BC, in Central and South America. As a treatment for stomach disorders, they go back to the Mayans. From the sixteenth century, when Spanish and Portuguese explorers brought them back to Europe, chilies became increasingly popular in Europe. The name is derived from a misspelling of the country where it grew—Chile. In 1498, the Portuguese explorer Vasco da Gama took chili to India, where it was immediately incorporated into Indian cuisine. Today it is the world's most popular spice, and India is the largest producer of chili.

A mixture of chili and chocolate was eaten by the Aztecs, though it was reserved for nobility and those in power. Chili has a long history of use as a stimulant for those suffering from fatigue. The ability to stimulate blood circulation throughout the body makes chili an excellent carrier for other herbs as it ensures speedy distribution of the herbal healing agents.

Gypsies used chilies in love charms, believing that tying two red chilies together and placing them under the pillow would keep a partner from straying from the loved one. It has also been applied to snakebites as a remedy, and added as neat powder to dog bites in India.

Chili stimulates digestion and the flow of saliva, and is used as a counter-irritant to treat itching or pain. Chili in soap liniment is applied to the skin to alleviate rheumatic pain and for chest conditions such as asthma and bronchitis. In a gargle, paste, or tincture form, chili has frequently been used to treat throat problems including tonsillitis. The gargle is prepared by adding chili powder to honey and water.

Chili is said to stimulate the heart, kidneys, nervous system, and skin. Being one of the world's most powerful natural stimulants, it has even been given to people suffering from heart attacks. The wide range of conditions chili can treat even includes hay fever, and, taken as snuff, it also aids seasickness and chronic diarrhea. Chili added to cinnamon and sugar has been used in the treatment of alcoholism.

Whole chilies cooked in milk are applied as a remedy to reduce swellings. Chili has anti-inflammatory, antirheumatic, antiseptic, and antispasmodic qualities, and can also equalize blood pressure and speed up the clotting process. For these reasons, it has been used for centuries to treat external and internal bleeding, including hemorrhaging.

A liniment made by combining half an ounce of chili powder with a pint of raspberry vinegar and a pint of water—then shaking it every day for ten days—can be used to treat bruises, burns, scalds, sprains, and sunburn. An excellent treatment for serious sprains is a liniment made by gently boiling a tablespoon of chili powder in a pint of cider vinegar for ten minutes and then storing unstrained.

Pepper

Pepper comes from peppercorns, and may be black, white, or green depending on their treatment. Black pepper comes from the baked immature peppercorns, whereas white pepper is from the ripened corns that need to be soaked to have the skins removed. Green pepper is from the ripe corns preserved in vinegar and other spices.

In India, its land of origin, pepper is used in remedies for treating asthma, bronchitis, and pneumonia. With a reputation as a protective spice, it has been used to banish evil influences and combat illnesses. Mexican healers used pepper to treat illnesses by brushing the patient with branches of the tree to absorb the sickness, and then burning the branches.

In recent years, pepper has been found in excavations in Egypt. The Copts used it in remedies mixed with questionable ingredients. The ancient Greeks and Romans also used pepper in their cooking, as evidenced by numerous recipes that have survived to today.

An old folk remedy says you should carry some black pepper in a small linen bag to relieve earache. Another remedy that may have roots in the actual healing properties is to put black pepper in cream and drink it for an upset stomach.

Black pepper has also been used in diets. An Ayurvedic recipe to help reduce the desire for food is to add a teaspoon of honey, two teaspoons of lime juice, and some black pepper to a cup of water to drink as a daily tonic.

Pepper is antiseptic and stimulates the circulatory system. It acts on the digestive system by stimulating the production of enzymes in the pancreas and small intestine, and also encouraging the secretion of bile. Pepper can also help with bloating, constipation, flatulence, nausea, and stomachache, and act as an appetite stimulator.

Enjoying the Sacred Seed

❧ by Stephanie Rose Bird ❧

In many cultures, seeds are the most sacred and celebrated of foods. In regions of Africa, food is scarce during parts of the year. Hunter-gatherers such as the Kalahari !Kung have learned over the centuries how to use all parts of plants to sustain life—including seeds. In some Native American cultures, sunflower seeds are used to pay tribute to their ancestors as well as for sustenance.

So it strikes me with a touch of irony when I go to the grocery store and find the appearance of increasingly more seedless melons and other produce. Typically, in America, if our produce is not seedless, we discard seeds. In this article, I hope to demonstrate the sacred nature of seeds in several cultures, as well as the numerous holistic health benefits contained in seeds.

Reverence for the seed crosses cultures and continents for practical and spiritual reasons. Many of the life-sustaining herbs of Africa and the Black Atlantic are in from the family Curcubitacea, the favorite plant group of Osayin, the Yoruban orisha (deity) responsible for knowledge of herbs. It is said that he stored this knowledge inside a calabash high atop a tree. Once this knowledge was knocked down to earth the seeds of herbal knowledge spread to the other orishas and eventually to humanity. The Curcubitacea family includes:

- *Cucumis* (cucumber and melon)
- *Momordica charantia* (African cucumber)
- *Cucurbita* (pumpkin and marrows)
- *Citrullus vulgaris* (watermelon)
- *Luffa cylindrical* (vegetable sponge)
- *Lagenaria* (gourd)

Along these lines, overlap between the vaunted seeds and disconnected cultures is unmistakable. In early Greece, the Four Great Cold Seeds of old Materia Medica were pumpkin, gourd, melon, and cucumber. These four great seeds were bruised and rubbed in water to form an emulsion. This healing formula was consumed and used to treat catarrhal infections, bowel disorders, and urinary infections. So the next time you are cleaning a member of the great seed family, perhaps you should think twice before throwing away such a precious cache of healing medicines. The pumpkin, our symbol of the harvest, is a very good case in point.

Pumpkin

Roast pumpkin seeds are an inexpensive, nutritious snack for many in Africa and the Americas. A good source of protein, the seeds also contain a reddish fixed oil, traces of a volatile oil, sugars, starches, and fiber. This snack has a shelf life of 30 days.

Beyond improving general health as part of a good diet, the seeds have several uses as a preventive treatment and to aid recovery. Pumpkin seed has been used medicinally and is a part of the official *German Pharmacoepia 10th Edition*. The Expanded Commission E of the American Botanical Council has approved the seeds for the treatment of irritable bladder. The seeds contain amino acids and curcurbitin. Consumption of pumpkin seeds may help reduce bladder stones in children. Other herbalists recommend pumpkin seed oil applied topically to the face or taken orally by the level teaspoon twice a day as a treatment for acne, particularly in teenagers.

Pumpkin (*Cucurbita pepo*) is an herbaceous plant called apakyi in Ghana. Fluted pumpkin (*Telfairia occidentalis*) is wildcrafted in Ghana, where it grows in the forests.

Watermelon

Watermelons flourish in many places worldwide. In Central Africa, native watermelons (*Citrullus lanatus*) are a vital source of water. The melons are a staple food that is refreshing for humans and animals in North Africa and parts of the Middle East. Almost always available in urban markets when in season, watermelons come in many varieties in terms of shape, size, and content. Burlus Delta Lake, east of the Rosetta channel of the Nile, is noted for its watermelon, which is yellow inside. Some varieties are grown just for the seeds. Though many varieties thrive in tropical Africa and the East Indies, many crops prosper in the Northern Hemisphere from May until November.

The food value of watermelon seeds, which are also used as a coffee substitute, is 45 percent fat, 54 percent protein. Watermelon has high amounts of lycopene and glutathione, antioxidant, and anticancer compounds. In Africa, egusi is made from ground melon seeds to add flavor and protein as well as to thicken stews. The Kalahari !Kung use watermelon as a survival food. Internationally today, we enjoy Kalahari seed oil in beauty treatments and as a fixed oil for making body care products.

Sunflowers

As a sun-loving culture, the ancient Egyptians would have loved the sunflower (*Helianthus annus*). The plant's name tells why, as helios means sun, and anthos means flower in Greek. The French word for it is tournesol or "turn with the sun," which is precisely what it does. The plant is called phototropic, meaning that it follows the sun.

As it stands, Native American people from various origins make great use of sunflowers by using them for healing poultices and skin washes as well as eating the seeds and working with the stalks to make life-preserving floatation devices. Bowls of the seeds are left on the graves of loved ones by certain groups—an interesting spiritual application of sunflower seeds.

Today, sunflowers are grown in the sunny climate of South Africa as well to create healing oils from the seeds for applications including use as an herbal infusion in massage and hot oil treatments. The oils are also used for cosmetic purposes, such as nail soaks to soothe cuticles and in formulating homemade cosmetics. However, South African sunflowers are also quite beneficial when simply eaten. Sunflower oil—useful in cooking, salad, dressings, and marinades—is inexpensive, helps boost the immune system, and provides some vitamin A, D, and E. Sunflower oil is an unsung hero in a market so saturated with saturated oils. Sunflowers are rich in unsaturated fatty acids, especially oleic (mono-unsaturated) and linoleic, which is di-unsatured. Polyunsaturated fatty acids are also found in sunflower. For those who consume seeds straight up, the nutritional breakdown of a cup of unshelled sunflower seeds indicates that they are a good source of nutrition, with 162 calories; 10.5 g protein; 8.6 g carbohydrate; 22.8 g fat (unsaturated); and 4.8 g fiber. And they are a good source of zinc with 2.3 mg.

Sunflowers are a special flower in the Midwest—so much so that they are the state flower of Kansas. They grow quite freely alongside the highways, beautify waste dumps, add color to fields, and, of course, grace our gardens. Basically, wherever their seeds blow, they take root unless they are disturbed. Called an annual, they reseed themselves so easily they are a perennial in many a garden.

Each year I almost look out at them with chagrin. Treelike in their massive ten-to-twelve foot splendor, they threaten to overtake my garden by choking out the light from the less aggressive or small-stature plants year after year. But every year, the ones I allow to grow share their metaphysical gifts. I can peer out of my front window at the most gorgeous sight. Green finches, the tiniest little critters, sing cheerfully as they eat the sunflower seeds. There are plenty to go around as well. In autumn, I cut the mature plants and take the seeds inside for my family and our bird—which absolutely loves them.

Holistic Healing with Sunflowers

1. The flowers are aesthetically pleasing; hence, the wide variety of artists who have dedicated canvases to them. Try painting or drawing sunflower plants, or press the leaves to use in collage.

2. The seeds invite wildlife that in turn share their magic and mystery with those who take time to enjoy.

3. The seeds are inexpensive, plentiful, and nutritious.

4. You can make a mildly antibacterial infusion from the leaves to treat scratches or minor irritations.

5. If you are truly industrious, you can utilize the stalks to make a very strong, textured, handmade paper. Sprinkle in the bright yellow petals for visual interest.

6. Cut a bunch of flowers and cheer up a sick room, dining room, or anywhere you please.

7. Last but not least, you can follow the example of our Nation's First People; put a bowl of the seeds on a grave, or adapt this rite by putting a bowl of them on your ancestral altar.

Benne (*Sesamum indicum*)

Commonly called sesame seed, benne (*Sesamum indicum*) is one of the herbs brought to the Americas by enslaved Africans. It is associated with one of the most feared and respected orishas, Sonponno, and his cult, who all wear red. Sonponno is a wind orisha who whips up evil storms dispersing smallpox. You can imagine the power of Sonponno by visualizing smallpox as the whelts left behind after a tornado blew sesame seeds at someone's face. Benne is eaten atop wafers, mixed into candies, and as cookies. The oil is used in cooking and massage. Benne has been used historically as a natural amulet, planted at the end of the rows of a garden to protect against thieves. This has been recorded in the American south, particularly in gardens tended by the Gullah people of South Carolina and Georgia's low country. (The Gullah are closely linked to the Mande people of West Africa). Benne also has a West Indian connection to the ADR, obeah, wherein it is believed to repel thieves and other intruders.

Black Seed Called Tepenen & Black Seed Oil

Black seed is a health amulet that is considered a panacea by many African people. Believed to be an indigenous Egyptian herb, black seed is used for a host of ailments when applied as a lotion or unguent. Ethiopians mix black cumin seeds (*Nigella sativa L*) with butter and then wrap the body in cloth or sniff for headaches. Strewn among linens, it serves as a moth repellent. Cumin remains an important African herb that is used for skin, nail, and hair care as well as for botanical cosmetic formulation. In short, black seed oil is multipurpose health oil.

Coneflower-Echinacea

Coneflower, commonly called echinacea, is a much-sought-after healing plant. Echinacea is growing more fragile in terms of sustainability because of overharvesting due to its popularity, but by working the seed, as I'll demonstrate in this section, you can use its healing medicine in good faith knowing that you are not depleting the herbal stock in a way that is unsustainable.

Some prevalent echinacea varieties you are likely to come across include:

Angustifolia, also called black sampson coneflower, has eight-inch leaves, large soft violet flowers, and a dark cone-shaped center. It is also known as Missouri snakeroot because the root is used to treat snakebites, detoxify the body, and treat rabies.

Pallida, also called pale purple coneflower, has rosy purple blossoms, and drooping flower petals. It boosts immunity by stimulating white blood cells and regulating red blood cells. It is considered an antitumor and antiallergenic herb.

Purpurea, also called purple coneflower, grows up to five feet tall and has large reddish or purple flowers four inches in diameter. Purple coneflower is used to stimulate the immune system, treat colds, and deter the flu.

The parts used include the root, rhizome, leaves, and flower petals. Its medicinal constituents are vitamins A, B complex, B3, C, E, iron, calcium, magnesium, manganese, potassium, selenium, silicon, sodium, essential oils, polyacetylenes, polysaccharide, glycoside, resin, betain, insulin, and sequiterpene.

There are numerous uses for this herb, which possesses antiallergenic, antiviral, antifungal, antimicrobial, and anti-inflammatory properties; and is an immunity booster and diaphoretic.

Echinacea tea is standard for infections and often used at the onset to stimulate immunity and speed recovery from colds, influenza, viruses, glandular swelling, lymphatic congestion, boils, abscesses, and inflammatory conditions.

Echinacea Tips

1. It is very easy to propagate echinacea. My local gardening neighbors and I cut down the plants in late autumn

(before a killing frost), shake out the seeds where we want more plants, and then set the flowers down as mulch. Inevitably, during the next growing season, there are lovely new echinacea plants. This practice is ecologically sound and saves money to boot.

2. Echinacea does not appreciate being transplanted, so be careful. You may well lose your plant in the process or stunt its growing season. It is worthwhile to make a plan about location and try to stick to it.

3. Other than the need for stability, you do not need a green thumb to grow echinacea. Like many prairie plants, echinaceas are happy if there is simply adequate sunlight and rainwater, though it does tolerate drought.

4. The decocted root of echinacea is commonly used, but leaves and even flowers offer some of the same medicinal qualities as well. Using varied parts helps sustain individual plants and protects the family echinacea from facing extinction. To decoct the root, dig up part of the root, wash it and chop into small pieces; put in a pot of water; bring water almost to a boil over medium heat; cover; simmer 25 minutes. Do not boil this or any other herb.

Do not use echinacea treatments continuously. If problems persist after one month, discontinue use and consult a health care professional.

As you can see from these few examples, seeds and the plants from which they stem provide us with important medicine that soothes the soul, mind, body, and spirit. Next time you are shopping for healing medicines found in herbs and produce, just say no to seedless.

The History of Curry

◈ by Cerridwen Iris Shea ◈

Curry. The word makes your mouth water. You can almost smell and taste it. There's both a sense of the exotic and a sense of the comfortable. The earliest text of a curry recipe was written in cuneiform, dates back to approximately 1700 BC. It's is a taste sensation that's been around so long, it is almost an archetype.

When we hear "curry," we usually think of the powdered spice mixed into cooking or the actual dish we refer to as "eating a curry." The term "curry" is used to denote a number of savory soup/stewlike dishes with flavorings indigenous to regions of India. Each region has its own particular take on curry. Most often, it is said to have descended from the Tamil word "kari," which means "spiced sauce."

As early as 1598, a Dutch traveler referred to "carriel," which may well have been a form of curry, and a seventeenth-century Portuguese cookbook mentions a chili-based curry powder called "caril." In 1390, 200 cooks employed by King Richard II, along with an assortment of philosophers and other interesting types, produced one of the first English cookbooks, compiled by a man named Samuel Pegge and called *The Forme of Cury*. "Cury" was the Old English derivative of the French "cuire"—to cook, and later evolved into "cuisine."

The text of the book is in Middle English. Of its 196 recipes, several included curry mixtures. In addition to flavoring the food, its power to aid digestion was useful in prerefrigeration times. Historians will continue to argue, as they have for hundreds of years, whether our word "curry" comes from "cury" or from "caril" or from "kari." It gives them something to do. I'll just go ahead and put it in the stew, thank you, and eat my dinner while they argue.

Because we travel so quickly via air and we communicate in a matter of seconds via the Internet, we forget that people in earlier centuries also traveled frequently, but differently. Because it took them much longer to get from point A to point B, once they got there they tended to stay for months rather than days. That gave travelers the opportunity to truly explore the region and bring back recipes and ideas and traditions. India was once part of the British Empire, and many of those who worked and lived for months and years in India brought back recipes and knowledge upon their return to Britain.

Of course, in days long gone and in the present, you always find people who travel and then want everything exactly the way it is at home, criticizing their way through the most beautiful scenery and the most delicious cooking. Fortunately, many world travelers throughout the centuries actually took an interest in their experiences and brought back ideas. And spices.

Curry leaves (*Chalcas koenigii*) grow on trees and look like bay leaves, but smaller. The smell given off these trees in a gentle breeze is beautiful and exotic. It is the merest curry-spiced whiff. The Botanical Garden in Adelaide, Australia, has some curry trees, and to walk past them is to get your spirits lifted, even if you don't know exactly why. The leaves are used in cooking, and dried leaves are one of the ingredients in curry powder.

The **curry plant** (*Helichrysum italicum*) is low to the ground, and a spiky, silvery green, with yellow flowers. Although it's a lovely addition to your garden, it's useless in the kitchen. Keep it in your borders, but don't put those bits of plant in the stew.

However, there is a more kitchen-friendly plant, often confused with the above, called the **daun salaam** (*Eugenia polyantha*). This plant is in the evergreen family, and used in Indonesian cooking. It loses its taste when dried, so it's best used when as fresh as possible.

Curry powders, what we toss in to perk up our stews, are complex concoctions, made up of an assortment of herbs and spices including coriander seeds, cumin seeds, fenugreek seeds, turmeric, cloves, garlic, dried and powdered curry leaves, galangal, fennel seeds, ginger, various chilies, mustard, red pepper, salt, cassia, black pepper, poppy seeds, anise, Bengal gram, cardamom, cassia buds, celery seed, cinnamon, dill seed, mace, nagkesar, nutmeg, and onion. There are thousands of recipes for this mix. It differs not only by region, but by family tradition. Cooks pass their special, secret mixtures down through the generations. Successive generations put their own spin on it. And the recipes evolve. One could devote a lifetime to the comparison of curry powder mixtures.

The medical world is starting to investigate curry's curative properties. King's College in London is working on extensive tests with galangal as an anticancer agent. Turmeric is an antibacterial. A solution containing it can be used to clean wounds (it hurts). Curry powder is an antioxidant, and now there are some studies to see if it can help with Alzheimer's disease. Tonics are made from curry leaves to treat digestive ailments. Curcumin, a main ingredient of turmeric, is reputed to be an anti-inflammatory. Modern medicine is coming back to the techniques used years ago, before it existed. And, finally, the healing properties of herbs are being taken more seriously, to work in tandem with modern medicine instead of outside of it. Always check with your doctor before working with natural remedies, especially if you take any sort of medication. And always read up thoroughly on the property of the herb or spice in which you're interested.

Although I haven't found fiction or music specifically dedicated to curry, the food itself appears in a wide range of artwork. And, William Makepeace Thackeray (best known for his novel *Vanity Fair*) wrote a "Poem to Curry" in his book *Kitchen Melodies*, published in 1846. I don't know if lovers ever died from lack of curry, but I'm sure many a romantic evening began with a meal of curry. It's a warm, fiery spice mix—passionate in its creation, and passionate in its use.

Next time you mix curry powder into your meal at home or order it in a restaurant, take a moment to savor that you are part of a tradition started no later than 1700 BC. And enjoy.

For Futher Reading

Boxer, Arabella. *The Herb Book*. Thunder Bay Press, 1996.

"Curry Powder: Ingredients." http://www.lionsgrip.com

Pegge, Samuel. (ed.) *The Forme of Cury*. 1390. Part of the Project Gutenberg Collection, http://www.gutenberg.org.

Smith, David W. "The Curry House FAQ." The Curry House, 1998-2000.

Sweet Nectar
of the Gods

⋙ by Sorita D'Este ⋙

*"Honey is the dew distilled
from stars and the rainbow."*

The bee is one of the most important creatures on our planet. In ancient times, it was seen as a symbol of the soul. Today it is said that if all the bees died, life would be irrevocably changed by the loss of their pollinating service. Bees produce a number of products, including honey, beeswax, and royal jelly. Honey, which has been called the nectar of the gods, has been used all over the world for a huge range of purposes since ancient times. As the food of the gods, it was believed that eating it conferred benefits such as long life and good health.

The image of the industrious bee working in harmony with its companions for the good of the hive has been held up as a model of an ideal society.

Of course, bees work within a strict hierarchy with the queen at the top. Nonetheless, the humble bee has fascinated man since the dawn of time, and it has often been seen as a symbol of the soul and of virtue. Some used to believe that bees would only sting people who had misbehaved or sinned.

Evidence suggests bees have been kept since at least 5000 BC, and records indicate that honey has been used medicinally since at least 2700 BC. Beekeeping might go back even further. Rock-art images from caves in Spain show men collecting honey from around 13,000 BC, and a cave painting from southern Spain shows a female figure with a bee as a head.

Honey is antibacterial, antiviral, and antifungal. It soothes the throat and digestion, and can be applied to the skin. It contains a wide range of vitamins and minerals, including vitamin K, which prevents acid bacteria from forming in the mouth, a major source of tooth decay. Hence, sweets with honey are far less harmful than those with sugar. Honey absorbs moisture and also draws dirt out of pores, two reasons it is so good for application to the skin. These effects have led to its use for millennia in application to wounds and burns.

Beekeeper, translator, and author Marna Pease said this of honey: "The more honey is used as a food, the less it will be needed as a remedy."

The flowers and tree blossoms that the bees forage determine the appearance and flavor of honey. Some popular honeys are those made from heather, thyme, white clover, lime, and other fruit blossoms.

Today, many varieties of honey are available worldwide. However, as in the past, the benefits of consuming local honey still apply, for it contains the local pollen that can help hay fever sufferers immunize their system and reduce sensitivity to the pollen that triggers attacks. Because of its localized differences, it is no surprise that while medicinal uses for honey cross over among cultures, each took a different path and developed distinct spiritual traditions, meanings, and attachments to the special nectar.

Early Connections

The Latin word for bee is Apis, which meant bull to the Egyptians. This connection of words may be no coincidence, for as the Greek poet Virgil recorded, it was believed that bees could be spontaneously generated from the carcasses of bulls, particularly if they were buried up to their horns. This belief was also described by Aristotle, and literary references have been made through the seventeenth century.

An Egyptian myth claims that when the sun god Ra cried, his tears turned into bees. An early title given to the Pharaohs was Bity, or "one of the bee," showing the importance of the bee, which represented the land of Lower Egypt to the ancient Egyptians. As a further tribute, the hieroglyph for the bee was also used to represent the title of "King of Lower Egypt." Bees were also associated with the primal Egyptian goddess Neith, whose temple was called "the house of the bee."

Large quantities of honey have been found in some Egyptian tombs as an offering, in one instance labeled as "good quality honey." Images of beekeepers and hives in ancient Egypt date back to 2400 BC, and one papyrus refers to honey collectors delivering the annual crop to the treasury.

The ancient Egyptians used honey for numerous purposes, notably as the most common ingredient used in medicine. Honey mixed with carob or ground-up frankincense was applied to burns. When mixed with oil and wax, honey was applied to insect bites. Ground-up bloodstone in honey was applied to wounds to stop bleeding. The herb fenugreek was added to honey for inducing childbirth. Honey was widely used as a base for ointments and cosmetics as well as in the embalming process.

Alexander the Great was buried in a coating of honey, a practice that also occurred elsewhere in the world. In Burma, bodies were steeped in honey to preserve them until money for the expensive funeral rites could be collected. Afterward, the honey was scraped off the bodies and reused, for it was believed to be incorruptible and therefore unaffected by the dead body it had coated. Another legend asserts that the honey helped the soul on its way, as bees were said to be able to travel to the underworld, prompting the practice of carving bees on tombs. Some Mycenaean tombs, called tholos, were even made in the shape of a beehive.

It was not just the ancient Egyptians who used honey medicinally. The Greek physician Hippocrates, widely regarded as the founder of modern medicine, said "I eat honey and use it in the treatment of many diseases because honey offers good food and good health."

The Greeks and Romans used honey as a base for powdered crystals to use in treating medical problems. Powdered malachite in honey was applied to wounds to stop bleeding and powdered hematite added to honey was applied to the eyelids for headaches and inflamed eyes. Roman soldiers carried honey in their packs for immediate application to wounds when more sophisticated treatment was not available.

The famous book *De Materia Medica*, written by the Greek surgeon Dioscorides in 77 AD, was the leading medical text in the West until the fifteenth century. He wrote that honey could be used as a treatment for stomach disease and hemorrhoids; for sealing wounds and for wounds that had pus. Drunk warm mixed with rose oil, honey was a treatment to stop coughing. Mixed with salt, honey was applied to the ear for earache, painted onto children's skin to kill lice, gargled to reduce tonsil swelling, and also said to improve vision.

Arab physician Al Razi wrote about the use of honey is his book, *The Encyclopaedia of Medicine*, which was translated from Arabic into Latin in the thirteenth century and used as a standard textbook until the eighteenth century. He declared that honey was the best treatment for gums and that mixing it with vinegar to use as a mouthwash would keep the teeth healthy. He also said it did not spoil and could be used to preserve corpses.

All the major medical texts, from the ancient Egyptian medical papyri to medieval Arabia and Renaissance Europe, mention honey and its beneficial effects. Even today, some cough sweets mirror the old remedy and contain honey and lemon, a combination still popular in hot water for an irritated throat.

Spiritual Inspiration

Pythagoras and his followers celebrated bees for the perfect hexagons they built in the hives, holding up the perfect symmetry as an example of the underlying order of the universe. The mathematician was not alone in heralding the precision associated with the industrious bees.

Priestesses of the Greek goddess Artemis were called Melissae, meaning bees, as the honey bee was sacred to her. The famous statues of Artemis of Ephesus and the many replicas all have bees on her robes. Bees were also known as "Birds of the Muses" due to the belief they could give eloquence or the ability to sing if they touched a baby's lips. The playwrights Plato, Sophocles, and Virgil were all said to have been blessed in this manner.

The priestesses of Cybele were also called Melissae, and Virgil wrote that playing the frame drum and cymbals of Cybele could help attract a swarm of bees to a new hive baited with herbs and flowers.

Melissae was originally a Cretan nymph who, with her sister Amalthea, weaned Zeus as a baby on honey and goat's milk. Milk and honey were frequently given as offerings to the gods, a practice which has survived into the modern Paganism of today. Pliny the Elder came up with some interesting ideas as to the origin of honey, suggesting it came from the sweat of the skies or the saliva of the stars.

The bee was very important to the Greeks. Another instance of sacred bees occurs with the Thriai, three bee maidens who were teachers of divination. When they ate yellow honey they spoke the truth, but when deprived of it, they spoke lies. The sun god Apollo, ruler of the Delphic Oracle, appointed them to Hermes, the messenger god and trickster. Apollo had another connection with bees through his son Aristaios, who was, amongst other roles, the god of beekeeping, bees, and honey.

Some Greek writers wrote of the king bee, though other cultures like the Minoans and Anglo-Saxons knew otherwise, as this charm to claim a swarm of bees demonstrates:

Stay, victorious women, sink to earth!
Never fly wild to the wood.
Be as mindful of my good
as each man is of food and home.

The Bible refers to honey several times, such as Moses leading his people to "the land of milk and honey," and in Judges 14:18 in the tale of the dead lion: "What is sweeter than honey? And what is stronger than a lion?" Honey was seen as pure because the bees were said to have swarmed out of Eden in disgust at the Fall, hence the reference to feeding Jesus in Isaiah 7:15: "Butter and honey shall he eat, that he may know to refuse the evil, and choose the good."

Honey was given in early christening ceremonies as a symbol of renewal and perfection, and bees were also revered for their ability to produce beeswax. From the wax, candles could be made, which produce light. The Catholic Church used to insist on pure beeswax candles made by the worker bees, which do not mate and are therefore virgin. Monks kept bees for the purity of the wax to use in essential products used by the church. Today, candles used by the Catholic Church still have to contain beeswax, though the quantity has been dropped to 25 percent.

There are even patron saints of bees. In Spain, St. John of the Nettles is the patron saint of bees, and women visit his tomb to pray for a male child. In Russia, Saint Sossima is the patron saint of beekeeping.

Legends Abound Worldwide

When Phoenician traders visited ancient Britain looking for lead and tin, they commented on the prominence of honey and called Britain the Isle of Honey. They may have taken this name from the Druids, who called Britain the Honey Isle of Bile, in honor of the Celtic Sun God whose golden light was mirrored in the golden honey made by the bees. By the time the Romans invaded Britain, it was said that every village in the land had beehives.

The Hindu gods Indra, Krishna, and Vishnu were all called Madhava, or "nectar-born ones," and were often represented as bees perched on a lotus flower, a symbol of perfection and of the chakras. In Tantra, the sound of the Kundalini (the fire serpent of sexual energy) rising was said to be that of bees buzzing.

The Celtic god of literature Ogma, who created writing and the Ogham, was also known as Cermait, meaning "Honey-mouthed." There are a number of expressions derived from this, such as being honey-mouthed and honey-tongued. And, of course, the term honey is used endearingly to partners and loved ones.

The idea of communication is strongly associated with bees. Across Europe, people would go to beehives and tell the bees about important events, especially deaths, recalling the idea of bees as souls. In southern Germany, beehives were decorated before weddings so the bees could join the celebrations.

In the Finnish epic, *the Kalevala*, the creation of the bee is described. A maiden, Kalevalatar, picked up a pea plant and rubbed it with her palms and her thighs, and from it a bee was produced. Bees were also responsible for alcohol, bringing honey to add to beer to make it ferment as all other attempts had failed.

The Aztecs practiced beekeeping and honey was considered one of the most important momentos they collected from the peoples they conquered. The Aztecs made drinks called atolli from corn dough mixed with water and flavored with honey and/or chili to aid digestion.

In the Middle East today, a decoction of fenugreek seeds with honey is used for upset stomachs, constipation, abdominal cramps, and menstrual pains. Some areas in India still follow the custom of giving the groom honey on his wedding day to ensure he will be fertile in the marriage. Feeding butter and honey to a baby with a golden spoon was thought to ensure long life.

In the West, dreaming of honey was thought to be a sign of suddenly overcoming a problem, or of domestic and social sweetness. In India, however, it was seen as a bad omen. Dreaming of a beehive tells of prosperity and happiness—unless the bees are upset, which suggests trouble of your own making. Bees buzzing in dreams is thought to indicate good news coming. Bee stings are also considered lucky, but a dead bee is a warning not to trust friends too much.

An old English saying goes, "Where there is the best honey there is also the best wool." Unplowed land produces flowers and is good pasture for sheep. Today bees can be kept in cities, though historically, beekeeping was much more a rural pastime.

Honey Wine

The ability of honey to absorb moisture means you should store it in airtight containers. Honey that absorbs too much moisture will start to ferment, which has been suggested as a possible discovery of alcohol. The first time this was consumed would have caused a few surprises and probably led to the popularity of honey-based alcoholic drinks.

A favorite drink in the ancient world was mead and its derivatives. Mead is a type of wine made with honey. It was an old Celtic and Teutonic custom for newly married couples to drink mead every day for a month after they had wed, leading to the name "honeymoon" to describe the postnuptial period.

The ancient Greeks made a whole range of honey drinks apart from mead, which they called hydromel and thought could disperse anger and sadness. They also made conditum, which was honey mixed with wine and pepper, oenomel from pure grape juice and honey, ompacomel with fermented grape juice and honey, and oxymel, made with honey, rainwater, sea salt, and vinegar.

The Romans made honey wine called muslum; the Russian

version was called Lipez. In medieval England, the mead was known as Piment or Clarre, and had spices added to it. Another popular drink was Morat, mead made with mulberry juice.

It is interesting to see how little the name of mead changes around the world. In Germany it is Meth, in Greece it is Methu, in India it is called Madhu, in Ireland it was called Mid, and in Lithuania it is Medus.

Old Cures

Honey was often used to disguise the taste of unpleasant herbs and had the added benefit of enhancing the effect of the herbs with its own positive qualities.

Burnt alum was added to pounded **bistort** (*Polygonum bistorta*) and **pellitory** (*Parietaria officinalis*) in honey to make a paste and used as a toothache cure by packing it into the cavity.

Honey and **garlic** (*Allium sativum*) were mixed as a cure for asthma, bronchitis, tuberculosis, and whooping cough.

Mousear (*Hieracium pilosella*) was infused in honey as a treatment for relieving whooping cough.

In the eighteenth century the British government once paid a woman the sum of £5,000 for her secret cure for bladder stones. This consisted of **parsley seeds** beaten up with snails in their shells and mixed with honey!

Poplar leaves still in bud, bruised and mixed with honey, were used to treat poor eyesight.

Culpepper prescribed rue boiled in equal amounts of wine and honey as a treatment for worms.

Hollowing out a large **radish** and filling it with honey was the way to make radish juice. After three hours the honey infused with radish juice was removed and used to treat coughs and hoarse throats.

The Romans made a mixture called **oxmel**, which consisted of lettuce preserved in honey and vinegar. This was used for constipation, insomnia, pain relief, and poor lactation.

Melrosette was a syrup made by simmering finely chopped red rose petals in honey until it turned red and smelled sweet. It was used to cleanse the body internally.

Honey Recipes
Face Packs

One teaspoon honey, one teaspoon glycerine or sour cream, and one raw egg yolk.

For oily skin add one teaspoon honey to one teaspoon apple cider vinegar or lemon juice.

Hand Lotion

Dissolve one dessertspoon honey, one dessertspoon glycerine, two tablespoons of witch hazel, and two tablespoons vegetable oil into a small quantity of warm water, then add a dessertspoon of fine oatmeal.

Parsley Honey

This is made by adding a large handful of chopped and washed parsley to a pan with 800 milliliters of boiling water. Boil until the quantity is reduced to a third of the original and strain. Then add 500 grams of pure honey and boil again for fifteen minutes. The resulting parsley honey is then used to treat indigestion and for heart and kidney problems.

Barefoot in the Wheel: Create a Sacred Garden

❧ by Patti Wigington ❧

Go back thousands of years and you'll find sacred circles in just about any civilization. From the standing stones of Scotland and France to the labyrinths of ancient Rome, from the mystical medicine wheels of the American west to the feng shui Zen garden, the circle is a space with no beginning and no end. It's a space in which positive energy can be retained, and negative can be repelled. A circle is a place for introspection, thought, meditation, and harmony.

What is it about the circle that is sacred? The Hopewell culture of the Ohio Valley understood its magic, and their great earthworks, which still exist today, celebrate the circle. The Native Americans of the Great Plains knew how important the circle was, and built the Big Horn Medicine Wheel in Wyoming and the Moose Medicine Wheel in Canada. The Celts left behind mysterious stone circles all over the British Isles and Western Europe. Although Stonehenge is the most famous of these standing stone circles, there are literally hundreds of megalithic monuments scattered through England, Scotland, Wales, Ireland, France, and Italy.

The circle represents, to many of us, the pathway that is the spiritual journey of life. We are born, we live, we die, and then we are reborn once more. Look at the many circular designs we see in nature. When a tree falls, what do you see in the trunk? Rings, each representing a year in the life. Examine a seashell, or a seed, or a flower. The circle is always present.

The philosopher Aristotle said, "In all things of nature, there is something marvelous." How right he was. Our ancestors knew that the gifts of nature transcended the physical. The land was more than just a place to grow vegetables, more than a patch of dirt with some leaves growing out of it. For them, a garden was a sacred and holy place, a place where the soul and spirit could thrive together.

There is something about plunging our hands into the dirt and watching things grow that calls out to us as spiritual beings. Gardening is a way to immerse ourselves in the changing of the seasons and the pathway of life. By developing a garden into a sacred circle, you allow yourself all the benefits that nature has to offer. Balance, renewal, and order are all part of the cycle of growth, both physical and spiritual.

Many ancient sacred spaces are vanishing as the sites once revered by our ancestors are replaced with strip malls and coffee shops. In a modern setting, people often have trouble finding a space they can consider sacred and special. With an increasingly urban landscape, it can be difficult to find a place that is quiet and peaceful. Often, the most earth-centered place we have access to is in our own yard. With a little planning and some hard work, you can create a circle garden, and build a sacred space of your own.

It's All About Location

Look at some of the best-known ancient circles. Stonehenge, the Big Horn Medicine Wheel, the Hopewell Mound City—all have one thing in common. All were placed at those sites for a reason. Whether it was because the spot was a place of natural spiritual resonance, or for celestial sky-watching, or because the site just seemed right for ritual work, all were very carefully planned out and designed.

Your sacred garden circle should be placed with as much effort as our ancestors used. How much property you have to work with will, of course, have some bearing on your location. If you're living in an apartment or condo, or have a small yard, that's also going to limit your choices. However, no matter how much—or how little—space you have to dedicate to your garden, it deserves attention and thought from you.

Go out in your yard and stand there for a moment. Try to pick a time of day that is quiet and peaceful. Sunrise is the perfect hour for examining your land—it's still pretty tranquil then, and if you're lucky, the kids are still asleep. If you're more of a night owl—and you can wander outside without tripping over objects in the dark—go out then.

Start by strolling the perimeter of your property. Walk all the way around it, preferably in a clockwise direction, the same path that the sun follows. As you walk, imagine a large circle. Envision it growing in your mind. Does it take the shape of a labyrinth or spiral? A simple ring around an open center? Is it perhaps a wheel with many spokes, or is it divided into four quadrants?

If you live in an apartment or don't have your own land, never fear. You can still create a sacred garden circle on your balcony with the use of containers. Imagine your terrace decorated with a ring of lovely pots, each overflowing with green herbs and flowers.

As you walk your property, reflect on which location feels best. The earth has natural vibrations within, and in a meditative state, you'll be able to say, "Oh, this is the perfect spot!" with little to no trouble. Carefully consider the chosen site. Do you want to be able to see it from your house, or would you prefer it be some distance away? Is the neighbors' swing set close enough to bother you when the kids are playing? Is it in a location that's easy to get to, or will you have to move the patio furniture to enjoy full use of the garden? What about that tree in the yard's west corner? Can you develop your garden around it?

Your sacred garden circle can be any size at all, from a simple tabletop tray to a thirty-foot ring of stones in the field behind your house. Get some graph paper and, before you start pulling up earth, map out the design and dimensions of your garden. Will it be a solid circle, or will paths crisscross the center? Perhaps it will take the form of that spiral you envisioned earlier, or maybe it will be a small circle with room for a statue or bench in the middle. Whatever you choose, be sure you draw it before you dig it.

Thanking Your Mother

Once you've designed your layout, there's an important step to take before you go mucking about in the soil. The earth is a sacred thing, and if you're going to take advantage of her gifts, it's nice to offer something in return. Your yard is something to approach with reverence like any other sacred space, so now is a good time to perform a blessing ritual around the site. The blessing may invoke one element, or all four. It's your choice.

Make an offering that returns to the earth what it once produced. Sprinkle cornmeal or sage around the circle, birdseed, or even tobacco. As you do this, offer a song or prayer of thanks to the earth. If you feel uncomfortable speaking or chanting out loud, it's OK to do it silently. [**Note**: Although salt is often used to represent the element of earth, don't use it in this situation. It will damage the soil you are preparing to plant.]

You can also perform a ritual called asperging, in which blessed water is sprinkled around the site. The best asperging water is rainwater collected in a small bowl. However, if you haven't had a chance to gather rainwater—or just live in a dry area—you can make your own blessed water by combining spring water with a little bit of lemon juice.

For an air-oriented consecration, do a ritual smudging for your garden circle. The Native Americans used cedar and sage bound together to purify an area. Light a smudge stick, available at nearly every New Age or Wiccan shop, and walk the space so that the smoke is dispersed throughout the area. In lieu of smudge sticks, burn some incense or dried herbs on a charcoal disc instead.

Another option is to walk the perimeter of the circle with a candle. As you do this, move slowly and meditatively, thinking of all the plants you will be able to grow with the power of the fiery sun above. You can do any or all of these blessings with your new garden. The point is, the earth is a gift that Nature bestows upon us, and we're fortunate to be able to use it. Try to show your appreciation.

Digging in the Dirt

Once you've marked out the outline of your garden, you can start digging. With each spadeful of soil you turn over, think about the rich black earth you are uncovering, and the strength your seedlings will gather from it. Don't throw away all those rocks you dig up, either. Stones make a perfect natural border for a garden, so save them in a pile until you're ready to outline the beds. Not only do they delineate the physical space, but they're also a potent source of power.

Part of being a successful gardener is knowing what kind of soil your area has. Healthy soil with equal proportions of sand, clay, and silt will promote healthy plant growth. To test your dirt, simply pick up a handful and squeeze it together. If it clumps together, keeping its shape, then your soil is probably good to use. Soil that is too dry or sandy will crumble apart.

You might also want to get a soil test kit from your local garden supply store to learn the pH factor of your dirt. If your soil is too acidic, it can be counterbalanced by adding such things as crushed eggshells and seashells, or powdered lime into the top few inches of dirt. Dirt that is too alkaline can be remedied by adding in coffee grounds and decayed leaves.

For the most part, unless the soil is severely unbalanced, you can usually make just about anything grow by using organic gardening methods. Such techniques as avoiding chemical pesticides, loosening the soil, and adding organic materials all will help your soil become strong and fertile. Regularly composting with grass clippings, newspaper, and kitchen scraps will add nutrients to the earth and bring you a bountiful garden.

Gardening by the Moon

Many ancient cultures believed that a Witch's power came, in part, from the Moon, and based their planting and harvesting schedules on its phases. Lunar cycles can be closely connected with the fertility of the earth.

During the first quarter, plant your annuals. This is also a good time to get your herbs into the ground, as well as green vegetables such as beans, lettuce, and broccoli. Rounded—Moon-shaped—crops seem to do best when planted during the second quarter. This is the time to put in your squashes, tomatoes, and melons.

In the third quarter, it's time to get your root crops in. Carrots, potatoes, and garlic do especially well when planted during this phase of the Moon, as do fruit-bearing bushes like strawberries. Finally, in the fourth quarter of the Moon cycle, let the soil take a break. Give it time to recover and rejuvenate. Now is the time to pull those stray weeds that have popped up, add some healthy organic fertilizer, and put in the compost.

How Does Your Garden Grow?

So you've drawn it out and dug it up . . . now it's time to figure out what goes in there. What sort of garden are you interested in? What plants call to you? Do you have only a few moments each week to devote to gardening, or can you spend hours each day tending plants and sticking your fingers in the dirt? Would you like your garden to grow edible plants, such as vegetables and herbs, or do you like fragrant flowers and long trails of ivy? Remember, this is your sacred space, so fill it with the things that bring you the most joy and serenity.

If you are doing a medicine-wheel style garden, the focus should be on the four primary directions—north, south, east, and west. East is the beginning of each day, the space in your garden that the sun greets first, and can be thought of as a place for new beginnings. West, on the other hand, is a place of completion and maturity, the end of each day's cycle. North is the direction of moonlight and stars, the endless cool night, and the wisdom of our ancestors. South holds the secrets of youth, warmth, and understanding.

In a classic medicine-wheel garden based on Native American traditions, plants are selected according to the colors of each cardinal direction. For example, east would be filled with a collection of yellow and gold plants—rue, witch hazel, St. John's wort, and summer squash, just to name a few. West is represented by reds and magentas, which makes it the perfect quadrant to plant your strawberries, chili peppers, tomatoes, and bergamot.

Blues and purples are the colors of the south, so here is the perfect place for your echinacea, blueberries, basil, and lobelias, while sweetgrass, cucumbers, and sage symbolize the whites and silvers of the north.

Perhaps you'd like to plant a garden that brings you closer to one or more of the four elements. Follow the same layout as the medicine wheel, but select your plants based upon their corresponding elements.

For example, earth-oriented plants include beets, corn, mugwort, peas, and potatoes. Air is represented by many of the edible plants such as clover, dandelion, anise, the mint family, parsley, and sage. Fire plants such as allspice, dill, mustard, and onion all work well together, as do the water plants—grapes, gourds, raspberries, and cucumbers.

If you're new to gardening or don't have a lot of space to work with, choose three or four kinds of plant for each quadrant, and then add a few each year as space permits. With either a traditional medicine-wheel garden or an elemental garden, be sure to leave paths between the quadrants, as well as a space in the center where you can sit and meditate.

Perhaps you've decided that a spiral or labyrinth shape would be the best to represent your sacred space. Consider arranging your crops so that early bloomers are at the outside of the spiral, working toward the middle, so that the last plants to bloom are in the center. As your herbs, flowers, and vegetables grow and bloom, so will your spiritual journey.

Another option that works nicely in a spiral layout is that of edible plants and flowers. As each season progresses, the growth will be consumed until you finally reach the center. Begin your spiral with low-growers like chamomile and clover, and gradually increasing the height of the plants as you progress to the middle. Add daisies and lilacs—yes, they're edible!—mixed in with strawberries and cherry tomato bushes. When you get to the center of the spiral, your meditation zone, place your tallest plants—pole beans and sweet peas, tulips, lavender and heather. Remember that if the idea of nibbling flowers doesn't appeal to you, they can be harvested and dried for use in decorating, potpourri, or incense.

Finally, if you've chosen to go with just a simple ring for your garden, one of the most beautiful arrangements is the flower clock. First designed by Swedish botanist Carolus Linnaeus in 1751, this garden incorporates plants that bloom at different times of day. Flowers like dandelion and evening primrose open early, even before sunrise, while chickweed and marigolds don't pop open until later in the morning. California poppies and chicory open in the early afternoon. Using this layout, you can actually tell the time of day by looking at your flowers.

Making the Space Your Own

Having a sacred circle garden is one thing, but claiming the space as your own is another. Personalize your garden, just like you do the inside of your home. Add statuary, gazing balls, wind chimes, or a fountain if you like. Perhaps all you want is a few stones to sit on, or a quiet bench where you can take time to reflect. The point is, it's your space, and so it needs to speak to you.

You may wish to incorporate a small table as an altar for ritual work. You can use a small household table or keep it natural with a large stump or a flat stone. If you honor a particular god or goddess, your sacred garden circle is a perfect place to make offerings to them. Add crystals, large stones, seashells, or interesting bits of wood depending on the tradition you follow.

Once the harvest season has come and gone, it's important not to forget about your garden during the cold weather. Be sure to clean out the beds and remove dead growth before winter arrives. Many of your plants will not die, but will instead lie dormant for a few months, so go out and visit them regularly. Tend them as carefully during the offseason as you did in the spring and summer.

If your family makes an annual Yule log, save the ashes and mix them into the dirt of your garden the following spring. You can also revitalize the soil by following one of the customs of the ancient Romans. Blend together equal parts olive oil, honey, and milk. Add this to your crop beds for fertility and enrichment.

Bless your garden, and be thankful for it. When the pressures of daily life get to be overwhelming, or your job and family are stressing you out, you will have a place where you can sit and meditate, reflect, and enjoy the gifts of the earth. It will be a place that brings you closer not only to nature but to your gods as well.

It will be a place that is yours, and because it is yours, it will be sacred.

For Further Reading

Dugan, Ellen. *Garden Witchery*. Llewellyn Worldwide, 2003.

Genders, Roy. *The Complete Book of Herbs and Herb Growing*. Sterling Publishing, 1980.

Kloss, Jethro. *Back to Eden*. Benedict Lust Publications, 1971.

Lennox-Boyd, Arabella. *Traditional English Gardens*. Orion Books, 2003.

Telesco, Patricia. *Gardening with the Goddess*. New Page Books 2001.

The Faerie Triad

Many trees are associated with the realm of Faerie in Celtic mythology. Faerie beings are said to flit among tree branches and inhabit hollowed-out trunks. They may bring a tree to life or move a tree from its normal position, confusing hapless travelers. Folklore and legend attribute the poem *Cad Goddeu*, *The Battle of the Trees*, to the Celtic poet Taliesin. In this poem, trees come to life and fight a battle (with varying skill). *Cad Goddeu* highlights the animistic elements, where animals and objects display human characteristics, of ancient Celtic beliefs. With this poem in the collective mindset of the people, faith in faerie tree sprites becomes a natural progression of cultural identity.

The Faerie Triad can be found in the phrase "By Oak and Ash and

Thorn," three trees of extreme power and might. When a grove or copse of oak trees, ash trees, and hawthorn trees grows together, intermingling their roots and energy, there you will see the faeries. These trees, with their branches in the sky and their roots underground, form a conduit between the Underworld (of faeries and mythology) and the Upperworld (of heaven and spirituality). Living in the Middle World (of earth and materialism) like men and women, these trees are physical representatives of humanity's reliance upon and connection to other places beyond the mist, the Otherworld of ancestors, faeries, and deities. The Faerie Triad is but one passageway into that Otherworld.

The Faerie Triad gains its power because of the trees' interdependence and synergy. Stumble upon only two of the trees, and you will simply be in the forest, with nary a faerie in sight. All three trees need to be present for the Path to Faerie to be revealed. In order to better understand the significance of these trees, it is necessary to know how each is independently connected to Faerieland.

The Oak Tree

The oak, quick moving, / Before him, tremble heaven and earth. / A valiant door-keeper against an enemy / His name is considered.
—*Cad Goddeu*, lines 117-120, Robert Williams, trans.

No other tree is so closely aligned to the ancient Celts as the mighty oak. The oak was considered one of the most sacred trees of the Druids, the spiritual and scholarly leaders of Celtic society. It is said that no spiritual conclave could take place except in the presence of an oak or, at least, an oak leaf. The Druids taught their young apprentices under the boughs of the oak tree. The very term "Druid" may derive from the Welsh words derw (oak) and ydd (a part of). In fact, the Gaelic words for oak (derw in Welsh and daur in Old Irish) may come from the Sanskrit word for door, duir. This Indo-European connection may help to explain the door reference in the *Cad Goddeu*, as quoted above.

In the nineteenth century, when writers, linguists, and cultural anthropologists were collecting the oral history of Ireland, Wales, and England, the Druids re-emerged in relation to the oak as the Welsh faeries, the Tylwyth Teg or "Fair Family." Many people believed that the faeries, or Tylwyth Teg, were actually the spirits of Druids who, although non-Christians, were too good to cast into Hell and so wandered freely on earth. It is quite common for the general term "faeries" to be expanded to include the spirits and souls of ancestors who are no longer living. In Cornwall, faeries (or pixies, as they term them) and ghosts are often interchangeable in the stories, inhabiting the same places and performing similar feats. The English folkrhyme "Fairy folks are in old Oaks" underscores the connection between faeries and spirits since, in the ancient past, the souls of the dead frequently took up residence inside a tree.

Another oak that serves as a channel for spirits is the Merlin's Oak in Carmarthen, Wales. Legend claims that the mythical magician Merlin, of the High Court of King Arthur, declared that when the oak tree fell, so too would the town of Carmarthen. The tree died in 1856 but was still standing (albeit with the help of cement and fencing) until 1978. The stump still rests in the town's civic hall, a testament to the power of Merlin, folk belief, and the mighty oak.

Tales and legends of the Land of Faerie follow the example set by the townspeople of Carmarthen, giving the oak tree mythical, magical power. Numerous stories, including the drinking tale *Faeries or no Faeries*, tell of wayfarers who stumble across a troop of the "good people" frolicking and playing around the trunk of an oak tree. (In *Faeries or No Faeries*, they turn into mushrooms upon closer inspection. Tricky faeries!) Hiding in an oak tree or sleeping against an oak tree in order to see the faeries are also common plot elements in Irish and British fairy tales. In fact, faeries appear to enjoy the oak tree so much that they cultivate forests of them in the "Happy Otherworld," Tir na Nog, or Faerieland.

Tir na Nog is populated by many types of faeries; however, the most well-known are those in the High Court of Faerie, the Sidhe or the Tuatha de Danann. The Tuatha de Danann are known as the children (or people) of Danu, an ancient Irish mythological figure who may derive from the Hindu water Goddess Danu, reflecting the Proto-Indo origins of the Celtic peoples. Danu's (sometime) partner in Celtic lands is the Dagda, an ancient God or faery king (depending on your point of view) who brings abundance, fertility, and good humor to the land. His tree is the oak, a forest of which grows at the heart of his home at Newgrange. He owns a harp called Dur-da-Bla or the Oak of Two Blossoms and he protects the Cauldron of Murias. The cauldron is one of four sacred faerie items that the Tuatha de Danann brought with them when they set sail for Ireland. Murias, in Irish legend, was one of four cities (along with Gorias, Falias, and Finias) from which the Tuatha de Danann hailed.

In one Irish legend, a shining being, most likely a member of the Tuatha de Danann (in some stories the being is a giant named Treochair), arrives at the court of King Conig at Tara with a single tree branch bearing apples, nuts, and acorns. The king planted each of the fruits from this mystical branch and they grew into the Three Ancient Marvel Trees of Erinn, or Old Ireland: the oak tree, the apple tree, and the hazel tree. The shining being claimed that these fruits would satisfy all of humanity's needs, connecting the fruit to the faery king, Dagda, and the Cauldron of Murias or the Cauldron of Plenty.

The Ash Tree

Cruel the ash tree / Turns not aside a foot-breath, / Straight at the heart runs he.
—*Cad Goddeu*, verse 14, Robert Graves' Interpretation.

The ash tree, like Tir na Nog or the Land of Faerie, is surrounded by confusion, mystery, and acrimony, for it is not included in every translation of the *Cad Goddeu*. Robert Graves, in his mythological treatise *The White Goddess*, re-wrote the epic

Battle of the Trees, adding his own significance and importance. The ash tree is barely mentioned in the D.W. Nash translation, as "Cruel the gloomy ash," and not at all in the Williams edition. Graves, layering modern research on ancient text, forges an identity for the ash out of thin air, out of the mists of Faerie.

Yet the transformation of the ash tree in the *Cad Goddeu* reflects its very nature in ancient Celtic thought. It was a tree that forced inner change while maintaining a strong outer appearance. In both Celtic and Norse mythology, the tree of life, the physical link between the upper, middle, and lower realms of existence, is an ash tree. The Norse belief system may seem irrelevant in an article concerning faeries but it is a fact that Northern peoples settled in England and Ireland. Over time, their myths mixed with the Celtic legends to form new stories that contained lore from both sources.

The Norse Tree of Life, Yggdrasil, stands at the center of the universe, uniting all of the worlds through its sturdy trunk, swaying branches, and strong roots. In Norse cosmology, the universe consists of nine worlds (instead of the Celtic three) that rest among the branches and the root system of the giant ash. Of these nine worlds, three house beings traditionally associated with the Realm of Faerie. Giants, contentious and daring, live in the land of Jotunheim directly above the Spring of Mimir. They continually harass the deities of the North, striving to attain worldly possessions (usually somebody else's). They are the forces of nature and of psyche that force change through their actions. In Svartalfheim, the dark elves and dwarves work hard, protective of their families and communities. Comfortable in the dark, they are usually found in deep forests or in caves, underground. The dark elves and dwarves are known for their abilities to work magic and metal. The final Faerie branch on Yggdrasil is Ljossalfheim, the land of the light elves. These beings are spiritual in nature and help humans attain more esoteric goals and desires. They understand the importance of thought in shaping our lives. With three realms dedicated to Faeries, it is obvious that Yggdrasil, the giant ash tree, is one of many ways to enter the Otherworld of Tir na Nog.

The concept of the World Tree as a pathway to Faerieland is continued in old folktales that surround the area around the Irish lake, Lough Gur. The Lough is thought to be an enchanted lake that dries up every seven years to reveal its true nature. During this time, a large tree, very much like the World Tree of Scandinavian myth, grows straight and true from the lake bottom. It is covered in a green cloth and a single woman sits underneath it, knitting, serving as the tree's guardian. (The woman under the tree has close ties to the three Norns who sit amid the roots of Yggdrasil, weaving. Both the Irish woman of the Lough and the Norns perform magic using cloth, bringing dissimilar strands of yarn or wool together to form one complete item.) Stories claim that when a child is stolen by the faeries of Munster, it is to Lough Gur that he is brought, in order to enter the enchanted state of Faerie.

Lough Gur is in the County of Limerick, in the Province of Munster, near Cnoc Aine or the Hill of Aine. Aine is a member of the Tuatha de Danann, a Faerie Queen who has been spotted leading faerie processions along her hill on Midsummer's Eve. She is said to have been sitting along the banks of Lough Gur when her connection to Faerie, her cloak, was seized by Maurice, the first Earl of the Fitzgerald family in Munster. Legend claims that Aine served as his wife and even bore him a son, Gearoid Iarla. Gearoid proved to be as magical as his mother and, upon popping into and out of a bottle at his father's dinner party, freed himself and his mother from his father's hold. (Maurice showed astonishment at Gearoid's antics, breaking a taboo placed on him by Aine.) Gearoid scampered into the waters of Lough Gur and is said to live there in an underwater palace. Every seven years, when the enchantment is lifted, he rides out on a white stallion shod with silver shoes. Local legends from the seventeenth, eighteenth, and nineteenth centuries claim that Gearoid will return to Ireland at the time of his family's greatest need, and several stories circulate around Munster telling of hapless wanderers or blacksmiths that have met and conversed with the famed Gearoid Iarla.

Gearoid Iarla's role as a protector and defender of his family links him to the strong and flexible ash tree. Ash was the wood most commonly used by ancient Celts for arrow shafts and spears. The tree could be cruel, utilizing the violence of battle to effect change and transformation. Ash is often described as a "check on peace" in ancient Irish manuscripts, giving it a decidedly warriorlike nature. So it is not surprising that three of the five sacred, protective trees of Ireland are ash trees. The Tree of Tortu (or Munga), the Tree of Dathi, and the Branching Tree of Uisnech protected the actual land of Ireland. They were praised for their sweeping branches and strong trunks—for their ability to shelter the people of Ireland. Eventually, in 665 AD, the trees were cut down to represent the end of Paganism in Ireland and the rising of a Christian nation. However, the power of the ash tree remained in the collective mindset of the people. Saint Patrick adopted the power of the ash tree and used its wood as his staff to drive the snakes (a symbol of Pagan beliefs) out of Ireland. Thus, the power of the ash tree lives on.

The Hawthorn Tree

The hawthorn, surrounded by prickles,
With pain at his hand
  —*Cad Goddeu*, lines 106-107, Robert Williams, trans.

Painful prickles and sharp thorns await the unwary traveler who thrusts his hand into a hawthorn bush or tree without thought or contemplation. As the *Cad Goddeu* suggests, the small and spindly hawthorn is a great protector. It is said to guard burial mounds, the dwelling places of the Sidhe or Faery. The word Sidhe literally means mound in Gaelic. When the Tuatha de Danann were driven out of Ireland by the Sons of Mil, legend states that they receded into the hills. In essence, they retreated into the very land itself. The idea of the Realm of Faery resting inside the ground is common. In Scotland, clergyman Robert Kirk espoused this belief in the seventeenth century, which has inspired numerous modern spiritualists and faery enthusiasts.

One of the most famous faery mounds in the British Isles is Glastonbury Tor, in the town of Glastonbury, England. Glastonbury has long been a seat of mysticism but its connection to Faery rests in the dark-faced Faery King Gwynn ap Nudd. Gwynn ap Nudd makes his home under the Tor. In many legends, Gwynn ap Nudd leads the tempestuous whirlwind known as The Wild Hunt. (The Wild Hunt is linked to other mythological figures as well, such as Cernunnos, Herne, and Woden/ Odin.) The Wild Hunt flies through the skies in the dark half of the year (usually autumn and winter), collecting the souls of those who have died. Faeries, ghosts, and apparitions trail behind Gwynn ap Nudd on magical flying horses, surrounded by a cacophony of barking hounds. The restless pack of dogs is known as Cwn Annwn or the Hounds of Annwn, and like many animals from the Land of Faerie, they are white with red ears. This coloration was a technique used by Celtic bards to suggest the touch of Faerie, without actually calling down the graces (either good or ill) of the "fair folk." Saint Brigid was sustained by milk from a white cow with red ears, when she couldn't eat anything else as a baby. And the hawthorn tree gifts the land with white five-petaled flowers in the spring and blood-red berries in the autumn, a sure sign of Faerie contact.

The most famous hawthorn tree in Glastonbury (and arguably in the British Isles) is the "Holy Thorn." Legend states that Joseph of Arimathea, merchant and acquaintance of Jesus of Nazareth, sailed to England shortly after the death of Jesus. At that time, Glastonbury was by the water and when Joseph stepped off the boat, his staff sunk into the ground and became the celebrated "Holy Thorn" (or hawthorn) of Glastonbury. (Other stories claim that Joseph brought the tree sapling with him and planted it himself.) However the tree came into existence, it rooted itself deep into British Isles folklore. This hawthorn tree was thought to be magical because it flowered two times during the year, once in the spring and then again at Yuletide or Christmas. (Botanists now believe that the tree was a variety from Greece, which typically flowers during those times.) Since the tree was seen as sacred and a direct link to the Otherworld, Glastonbury Abbey was built next to it and became a site for pilgrimages and adoration. Unfortunately, Cromwell's army chopped down the original Glastonbury thorn during the Reformation. However, numerous hawthorns thrive in Britain, thought to be descendents of the original tree through the transplanting of cuttings. Today, one such hawthorn grows in Glastonbury, west of the center of town, on Wearyall Hill.

It is no wonder that Cromwell's Puritan reign in England lasted such a short time, since he chose to ignore the taboo against cutting down a hawthorn tree. In Ireland, according to legend, a person who chops down a hawthorn tree will lose his cattle (or financial security), his children, and all well-being. Lady Wilde, Irish poet, translator, and mother of Irish playwright Oscar Wilde, records that the favorite resting place and dwelling for Irish faeries is the hawthorn tree and that the peasantry would rather die than cut down one of these sacred ancient icons. When John DeLorean planned to expand his business to include the site of an Irish mound with a single hawthorn, the construction workers refused to destroy the tree. Undeterred by their admonishments, DeLorean eventually bulldozed the tree into the ground himself! The faeries undoubtedly felt much satisfaction when he experienced financial devastation shortly thereafter. (Is that laughter I hear on the wind?)

If faeries can destroy on a whim, they can also provide abundance. One popular Irish folk story tells of two young men who were plowing a field in which a single hawthorn grew. One boy created a circle around the tree, indicating that it should be left alone. Immediately he was rewarded for honoring the ways of Faerie. Some stories state that a table overflowing with food appeared within the circle. After the young man ate of the food, he was wise ever after.

While hawthorn branches serve as a favorite place for faeries to play, the trunks and roots of the tree provide a direct pathway to Tir na Nog or the Land of Faerie. Isolated hawthorn trees are known as "faery trees," and are haunted by ghosts and apparitions, Otherworldly beings that are interchangeable for faeries, in some stories. Thomas the Rhymer and Sir Crawline, main characters in Scottish ballads of the thirteenth century, both attend to a single hawthorn tree in the wilds of Scotland in order to be visited by the "good neighbors." Single hawthorn trees that grow near a well or a natural spring are especially magical, having been planted by the faeries themselves. In the past, people would tie bits of cloth to such a sacred hawthorn tree, sending their wishes to the faeries, as well as to the spiritual Upperworld. Even today, ribbons can be seen fluttering in the breeze, securely tied to the branches of a lone hawthorn tree.

The Faerie Triad

And so we come full circle, which is only fitting in a discussion of Faery, returning to the growth of three dissimilar trees in close proximity. Finding a Faery Triad will not be easy as hawthorn trees fare best in open terrain, isolated and alone, or grouped together as a hedge while oaks thrive in dense forests, clumped in copses, in the shadows of the woods. The ash, flexible, mutable, useful for ships or spears, links the oak and the hawthorn together as it can grow in wild woodlands or in cultivated towns and parks. The variable nature of the ash tree, the steadfast attitude of the oak, and the protective stance of the hawthorn resemble the many layers of the folklore and legends of the British Isles. Faerie is as changeable as the wind and as fleeting as a moment of time. Yet certain taboos and warnings remain through time and space, through the advent of automobiles and computers. (Just ask Mr. DeLorean!) The Oak, Ash, and Thorn evoke the wonder and mysticism at the heart of the

Sidhe, the Tuatha de Danann, the Tylwyth Teg. They suggest a connection between the world of humankind and the world of faerie, for without all three trees, the magic is lost. So too is our wonder lost when the Realm of Faerie recedes from our collective beliefs.

An old wives' tale from Cornwall states that if you hold a dried leaf from each of the oak, ash, and hawthorn trees, and chant a poem, you will be able to call up the faeries. (In particular a certain troll at the Newlyn Tolcarne, considered to be a Puck or Robin Goodfellow figure in the English Midlands.) Unfortunately, the poem has been lost but that does not mean that the magic is gone. Try it for yourself. Gather some leaves, find a poem (or create one of your own) and see what appears through the mists of Tir na Nog.

For Further Reading

Evans-Wentz, W.Y. *The Fairy-Faith in Celtic Counties*. New York: H. Froude, 1911. Found online at: http://www.sacred-texts.com/index.htm.

Gifford, Jane. *The Wisdom of Trees*. New York: Sterling Publishing Company, 2001.

Hopman, Ellen Evert. *Tree Medicine, Tree Magic*. Blaine, WA: Phoenix Publishing, 1991.

Mountfort, Paul Rhys. *Ogam – The Celtic Oracle of the Trees*. Rochester, VT: Destiny Books, 2002.

Spence, Lewis. *The Fairy Tradition in Britain*. Montana: Kessinger Publishing Company, re-print.

The
Quarters and
Signs of the
Moon and
Moon
Tables

The Quarters and Signs
of the Moon

Everyone has seen the Moon wax and wane through a period of approximately twenty-nine-and-a-half days. This circuit from New Moon to Full Moon and back again is called the lunation cycle. The cycle is divided into parts called quarters or phases. There are several methods by which this can be done, and the system used in the *Herbal Almanac* may not correspond to those used in other almanacs.

The Quarters

First Quarter

The first quarter begins at the New Moon, when the Sun and Moon are in the same place, or conjunct. (This means that the Sun and Moon are in the same degree of the same sign.) The Moon is not visible at first, since it rises at the same time as the Sun. The New Moon is the time of new beginnings, beginnings of projects that favor growth, externalization of activities, and the growth of ideas. The first quarter is the time of germination, emergence, beginnings, and outwardly directed activity.

Second Quarter

The second quarter begins halfway between the New Moon and the Full Moon, when the Sun and Moon are at right angles, or a ninety-degree square to each other. This half Moon rises around noon and sets around midnight, so it can be seen in the western sky during the first half of the night. The second quarter is the time of growth and articulation of things that already exist.

Third Quarter

The third quarter begins at the Full Moon, when the Sun and Moon are opposite one another and the full light of the Sun can shine on the full sphere of the Moon. The round Moon can be seen rising in the east at sunset, and then rising a little later each evening. The Full Moon stands for illumination, fulfillment, culmination, completion, drawing inward, unrest, emotional expressions, and hasty actions leading to failure. The third quarter is a time of maturity, fruition, and the assumption of the full form of expression.

Fourth Quarter

The fourth quarter begins about halfway between the Full Moon and New Moon, when the Sun and Moon are again at ninety degrees, or square. This decreasing Moon rises at midnight and can be seen in the east during the last half of the night, reaching the overhead position just about as the Sun rises. The fourth quarter is a time of disintegration, drawing back for reorganization and reflection.

The Signs

Moon in Aries

Moon in Aries is good for starting things, but lacking in staying power. Things occur rapidly, but also quickly pass.

Moon in Taurus

With Moon in Taurus, things begun during this sign last the longest and tend to increase in value. Things begun now become habitual and hard to alter.

Moon in Gemini

Moon in Gemini is an inconsistent position for the Moon, characterized by a lot of talk. Things begun now are easily changed by outside influences.

Moon in Cancer

Moon in Cancer stimulates emotional rapport between people. It pinpoints need and supports growth and nurturance.

Moon in Leo

Moon in Leo accents showmanship, being seen, drama, recreation, and happy pursuits. It may be concerned with praise and subject to flattery.

Moon in Virgo

Moon in Virgo favors accomplishment of details and commands from higher up, while discouraging independent thinking.

Moon in Libra

Moon in Libra increases self-awareness. It favors self-examination and interaction with others, but discourages spontaneous initiative.

Moon in Scorpio

Moon in Scorpio increases awareness of psychic power. It precipitates psychic crises and ends connections thoroughly.

Moon in Sagittarius

Moon in Sagittarius encourages expansionary flights of imagination and confidence in the flow of life.

Moon in Capricorn

Moon in Capricorn increases awareness of the need for structure, discipline, and organization. Institutional activities are favored.

Moon in Aquarius

Moon in Aquarius favors activities that are unique and individualistic, concern for humanitarian needs and society as a whole, and improvements that can be made.

Moon in Pisces

During Moon in Pisces, energy withdraws from the surface of life and hibernates within, secretly reorganizing and realigning.

January Moon Table

Date	Sign	Element	Nature	Phase
1 Mon	Gemini	Air	Barren	2nd
2 Tue 10:14 am	Cancer	Water	Fruitful	2nd
3 Wed	Cancer	Water	Fruitful	Full 8:57 am
4 Thu 4:14 pm	Leo	Fire	Barren	3rd
5 Fri	Leo	Fire	Barren	3rd
6 Sat	Leo	Fire	Barren	3rd
7 Sun 1:18 am	Virgo	Earth	Barren	3rd
8 Mon	Virgo	Earth	Barren	3rd
9 Tue 1:15 pm	Libra	Air	Semi-fruitful	3rd
10 Wed	Libra	Air	Semi-fruitful	3rd
11 Thu	Libra	Air	Semi-fruitful	4th 7:44 am
12 Fri 2:08 am	Scorpio	Water	Fruitful	4th
13 Sat	Scorpio	Water	Fruitful	4th
14 Sun 1:11 pm	Sagittarius	Fire	Barren	4th
15 Mon	Sagittarius	Fire	Barren	4th
16 Tue 8:49 pm	Capricorn	Earth	Semi-fruitful	4th
17 Wed	Capricorn	Earth	Semi-fruitful	4th
18 Thu	Capricorn	Earth	Semi-fruitful	New 11:01 pm
19 Fri 1:15 am	Aquarius	Air	Barren	1st
20 Sat	Aquarius	Air	Barren	1st
21 Sun 3:48 am	Pisces	Water	Fruitful	1st
22 Mon	Pisces	Water	Fruitful	1st
23 Tue 5:52 am	Aries	Fire	Barren	1st
24 Wed	Aries	Fire	Barren	1st
25 Thu 8:28 am	Taurus	Earth	Semi-fruitful	2nd 6:01 pm
26 Fri	Taurus	Earth	Semi-fruitful	2nd
27 Sat 12:10 pm	Gemini	Air	Barren	2nd
28 Sun	Gemini	Air	Barren	2nd
29 Mon 5:16 pm	Cancer	Water	Fruitful	2nd
30 Tue	Cancer	Water	Fruitful	2nd
31 Wed	Cancer	Water	Fruitful	2nd

February Moon Table

Date	Sign	Element	Nature	Phase
1 Thu 12:14 am	Leo	Fire	Barren	2nd
2 Fri	Leo	Fire	Barren	Full 12:45 am
3 Sat 9:34 am	Virgo	Earth	Barren	3rd
4 Sun	Virgo	Earth	Barren	3rd
5 Mon 9:15 pm	Libra	Air	Semi-fruitful	3rd
6 Tue	Libra	Air	Semi-fruitful	3rd
7 Wed	Libra	Air	Semi-fruitful	3rd
8 Thu 10:09 am	Scorpio	Water	Fruitful	3rd
9 Fri	Scorpio	Water	Fruitful	3rd
10 Sat 10:01 pm	Sagittarius	Fire	Barren	4th 4:51 am
11 Sun	Sagittarius	Fire	Barren	4th
12 Mon	Sagittarius	Fire	Barren	4th
13 Tue 6:42 am	Capricorn	Earth	Semi-fruitful	4th
14 Wed	Capricorn	Earth	Semi-fruitful	4th
15 Thu 11:34 am	Aquarius	Air	Barren	4th
16 Fri	Aquarius	Air	Barren	4th
17 Sat 1:30 pm	Pisces	Water	Fruitful	1st 11:14 am
18 Sun	Pisces	Water	Fruitful	1st
19 Mon 2:06 pm	Aries	Fire	Barren	1st
20 Tue	Aries	Fire	Barren	1st
21 Wed 3:03 pm	Taurus	Earth	Semi-fruitful	1st
22 Thu	Taurus	Earth	Semi-fruitful	1st
23 Fri 5:42 pm	Gemini	Air	Barren	1st
24 Sat	Gemini	Air	Barren	2nd 2:56 am
25 Sun 10:47 pm	Cancer	Water	Fruitful	2nd
26 Mon	Cancer	Water	Fruitful	2nd
27 Tue	Cancer	Water	Fruitful	2nd
28 Wed 6:29 am	Leo	Fire	Barren	2nd

March Moon Table

Date	Sign	Element	Nature	Phase
1 Thu	Leo	Fire	Barren	2nd
2 Fri 4:32 pm	Virgo	Earth	Barren	2nd
3 Sat	Virgo	Earth	Barren	Full 6:17 pm
4 Sun	Virgo	Earth	Barren	3rd
5 Mon 4:25 am	Libra	Air	Semi-fruitful	3rd
6 Tue	Libra	Air	Semi-fruitful	3rd
7 Wed 5:16 pm	Scorpio	Water	Fruitful	3rd
8 Thu	Scorpio	Water	Fruitful	3rd
9 Fri	Scorpio	Water	Fruitful	3rd
10 Sat 5:37 am	Sagittarius	Fire	Barren	3rd
11 Sun	Sagittarius	Fire	Barren	4th 11:54 pm
12 Mon 4:34 pm	Capricorn	Earth	Semi-fruitful	4th
13 Tue	Capricorn	Earth	Semi-fruitful	4th
14 Wed 10:52 pm	Aquarius	Air	Barren	4th
15 Thu	Aquarius	Air	Barren	4th
16 Fri	Aquarius	Air	Barren	4th
17 Sat 1:30 am	Pisces	Water	Fruitful	4th
18 Sun	Pisces	Water	Fruitful	New 10:42 pm
19 Mon 1:41 am	Aries	Fire	Barren	1st
20 Tue	Aries	Fire	Barren	1st
21 Wed 1:15 am	Taurus	Earth	Semi-fruitful	1st
22 Thu	Taurus	Earth	Semi-fruitful	1st
23 Fri 2:06 am	Gemini	Air	Barren	1st
24 Sat	Gemini	Air	Barren	1st
25 Sun 5:49 am	Cancer	Water	Fruitful	2nd 2:16 pm
26 Mon	Cancer	Water	Fruitful	2nd
27 Tue 1:04 pm	Leo	Fire	Barren	2nd
28 Wed	Leo	Fire	Barren	2nd
29 Thu 11:27 pm	Virgo	Earth	Barren	2nd
30 Fri	Virgo	Earth	Barren	2nd
31 Sat	Virgo	Earth	Barren	2nd

April Moon Table

Date	Sign	Element	Nature	Phase
1 Sun 11:43 am	Libra	Air	Semi-fruitful	2nd
2 Mon	Libra	Air	Semi-fruitful	Full 1:15 pm
3 Tue	Libra	Air	Semi-fruitful	3rd
4 Wed 12:35 am	Scorpio	Water	Fruitful	3rd
5 Thu	Scorpio	Water	Fruitful	3rd
6 Fri 12:56 pm	Sagittarius	Fire	Barren	3rd
7 Sat	Sagittarius	Fire	Barren	3rd
8 Sun 11:36 pm	Capricorn	Earth	Semi-fruitful	3rd
9 Mon	Capricorn	Earth	Semi-fruitful	3rd
10 Tue	Capricorn	Earth	Semi-fruitful	4th 2:04 pm
11 Wed 7:23 am	Aquarius	Air	Barren	4th
12 Thu	Aquarius	Air	Barren	4th
13 Fri 11:38 am	Pisces	Water	Fruitful	4th
14 Sat	Pisces	Water	Fruitful	4th
15 Sun 12:46 pm	Aries	Fire	Barren	4th
16 Mon	Aries	Fire	Barren	4th
17 Tue 12:11 pm	Taurus	Earth	Semi-fruitful	New 7:36 am
18 Wed	Taurus	Earth	Semi-fruitful	1st
19 Thu 11:51 am	Gemini	Air	Barren	1st
20 Fri	Gemini	Air	Barren	1st
21 Sat 1:50 pm	Cancer	Water	Fruitful	1st
22 Sun	Cancer	Water	Fruitful	1st
23 Mon 7:38 pm	Leo	Fire	Barren	1st
24 Tue	Leo	Fire	Barren	2nd 2:35 am
25 Wed	Leo	Fire	Barren	2nd
26 Thu 5:24 am	Virgo	Earth	Barren	2nd
27 Fri	Virgo	Earth	Barren	2nd
28 Sat 5:44 pm	Libra	Air	Semi-fruitful	2nd
29 Sun	Libra	Air	Semi-fruitful	2nd
30 Mon	Libra	Air	Semi-fruitful	2nd

May Moon Table

Date	Sign	Element	Nature	Phase
1 Tue 6:41 am	Scorpio	Water	Fruitful	2nd
2 Wed	Scorpio	Water	Fruitful	Full 6:09 am
3 Thu 6:47 pm	Sagittarius	Fire	Barren	3rd
4 Fri	Sagittarius	Fire	Barren	3rd
5 Sat	Sagittarius	Fire	Barren	3rd
6 Sun 5:21 am	Capricorn	Earth	Semi-fruitful	3rd
7 Mon	Capricorn	Earth	Semi-fruitful	3rd
8 Tue 1:48 pm	Aquarius	Air	Barren	3rd
9 Wed	Aquarius	Air	Barren	3rd
10 Thu 7:31 pm	Pisces	Water	Fruitful	4th 12:27 am
11 Fri	Pisces	Water	Fruitful	4th
12 Sat 10:19 pm	Aries	Fire	Barren	4th
13 Sun	Aries	Fire	Barren	4th
14 Mon 10:48 pm	Taurus	Earth	Semi-fruitful	4th
15 Tue	Taurus	Earth	Semi-fruitful	4th
16 Wed 10:34 pm	Gemini	Air	Barren	New 3:27 pm
17 Thu	Gemini	Air	Barren	1st
18 Fri 11:38 pm	Cancer	Water	Fruitful	1st
19 Sat	Cancer	Water	Fruitful	1st
20 Sun	Cancer	Water	Fruitful	1st
21 Mon 3:56 am	Leo	Fire	Barren	1st
22 Tue	Leo	Fire	Barren	1st
23 Wed 12:26 pm	Virgo	Earth	Barren	2nd 5:02 pm
24 Thu	Virgo	Earth	Barren	2nd
25 Fri	Virgo	Earth	Barren	2nd
26 Sat 12:16 am	Libra	Air	Semi-fruitful	2nd
27 Sun	Libra	Air	Semi-fruitful	2nd
28 Mon 1:11 pm	Scorpio	Water	Fruitful	2nd
29 Tue	Scorpio	Water	Fruitful	2nd
30 Wed	Scorpio	Water	Fruitful	2nd
31 Thu 1:06 am	Sagittarius	Fire	Barren	Full 9:04 pm

June Moon Table

Date	Sign	Element	Nature	Phase
1 Fri	Sagittarius	Fire	Barren	3rd
2 Sat 11:09 am	Capricorn	Earth	Semi-fruitful	3rd
3 Sun	Capricorn	Earth	Semi-fruitful	3rd
4 Mon 7:15 pm	Aquarius	Air	Barren	3rd
5 Tue	Aquarius	Air	Barren	3rd
6 Wed	Aquarius	Air	Barren	3rd
7 Thu 1:24 am	Pisces	Water	Fruitful	3rd
8 Fri	Pisces	Water	Fruitful	4th 7:43 am
9 Sat 5:26 am	Aries	Fire	Barren	4th
10 Sun	Aries	Fire	Barren	4th
11 Mon 7:29 am	Taurus	Earth	Semi-fruitful	4th
12 Tue	Taurus	Earth	Semi-fruitful	4th
13 Wed 8:24 am	Gemini	Air	Barren	4th
14 Thu	Gemini	Air	Barren	New 11:13 pm
15 Fri 9:45 am	Cancer	Water	Fruitful	1st
16 Sat	Cancer	Water	Fruitful	1st
17 Sun 1:25 pm	Leo	Fire	Barren	1st
18 Mon	Leo	Fire	Barren	1st
19 Tue 8:45 pm	Virgo	Earth	Barren	1st
20 Wed	Virgo	Earth	Barren	1st
21 Thu	Virgo	Earth	Barren	1st
22 Fri 7:43 am	Libra	Air	Semi-fruitful	2nd 9:15 am
23 Sat	Libra	Air	Semi-fruitful	2nd
24 Sun 8:26 pm	Scorpio	Water	Fruitful	2nd
25 Mon	Scorpio	Water	Fruitful	2nd
26 Tue	Scorpio	Water	Fruitful	2nd
27 Wed 8:23 am	Sagittarius	Fire	Barren	2nd
28 Thu	Sagittarius	Fire	Barren	2nd
29 Fri 6:05 pm	Capricorn	Earth	Semi-fruitful	2nd
30 Sat	Capricorn	Earth	Semi-fruitful	Full 9:49 am

July Moon Table

Date	Sign	Element	Nature	Phase
1 Sun	Capricorn	Earth	Semi-fruitful	3rd
2 Mon 1:24 am	Aquarius	Air	Barren	3rd
3 Tue	Aquarius	Air	Barren	3rd
4 Wed 6:52 am	Pisces	Water	Fruitful	3rd
5 Thu	Pisces	Water	Fruitful	3rd
6 Fri 10:56 am	Aries	Fire	Barren	3rd
7 Sat	Aries	Fire	Barren	4th 12:53 pm
8 Sun 1:54 pm	Taurus	Earth	Semi-fruitful	4th
9 Mon	Taurus	Earth	Semi-fruitful	4th
10 Tue 4:10 pm	Gemini	Air	Barren	4th
11 Wed	Gemini	Air	Barren	4th
12 Thu 6:39 pm	Cancer	Water	Fruitful	4th
13 Fri	Cancer	Water	Fruitful	4th
14 Sat 10:43 pm	Leo	Fire	Barren	New 8:04 am
15 Sun	Leo	Fire	Barren	1st
16 Mon	Leo	Fire	Barren	1st
17 Tue 5:39 am	Virgo	Earth	Barren	1st
18 Wed	Virgo	Earth	Barren	1st
19 Thu 3:53 pm	Libra	Air	Semi-fruitful	1st
20 Fri	Libra	Air	Semi-fruitful	1st
21 Sat	Libra	Air	Semi-fruitful	1st
22 Sun 4:18 am	Scorpio	Water	Fruitful	2nd 2:29 am
23 Mon	Scorpio	Water	Fruitful	2nd
24 Tue 4:29 pm	Sagittarius	Fire	Barren	2nd
25 Wed	Sagittarius	Fire	Barren	2nd
26 Thu	Sagittarius	Fire	Barren	2nd
27 Fri 2:21 am	Capricorn	Earth	Semi-fruitful	2nd
28 Sat	Capricorn	Earth	Semi-fruitful	2nd
29 Sun 9:13 am	Aquarius	Air	Barren	Full 8:48 pm
30 Mon	Aquarius	Air	Barren	3rd
31 Tue 1:40 pm	Pisces	Water	Fruitful	3rd

August Moon Table

August	Sign	Element	Nature	Phase
1 Wed	Pisces	Water	Fruitful	3rd
2 Thu 4:43 pm	Aries	Fire	Barren	3rd
3 Fri	Aries	Fire	Barren	3rd
4 Sat 7:16 pm	Taurus	Earth	Semi-fruitful	3rd
5 Sun	Taurus	Earth	Semi-fruitful	4th 5:19 pm
6 Mon 10:01 pm	Gemini	Air	Barren	4th
7 Tue	Gemini	Air	Barren	4th
8 Wed	Gemini	Air	Barren	4th
9 Thu 1:36 am	Cancer	Water	Fruitful	4th
10 Fri	Cancer	Water	Fruitful	4th
11 Sat 6:42 am	Leo	Fire	Barren	4th
12 Sun	Leo	Fire	Barren	New 7:02 pm
13 Mon 2:03 pm	Virgo	Earth	Barren	1st
14 Tue	Virgo	Earth	Barren	1st
15 Wed	Virgo	Earth	Barren	1st
16 Thu 12:04 am	Libra	Air	Semi-fruitful	1st
17 Fri	Libra	Air	Semi-fruitful	1st
18 Sat 12:13 pm	Scorpio	Water	Fruitful	1st
19 Sun	Scorpio	Water	Fruitful	1st
20 Mon	Scorpio	Water	Fruitful	2nd 7:54 pm
21 Tue 12:44 am	Sagittarius	Fire	Barren	2nd
22 Wed	Sagittarius	Fire	Barren	2nd
23 Thu 11:20 am	Capricorn	Earth	Semi-fruitful	2nd
24 Fri	Capricorn	Earth	Semi-fruitful	2nd
25 Sat 6:35 pm	Aquarius	Air	Barren	2nd
26 Sun	Aquarius	Air	Barren	2nd
27 Mon 10:34 pm	Pisces	Water	Fruitful	2nd
28 Tue	Pisces	Water	Fruitful	Full 6:35 am
29 Wed	Pisces	Water	Fruitful	3rd
30 Thu 12:24 am	Aries	Fire	Barren	3rd
31 Fri	Aries	Fire	Barren	3rd

September Moon Table

Date	Sign	Element	Nature	Phase
1 Sat 1:35 am	Taurus	Earth	Semi-fruitful	3rd
2 Sun	Taurus	Earth	Semi-fruitful	3rd
3 Mon 3:30 am	Gemini	Air	Barren	4th 10:32 pm
4 Tue	Gemini	Air	Barren	4th
5 Wed 7:08 am	Cancer	Water	Fruitful	4th
6 Thu	Cancer	Water	Fruitful	4th
7 Fri 12:59 pm	Leo	Fire	Barren	4th
8 Sat	Leo	Fire	Barren	4th
9 Sun 9:10 pm	Virgo	Earth	Barren	4th
10 Mon	Virgo	Earth	Barren	4th
11 Tue	Virgo	Earth	Barren	New 8:44 am
12 Wed 7:31 am	Libra	Air	Semi-fruitful	1st
13 Thu	Libra	Air	Semi-fruitful	1st
14 Fri 7:37 pm	Scorpio	Water	Fruitful	1st
15 Sat	Scorpio	Water	Fruitful	1st
16 Sun	Scorpio	Water	Fruitful	1st
17 Mon 8:21 am	Sagittarius	Fire	Barren	1st
18 Tue	Sagittarius	Fire	Barren	1st
19 Wed 7:51 pm	Capricorn	Earth	Semi-fruitful	2nd 12:48 pm
20 Thu	Capricorn	Earth	Semi-fruitful	2nd
21 Fri	Capricorn	Earth	Semi-fruitful	2nd
22 Sat 4:18 am	Aquarius	Air	Barren	2nd
23 Sun	Aquarius	Air	Barren	2nd
24 Mon 8:55 am	Pisces	Water	Fruitful	2nd
25 Tue	Pisces	Water	Fruitful	2nd
26 Wed 10:22 am	Aries	Fire	Barren	Full 3:45 pm
27 Thu	Aries	Fire	Barren	3rd
28 Fri 10:17 am	Taurus	Earth	Semi-fruitful	3rd
29 Sat	Taurus	Earth	Semi-fruitful	3rd
30 Sun 10:34 am	Gemini	Air	Barren	3rd

October Moon Table

Date	Sign	Element	Nature	Phase
1 Mon	Gemini	Air	Barren	3rd
2 Tue 12:57 pm	Cancer	Water	Fruitful	3rd
3 Wed	Cancer	Water	Fruitful	4th 6:06 am
4 Thu 6:27 pm	Leo	Fire	Barren	4th
5 Fri	Leo	Fire	Barren	4th
6 Sat	Leo	Fire	Barren	4th
7 Sun 3:03 am	Virgo	Earth	Barren	4th
8 Mon	Virgo	Earth	Barren	4th
9 Tue 1:57 pm	Libra	Air	Semi-fruitful	4th
10 Wed	Libra	Air	Semi-fruitful	4th
11 Thu	Libra	Air	Semi-fruitful	New 1:01 am
12 Fri 2:13 am	Scorpio	Water	Fruitful	1st
13 Sat	Scorpio	Water	Fruitful	1st
14 Sun 2:58 pm	Sagittarius	Fire	Barren	1st
15 Mon	Sagittarius	Fire	Barren	1st
16 Tue	Sagittarius	Fire	Barren	1st
17 Wed 3:03 am	Capricorn	Earth	Semi-fruitful	1st
18 Thu	Capricorn	Earth	Semi-fruitful	1st
19 Fri 12:52 pm	Aquarius	Air	Barren	2nd 4:33 am
20 Sat	Aquarius	Air	Barren	2nd
21 Sun 7:02 pm	Pisces	Water	Fruitful	2nd
22 Mon	Pisces	Water	Fruitful	2nd
23 Tue 9:24 pm	Aries	Fire	Barren	2nd
24 Wed	Aries	Fire	Barren	2nd
25 Thu 9:07 pm	Taurus	Earth	Semi-fruitful	2nd
26 Fri	Taurus	Earth	Semi-fruitful	Full 12:51 am
27 Sat 8:11 pm	Gemini	Air	Barren	3rd
28 Sun	Gemini	Air	Barren	3rd
29 Mon 8:49 pm	Cancer	Water	Fruitful	3rd
30 Tue	Cancer	Water	Fruitful	3rd
31 Wed	Cancer	Water	Fruitful	3rd

November Moon Table

Date	Sign	Element	Nature	Phase
1 Thu 12:48 am	Leo	Fire	Barren	4th 5:18 pm
2 Fri	Leo	Fire	Barren	4th
3 Sat 8:44 am	Virgo	Earth	Barren	4th
4 Sun	Virgo	Earth	Barren	4th
5 Mon 6:47 pm	Libra	Air	Semi-fruitful	4th
6 Tue	Libra	Air	Semi-fruitful	4th
7 Wed	Libra	Air	Semi-fruitful	4th
8 Thu 7:18 am	Scorpio	Water	Fruitful	4th
9 Fri	Scorpio	Water	Fruitful	New 6:03 pm
10 Sat 7:59 pm	Sagittarius	Fire	Barren	1st
11 Sun	Sagittarius	Fire	Barren	1st
12 Mon	Sagittarius	Fire	Barren	1st
13 Tue 8:00 am	Capricorn	Earth	Semi-fruitful	1st
14 Wed	Capricorn	Earth	Semi-fruitful	1st
15 Thu 6:30 pm	Aquarius	Air	Barren	1st
16 Fri	Aquarius	Air	Barren	1st
17 Sat	Aquarius	Air	Barren	2nd 5:32 pm
18 Sun 2:14 am	Pisces	Water	Fruitful	2nd
19 Mon	Pisces	Water	Fruitful	2nd
20 Tue 6:24 am	Aries	Fire	Barren	2nd
21 Wed	Aries	Fire	Barren	2nd
22 Thu 7:18 am	Taurus	Earth	Semi-fruitful	2nd
23 Fri	Taurus	Earth	Semi-fruitful	2nd
24 Sat 6:29 am	Gemini	Air	Barren	New 9:30 am
25 Sun	Gemini	Air	Barren	3rd
26 Mon 6:07 am	Cancer	Water	Fruitful	3rd
27 Tue	Cancer	Water	Fruitful	3rd
28 Wed 8:23 am	Leo	Fire	Barren	3rd
29 Thu	Leo	Fire	Barren	3rd
30 Fri 2:44 pm	Virgo	Earth	Barren	3rd

December Moon Table

Date	Sign	Element	Nature	Phase
1 Sat	Virgo	Earth	Barren	4th 7:44 am
2 Sun	Virgo	Earth	Barren	4th
3 Mon 1:01 am	Libra	Air	Semi-fruitful	4th
4 Tue	Libra	Air	Semi-fruitful	4th
5 Wed 1:31 pm	Scorpio	Water	Fruitful	4th
6 Thu	Scorpio	Water	Fruitful	4th
7 Fri	Scorpio	Water	Fruitful	4th
8 Sat 2:11 am	Sagittarius	Fire	Barren	4th
9 Sun	Sagittarius	Fire	Barren	New 12:40 pm
10 Mon 1:50 pm	Capricorn	Earth	Semi-fruitful	1st
11 Tue	Capricorn	Earth	Semi-fruitful	1st
12 Wed	Capricorn	Earth	Semi-fruitful	1st
13 Thu 12:01 am	Aquarius	Air	Barren	1st
14 Fri	Aquarius	Air	Barren	1st
15 Sat 8:15 am	Pisces	Water	Fruitful	1st
16 Sun	Pisces	Water	Fruitful	1st
17 Mon 1:52 pm	Aries	Fire	Barren	2nd 5:17 am
18 Tue	Aries	Fire	Barren	2nd
19 Wed 4:38 pm	Taurus	Earth	Semi-fruitful	2nd
20 Thu	Taurus	Earth	Semi-fruitful	2nd
21 Fri 5:14 pm	Gemini	Air	Barren	2nd
22 Sat	Gemini	Air	Barren	2nd
23 Sun 5:18 pm	Cancer	Water	Fruitful	Full 8:15 pm
24 Mon	Cancer	Water	Fruitful	3rd
25 Tue 6:52 pm	Leo	Fire	Barren	3rd
26 Wed	Leo	Fire	Barren	3rd
27 Thu 11:44 pm	Virgo	Earth	Barren	3rd
28 Fri	Virgo	Earth	Barren	3rd
29 Sat	Virgo	Earth	Barren	3rd
30 Sun 8:37 am	Libra	Air	Semi-fruitful	3rd
31 Mon	Libra	Air	Semi-fruitful	4th 2:51 am

About the Authors

ELIZABETH BARRETTE serves as the Managing Editor of PanGaia. She has been involved with the Pagan community for more than seventeen years, including coffeehouse meetings and open sabbats. Her other writing fields include speculative fiction and gender studies. She lives in central Illinois and enjoys herbal landscaping and gardening for wildlife. Visit her website at: http://www.worthlink.net/~ysabet/sitemap.html.

CHANDRA MOIRA BEAL is a freelance writer currently living in England. She has authored three books and published hundreds of articles, all inspired by her day-to-day life and adventures. She has been writing for Llewellyn since 1998. Chandra is also a massage therapist. To learn more, visit www.beal-net.com/laluna.

NANCY BENNETT has been published in Llewellyn's annuals, *We'moon*, *Circle Network*, and many mainstream publications. Her pet projects include reading and writing about history and creating ethnic dinners to test on her family. She lives near a protected salmon stream where deer and bears often play.

STEPHANIE ROSE BIRD is an artist, writer, herbalist, healer, mother, and companion. She studied art at the Tyler School of Art and at the University of California at San Diego, and she researched Australian Aboriginal art, ritual, and cermonial practices as a Fulbright senior scholar. Her column "Ase! from the Crossroads" is featured in *SageWoman*. Her book *Four Seasons of Mojo* was published by Llewellyn in 2006.

KAAREN CHRIST is a self-employed consultant providing research and writing services to social service organizations. She also writes children's stories, crafts poetry, and writes freelance articles about social issues. She lives in beautiful Prince Edward County, Ontario, where she shares her world with two beautiful children named Indigo and Challian, a Super-Dog called Lukki, and a magical boy-rabbit who answers to "Nana."

DALLAS JENNIFER COBB lives in an enchanted waterfront village. She's freed up resources for what she loves: family, gardens, fitness, and fabulous food. She's forever scheming novel ways to pay the bills when she's not running country roads or wandering the beach. Her essays are in Llewellyn's almanacs, and recent Seal Press anthologies *Three Ring Circus* and *Far From Home*. Her video documentary, *Disparate Places*, appeared on TV Ontario's Planet Parent. Contact her at Jennifer.Cobb@Sympatico.ca.

SALLY CRAGIN writes the astrological forecast, "Moon Signs," for the Boston Phoenix and other newspapers, which can be found online. A regular arts reviewer and feature writer for the Boston Globe, she also edits *Button*, New England's Tiniest Magazine of poetry, fiction, and gracious living since 1993. More on everything, including your personal forecast, at moonsigns.net.

SORITA D'ESTE is an author, researcher, and Priestess. She is the author of *Artemis Virgin Goddess of the Sun & Moon* and coauthor of *Circle of Fire* and *The Guises of the Morrigan*. She regularly contributes to MBS publications and community magazines. She spends most of her time in London (UK) from where she writes. For more information, please visit www.avalonia.co.uk.

MICHELLE HIGGINS is an Australian gardener (now in New York), herbalist, astrologer, writer, and amateur Wiccan. Studying these topic over three decades has led her on a road of preventative medicine and good nutrition, blended with a belief in self mediation and power via natural charms, spells, and magic.

ROBIN IVY is an astrologer, radio host, educator, and writer in Portland, Maine. View her astrology reports at www.robinszodiaczone.com. Robin dedicates her article, "Remedies for Domestic Animals," to Sully, her border collie, who taught us about love, health, and life. December 13, 2001-August 23, 2005.

JAMES KAMBOS is an herbalist, writer, and painter. He celebrates the changing seasons by tending his herb and flower gardens at his home in the beautiful Appalachian hills of southern Ohio. He is a regular contributor to Llewellyn's annuals.

DOROTHY J. KOVACH is a practicing astrologer, writer, and timing expert whose home is perched in a sea of nettles. She helps businesses and individuals find the best time to start projects—everything from starting a business, having surgery, and saying "I do." Her specialty is interrogatory (a.k.a. "horary") astrology, the branch that answers specific questions. She has been predicting the markets in Llewellyn's *Moon Signs Book* since 2003. Reach her via e-mail, dstar@mcn.org or at www.worldastrology.net.

SALLY MCSWEENEY has been "digging in the dirt" since childhood. Many plants later, she is a master herbalist specializing in aromatherapy and creating blended teas. She also owns Triple Aspect Herbs, a metaphysical herbal apothecary. As a Pagan hedge Witch with leanings toward Celtic and Norse traditions, she is working on a book about healing with the energies of the Moon throughout the wheel of the year. She lives in Oregon with her husband and grows a multitude of catnip for her two cats.

LAUREL REUFNER has been a solitary Pagan for more than a decade. She is active in the Circle of Gaia Dreaming and is often attracted to bright and shiny ideas. Southeaster Ohio has always been home. She currently lives in Athens County witth her husband and two adorable heathers, er, daughters. Her website may be found at www.spiritrealm.com/Melinda/paganism.html.

MICHELLE SANTOS has been a practicing Witch for over nine years and has been working with the fey since she was a child. Founding member of the Sisterhood of the Crescent Moon, she is active in the Pagan community in southeastern Massachusetts, where she shares her home with elfy husband Michael and little Witch-in-training Neisa. Michelle presents various workshops, classes, and apprenticeship programs near her home. An ordained minister through the Universal Life Church, she performs legal handfastings, weddings, and other spiritual rites of passage.

CERRIDWEN IRIS SHEA is a writer, teacher, and tarot reader who loves ice hockey and horse racing. Visit her website at: www.cerridwenscottage.com; visit her blog Kemmyrk, which discusses working with tarot and oracles at: tarotkemmyrk.blogspot.com. She also wrote the magical realism serial "Angel Hunt."

LYNN SMYTHE is a freelance writer living in south Florida with her husband, son, and daughter. She has written a variety of articles for publications such as the *Herb Quarterly*, *Back Home*, and Llewellyn's annual *Herbal Almanac*. Lynn is also the founder and manager of the online community Herb Witch, which is located at http://groups.msn.com/herbwitch.

TAMMY SULLIVAN is a full-time writer and solitary Witch who writes from home in the foothills of The Great Smokey Mountains. Author of *Pagan Anger Magic: Positive Transformations from Negative Energies* and *Elemental Witch*, her work has also appeared in the Llewellyn Almanacs and *Circle Magazine*.

PATTI WIGINGTON is a staff writer for a central Ohio newspaper, as well as a contributing editor for Garden and Hearth. Her articles have appeared in *Gaea's Cauldron*, *Twinshelp*, *Pediatrics for Parents*, and *The Witches Tutorial*. She is also the author of an historical adventure novel, a children's book, and *Summer's Ashes*, the first book in a series about teen Witches. Patti has followed an eclectic Pagan path since 1987, and lives in Ohio with her husband and three children.

S. Y. ZENITH is three-quarters Chinese, one tad Irish, and a lifelong solitary eclectic Pagan, although her main path is of Shaivite Tradition. She has lived and traveled extensively in many parts of Asia such as India, Nepal, Thailand, Malaysia, Singapore, Borneo, and Japan. Currently based in Australia, her time is divided between travel, writing, experimenting with alternative remedies, and teaching the use of gems, crystals, holy beads, and sacraments from India and the Himalayas.